CH Neely

143 Welsh Rd

Lansdowne

Pa

3/24/61

Sims.

THE LIBRARY OF
PHILOSOPHY AND THEOLOGY
Edited by
JOHN MCINTYRE and IAN T. RAMSEY

THE SCOPE OF DEMYTHOLOGIZING

LIBRARY OF PHILOSOPHY AND THEOLOGY

Titles in the Series

THE SCOPE OF DEMYTHOLOGIZING

Bultmann and his Critics

JOHN MACQUARRIE

SCM PRESS LTD
56 BLOOMSBURY STREET
LONDON

FIRST PUBLISHED 1960
© SCM PRESS LTD 1960
PRINTED IN GREAT BRITAIN BY
THE CAMELOT PRESS LTD
LONDON AND SOUTHAMPTON

To Jenny

CONTENTS

PREFACE

THIS book is a revised and much expanded version of a series of lectures given in March, 1957, at Union Theological Seminary, New York. I wish to thank the President and Faculty of the Seminary not only for the honour which they did me in the invitation to give these lectures, but also for their friendly welcome and for the opportunities of discussion which were, to me, very helpful. Especially I wish to thank the President, Dr Van Dusen, and Mrs Van Dusen, for the generous hospitality which they accorded me during my stay in New York.

The present volume may be regarded as a companion to my earlier book on Bultmann and Heidegger, *An Existentialist Theology* (SCM Press, 1955). The earlier book was, in the main, expository, whilst the present one is concerned with assessment and evaluation. It takes up what I regard as the central problem presented by Bultmann's theology—what I have called 'the limit to demythologizing'. This problem is discussed in relation to the main points of criticism to which Bultmann's views have been subjected in the course of the demythologizing controversy. Some of the critics discussed here—such as Professor Buri of Basle—are perhaps as yet little known among English-speaking readers. To show the limit of anything is, however, to demonstrate its scope. And since the aim of this book is positive rather than negative, I should like to stress the scope as much as the limits of demythologizing.

I wish to express my warm thanks to Professor Bultmann for sending me, unsolicited, his detailed comments on my earlier book. These comments have proved most useful to me, and have, I hope, led me to a much clearer understanding of his views on many topics. I wish also to thank the Editor of the SCM Press and the Editors of 'The Library of Philosophy and Theology' for their help in preparing the manuscript for publication.

J. M.

University of Glasgow,
October, 1959

I

THE PARADOX IN BULTMANN

1 *The Problem Stated*

IT may be useful for us to begin by conjuring up in our imaginations a little tableau, which will help to illustrate the problem confronting us and will also serve as a point of departure for the discusssion of it. Let us picture to ourselves a motorist who has been driving his vehicle at a fairly brisk speed down a long steady incline. At the bottom of the slope the road dips suddenly out of sight. We cannot as yet tell what lies beyond the dip, though it looks as if there may well be a precipitous fall into an abyss of some sort. But the motorist has also noticed the sharp declivity in front of him. Almost at the last moment, as it appears, he has pulled strongly on his wheel, the car has slewed violently round, and instead of going over the dip it now follows a different road in quite a new direction.

Our picture is easily interpreted. Rudolf Bultmann is the motorist, and his vehicle is the Christian message as he understands it. The road by which he has come is the way of demythologizing. The sudden change of direction before the point at which the road dips out of sight is what we propose to call the limit to demythologizing—a limit which has been set by Bultmann himself. It is this limit which will engage our attention. It may be said to constitute the basic paradox in Bultmann's thought. Some would go so far as to say that it is a fundamental inconsistency and that it vitiates his whole theological position. Why does he set a limit? Why does he not pursue the method of demythologizing to the very end?

From its formation, the word 'demythologizing' would seem to mean something like 'the removal of mythology', just as 'decarbonizing', for instance, means 'the removal of carbon'.

In the specialized sense in which Bultmann speaks of 'demythologizing', the word denotes a process of translation or interpretation. Mythical language is to be interpreted in existential terms. This will serve as a preliminary definition of 'demythologizing', though clearly it is no more than preliminary, since the reader is now entitled to demand of us what exactly we mean by 'myth' and 'existential interpretation'. These terms will be discussed in detail later. For the present, it is enough to notice that, in Bultmann's view, the teaching of the Bible is given largely in the form of myth, and that the meaning of such mythical language is to be elucidated by asking what it says about this human existence of ours.

Thus Bultmann sets out by asking of the New Testament questions which relate to human existence. As a consequence, he obtains answers which relate to human existence. The teaching of the New Testament is thus translated into terms of what it says about the possibilities of human existence. In the course of making this translation Bultmann sets aside many beliefs which have been traditionally held in the Church and which were supposed to rest on the evidence of the New Testament. For instance, the traditional christological teaching of the Church pretty well disappears in the course of the radical reinterpretation which Bultmann gives to it. As his negations mount up, it seems as if the Christian faith as handed down by the Church is to be dissolved into a philosophy of existence, in which one will no longer need to speak of Christ and his work at all, but only of possible ways of being or modes of existence between which men are summoned to decide.

But if we were expecting that such a dissolution of the faith would take place, we find this expectation falsified as we read further in Bultmann. He strongly denies that the Christian faith can be so dissolved, and it is certainly not his intention that it should. For him, despite what we might have expected, the teaching of the New Testament is not another philosophy, but a 'kerygma'—a proclamation in which God addresses us through Christ. In Bultmann's own words, this kerygma is 'the proclamation of the decisive act of God in Christ'.[1] When he says this, Bultmann sets a limit to demythologizing. A 'decisive act of

---

[1] 'New Testament and Mythology', in Kerygma and Myth, ed. H. W. Bartsch, trans. R. H. Fuller (S.P.C.K., London, 1953), p. 13.

God' is something radically different from and irreducible to a possibility of human existence, and with the recognition of such an act Bultmann's thought moves in a different direction. This is the paradox with which we are presented in Bultmann. The method of demythologizing calls for the translation of the New Testament teaching into statements concerning human existence, yet at the same time Bultmann insists upon speaking of God's decisive act in Christ. The analysis of human possibilities thus gives place to the proclamation of a divine act. Indeed, the whole aim of Bultmann's demythologizing is to set the *kerygma* free so that we may be genuinely addressed by it. Can this make sense? Can the two sides of his thinking be properly held together?

Such questions are crucial when it comes to making an assessment of the value of demythologizing; and demythologizing has received such prominence in recent discussion that the contemporary theologian can hardly avoid making some assessment of it. When Paul Tillich revisited Europe after the Second World War, he summed up his impression of the theological scene in these words: 'When you come to Europe to-day, it is not as it was before, with Karl Barth in the centre of discussion; it is now Rudolf Bultmann who is in the centre'.[1] It is certainly the case that Bultmann's demythologizing has made a most remarkable impact upon the theological world—an impact comparable in its magnitude to that made by Barth's theology of crisis after the First World War. Since the appearance of Bultmann's essay, quoted above, there has been a steady and voluminous stream of books and articles in which the merits and demerits of demythologizing have been debated with varying degrees of penetration. This stream has poured forth not only in Germany but in France, Britain and America; not only among Lutherans but among Presbyterians, Anglicans and Roman Catholics; indeed, not only among theologians but in some philosophical circles as well. Whatever we may make of it, demythologizing is not to be ignored.

It seems true to say that up till now Bultmann's views have earned him more kicks than halfpence from those who have written on the subject. There is admittedly general agreement

[1] In an Auburn Lecture delivered at Union Theological Seminary, November 10, 1952.

that he does have something important and perhaps valuable to say. There is also widespread admiration for the courage and honesty with which he has faced up to the task of trying to make the Christian gospel meaningful in a world where it seems largely to have lost its relevancy. But on the other hand there is a certain fear of demythologizing, and this fear has usually outweighed the factors on the other side. Few theologians have been willing to go for a ride in Bultmann's car. And the reason for their reluctance lies in the fact that no clear answers are available to the kind of questions which we have raised in connection with the limit to demythologizing. Where does this way of demythologizing eventually lead us? If pursued to its end, does it not mean the disappearance of everything that is distinctive in Christianity? How far does Bultmann himself invite us to go with him along this way? Can he stop once he has begun to travel along it? Our aim in the following pages will be to clarify questions such as these, and to seek some answers to them. It may be that in the course of the discussion we shall allay some of the fears and suspicions which the very mention of demythologizing seems to arouse.

And as a first step towards this, it may be worth pointing out that the kind of paradox which we have noted in Bultmann was already present in the earliest propagation of the gospel. In the New Testament[1] we read how Saint Philip the Evangelist, on the road leading south from Jerusalem, fell in with an Ethiopian official who was returning to his own country. The Ethiopian was reading in his chariot a passage from the Hebrew prophets. The evangelist asked, 'Do you understand what you are reading?' The man replied, 'How can I, unless someone guides me?' And he goes on to ask: 'About whom does the prophet say this, about himself or about someone else?' Now it is interesting to notice how Saint Philip answered the Ethiopian's questions. On the one hand, he connected the passage of scripture with the person and work of Christ, and expounded it accordingly. On the other hand, when they came to some water, he took the Ethiopian down to it and baptized him. If we regard this story as showing us how a man is brought into the Christian faith, it would seem that something twofold is involved. On one side there is the proclaiming and hearing

[1] Acts 8.26-39.

of what Bultmann calls a 'decisive act of God'. On the other side there is the unfolding of the possibilities of human existence in the commitment to a new way of life. This, however, is a prototype of the kind of paradox which we find in Bultmann.

2 Bultmann's Negations

We must examine the structure of Bultmann's theology in more detail, so that the full range of the paradox in his thinking may become evident to us. We shall consider first the method of demythologizing and the negations which it involves. Friedrich Gogarten has lamented the fact that Bultmann's approach to the meaning of the Christian message has been designated by the negative term 'demythologizing'.[1] He thinks that it would be better to speak of it positively as 'existential interpretation'. Gogarten is right in drawing attention to the fact that de-mythologizing has a positive end in view, and that it seeks to interpret rather than to eliminate. Yet his claim must be treated with caution, for it is valid only up to a point. Bult-mann's demythologizing does involve negative attitudes which do not necessarily follow from a simple existential interpretation as such. In the widest sense, existential interpretation of the New Testament occurs whenever a hearer understands the text as presenting him with a possibility of decision in the situa-tion in which he finds himself. We have already suggested that such existential interpretation is as old as the New Testa-ment itself—or older—and is to be found in the earliest preach-ing and hearing of the gospel. But demythologizing is some-thing much more sophisticated. Bultmann indeed gives his assent to existential interpretation in general, but it is important to notice where demythologizing differs from simple existential interpretation. Three distinguishing marks call for notice.

In the first place, demythologizing is more restricted than existential interpretation. Demythologizing is directed upon those parts of the New Testament which are more or less mythical in their form. But not all of the New Testament is myth. For instance, there is a good deal of ethical teaching in the New Testament, and a moral precept, whatever it may be, is not a myth. But a moral precept is capable of being existen-tially interpreted. As an illustration, we may recall that Saint

[1] *Demythologizing and History*, trans. N. H. Smith (SCM Press, London, 1955), p. 9.

Athanasius tells us how Saint Antony, when he first contemplated the ascetic life, decided to hold on to some of his possessions in case they might be needed at some future time for his sister. But 'as he went into the church, hearing the Lord say in the gospel, "Be not anxious for the morrow",[1] he could stay no longer, but went out and gave those things also to the poor'.[2] We could describe what happened to Saint Antony by saying that for him the words of the gospel ceased to be just a universal precept to which he might give a general assent and became a word addressed to him in his situation about which he had to decide. This is existential interpretation, but it is not demythologizing. Of course, it need hardly be added that when Bultmann speaks of such New Testament commands as that we should love our neighbours, he too insists that they should be understood in a concrete existential way and not just as general precepts or sentimental ideals. But even though this is the case, it can lead only to confusion if we fail to recognize that there is and always has been much existential interpretation which cannot properly be called demythologizing.

But even when a more or less mythical passage of the New Testament is involved, it is not necessarily the case that an existential interpretation of it should be also a demythologizing of it in the strict sense. A second distinction has to be made, and this one concerns the manner of the interpretation. Existential interpretation takes place whenever a text is understood as disclosing a possibility of human existence. Such a possibility may be disclosed as belonging to an individual in his own concrete situation, and in that case one should really speak of an *existentiell* possibility, and thus of *existentiell* interpretation of the text.[3] But demythologizing aims to go beyond such *existentiell* interpretation to a strictly existential or even existentialist understanding of the text. Such an understanding would be concerned with the horizons of human existence in general, and in order to reach it we would need to call to our aid the concepts in which existentialist philosophy has analysed the structures of man's being. It is obvious that here we have to do with something much more complicated than a concrete *existentiell* interpretation.

[1] Matt. 6.34.   [2] *Vita S. Antoni*, 3.
[3] For the distinction between the terms 'existential' and '*existentiell*', see the present writer's earlier book on Bultmann, *An Existentialist Theology* (SCM Press, London, 1955), p. 34. See also below, pp. 148-50.

Thus Albert Schweitzer drew the initial inspiration for his work from a New Testament story which is not lacking in mythical features—the story of Lazarus and the rich man.[1] Schweitzer tells us that his reading led him to understand that we in the Western world are the rich men of the earth, taking for granted the gifts of medical science. 'Out there in the colonies, however, sits wretched Lazarus who suffers from illness and pain just as much as we do, nay, much more, and has absolutely no means of fighting them'.[2] This is an existential understanding of the story in so far as it brings the reader to confront a possibility of his own existence. More strictly, however, it is an *existentiell* understanding, and therefore to be distinguished from demythologizing, which would seek to interpret the story in terms of the structures of human existence in general. And while most people might applaud the *existentiell* interpretation, and acknowledge the necessity for such interpretation, they would find more problematical the demand for an interpretation in terms of existentialist concepts.

A third distinction between demythologizing and existential interpretation arises from the fact that demythologizing displays a radical scepticism towards any objective understanding of the stories which it seeks to interpret. This scepticism which distinguishes demythologizing and which earns for it its negative description is not a necessary concomitant of existential interpretation. It is derived from various elements in Bultmann's thought, not least from his concept of modernity, to which we must pay attention at a later stage.[3] Once again, we may clarify the distinction by means of an illustration.

Here we may compare an ancient example of existential interpretation with a contemporary example of demythologizing. There is a Greek hymn of the eighth century which is based on the story in the Gospels of Christ's stilling of the storm.[4] The hymn is familiar to us in John Mason Neale's English translation which begins, 'Fierce was the wild billow'. The first and second verses give a description of the storm and of the calm which followed at the Master's word. But the third verse is a prayer in which the hymn-writer and those who sing

---

[1] Luke 16.19-31.
[2] *On the Edge of the Primeval Forest*, trans. C. T. Campion (A. & C. Black, London, 1922), pp. 1-2.
[3] See pp. 230ff.   [4] Mark 4.35-41; Matt. 8.23-7; Luke 8.22-5.

B

his hymn interpret that word as a word addressed to themselves in their situation in the world. The prayer gives expression to the conviction that Christ can give peace and confidence to men in the storms of life and in the final storm of death. For a modern counterpart we go to Hans-Werner Bartsch who has published a volume of sermons[1] designed to show how the method of demythologizing can serve the cause of preaching. Among the themes which he has selected, we come once more upon the stilling of the storm. The interpretation given is similar to that found in the old hymn-writer—and no doubt in many preachers through the centuries. Christ's word of peace is a word addressed to us now, and through hearing it we can overcome fear and anxiety.

There is both similarity and difference in these two interpretations. The similarity lies in this, that both interpreters understand that the bare record of a past event has no religious significance in itself. Regarded simply as an account of something that once happened, the story of the stilling of the storm might as well occur in the Arabian Nights as in the gospels for all the religious value it would have. It has religious significance only when it speaks to men existing in the world, presenting them with a possibility of existence, and both interpreters have let it speak in that way. The difference between the two interpreters lies in their attitude to the reported event itself. Presumably the old hymn-writer did not doubt for a moment that Christ had in fact stilled a storm on the lake— the opening verses of his hymn seem to make that clear. On the other hand, the modern demythologizer denies that anything of the kind ever happened, or ever could happen. He is not even interested in rationalized versions of the story which would seek to explain what happened in terms of some remarkable coincidence, such as a freak of the weather—and probably he is very right to reject such speculations. They might give the story greater plausibility so far as its factual content is concerned, but they would do so at the expense of taking from it any religious content that it may be supposed to have. For the demythologizer, the story is purely a legend and its meaning lies wholly in the existential interpretation of it.

One point emerges very clearly when we look at the difference

---

[1] *Die Anrede Gottes* (Evangelischer Verlag, Hamburg, 1953).

between the two interpretations before us. It is that an existential interpretation in itself makes no pronouncement whatever concerning the factual content of the story which it professes to interpret. It leads us neither to affirm nor to deny any objective reference and, as we have seen, it may without inconsistency be accompanied by either an affirmation or a denial of such a reference. Demythologizing therefore adds something to simple existential interpretation when it goes on to deny any objective reference in the story, and this overplus of negation must be derived from some other source, such as a world-view which does not admit of the possibility of the kind of events narrated in the story.

But although existential interpretation of a story does not in itself deny the factual content of the story, it certainly does put that content 'in brackets', so to speak. The objective reference becomes bracketed in the sense that interest has shifted away from it to the existential significance. The question of fact is no longer being raised. We are not asking about what happened but about what the story says to us in our situation now. The objective reference has somehow become irrelevant. Whether we affirm it or whether we deny it or whether we suspend judgement about it, the existential significance appears to remain quite unaffected. The essential religious message of the story can still speak home to us, as we have seen.

The view that the objective reference of a religious story is irrelevant may not give rise to much concern so long as we are thinking of such stories as that of the stilling of the storm. Apart altogether from Bultmann's demythologizing, many people to-day would have difficulty in believing that such a story describes an event which actually happened, or even that it is meant to describe one. But we soon find that much more is being called in question—indeed, the whole objective reference of the gospel narrative is affected.

The first distinction which we made between demythologizing and existential interpretation in the wide sense was that demythologizing is properly restricted to the interpretation of myth while existential interpretation can operate on a much wider front. But we were careful to speak of the 'more or less' mythical parts of the New Testament, and it very quickly becomes evident that it is extremely difficult, if not impossible, to isolate the mythical from the non-mythical. We may think demythologizing appropriate when the New Testament speaks of the last days, of the end of the age, of final judgment, and of the urgency of decision before the approaching catastrophe, for here the language is definitely mythical and the ideas can be traced in Jewish apocalyptic. Even if the first Christians believed that they would see these events come to pass in the near future, we may believe that the significance of such passages for us lies in what they say to the individual existence. Decision, judgment, the end—these belong to the existence of the finite individual whose being, as Martin Heidegger expresses it, is a being-towards-death. But demythologizing claims its say also when it comes to such an event as the crucifixion, for though this is a factual happening in world-history, the New Testament sets it in a cosmic drama involving pre-existence, incarnation, resurrection and exaltation. The mythical elements cannot be sealed off, as it were. And it might be added that even those moral precepts which we took to be furthest from myth in their form must be understood in the light of the eschatological expectations of the first Christians which brought about a transvaluation of values in face of the coming end. Thus the bracketing of existential interpretation and perhaps even the added negation of demythologizing threatens to impinge in one way or another upon the whole content of the Christian gospel. Just how irrelevant can the factual content of the gospel become without its ceasing to be a gospel?

Is the record of events contained in the gospel narrative to be regarded as a kind of ladder, by way of which we can be brought into an understanding of religious truth? Is this understanding reached when the record ceases to be a record and is translated into a possibility of existence? The cross of Christ, for instance, may cease to be understood as an event of two thousand years ago and may become understood as a possibility confronting us now. Bultmann expresses this by saying that the cross is an eschatological event (in his sense of the term) which brings one into a self-understanding. But when this self-understanding is attained, does the objective event of which the record speaks no longer matter? Has it become totally irrelevant, so that it is a matter of indifference whether its factuality is affirmed or denied or simply bracketed? Is it completely swallowed up in the eschatological event?

It is because there is no clear answer to questions such as these that demythologizing arouses the fears of which we spoke, and gives rise to the suspicion that an existential—and still more, an existentialist—approach to the New Testament must lead to a kind of *gnosis*. Those who have attained to it, like the Gnostics of the early centuries, have, it is supposed, no need for a human Jesus who actually lived and suffered in the flesh, but put in his place a purely mythical redeemer. Bultmann, as is well-known, believes that as a matter of fact Gnostic influences entered deeply into the thought of the New Testament.[1] But the early Church set its face resolutely against the transformation of the gospel into a pure *gnosis*. It was maintained that only one who has been 'made like his brethren in every respect' can be a high priest for men.[2] Where does demythologizing take us in this matter?

It was suggested that the gospel record may be compared to a ladder, in so far as it is the way by which men are brought into an understanding of a religious truth—a truth which has to do with their own being and is not just the truth which may be asserted of objective facts. When a man has obtained access by way of a ladder to a new situation, there are two things which he may do with the ladder itself. He may kick it away or he may leave it in position. To kick it away has its own attractiveness—it means at least that the man has committed himself finally to the new level on to which the ladder has brought him, and has no thought of going down again. On the other hand, to leave the ladder where it is has its own wisdom. A time may come when the man wishes to show other people or even to assure himself that he has some right to stand where he does. If he can still point to a sure way of access, that may be both important and relevant for his situation. If he can indicate no such way of access, then he may well begin to wonder whether he is dreaming it all and is lost in a realm of illusion. At first sight, it might seem that demythologizing tends to kick away the ladders pretty freely.

---

[1] See, for instance, his *Gnosis*, trans. J. R. Coates (A. & C. Black, London, 1952), p. 41ff.
[2] Heb. 2.17.

We have noted how any objective reference in the stories of nature miracles is ruled out, but Bultmann's negations go far beyond that. There is to be no selection. Along with the nature miracles go the healing miracles, and along with them the eschatological teaching, the birth stories and the resurrection stories, so far as any objective reference is concerned. Negation moves into the field of doctrine. 'What a primitive mythology it is', says Bultmann, 'that a divine being should become incarnate, and atone for the sins of men through his own blood!'[1] But Bultmann's scepticism does not halt even there. It calls in question the record of facts which have nothing miraculous or mythical about them. For instance, it is denied that Jesus had any belief that he was the Messiah. Jesus becomes indeed a very shadowy figure. We know something of his teaching but 'we can now know almost nothing concerning the life and personality of Jesus'.[2] When we look at this series of negations, we may think that the fears which demythologizing has aroused are not groundless, and that there is only one possible end to the road upon which we have started. The whole record of events in the New Testament is going to be reduced to the status of a myth. Its sole meaning will lie in the existential interpretation which we put upon it. And since this interpretation can be expressed in terms of possibilities of human existence without referring any longer to the symbols of the myth, we shall end up by replacing the Christian gospel with a philosophy of man's being. It looks as if that must happen if we follow out Bultmann's demythologizing to the end. It looks as if it has almost happened already at this stage to which we have been brought. It was not just a rhetorical way of speaking when it was said at the beginning that 'almost at the last moment' the motorist pulls upon his wheel. But to our surprise, Bultmann does pull on his wheel, and he pulls very strongly. A limit is set; demythologizing is not pursued to the end which we envisaged. It is claimed on the contrary that Christianity is so far from having been dissolved that it can now properly assert itself.

3 Bultmann's Affirmations

Having considered demythologizing and its negations, we

---

[1] *Kerygma and Myth*, p. 7.
[2] *Jesus and the Word*, trans. L. P. Smith and E. Huntress (Nicholson & Watson London, 1935), p. 8.

must turn in the next place to look at Bultmann's equally strong affirmations. It is he himself who poses the question concerning the possible merging of Christian theology into a philosophy of existence. 'Is theology simply the precursor of existentialism?' he asks. 'Is it no more than an antiquated survival and an unnecesssary incubus?'[1] And to these questions he returns a decided and unhesitating negative. The work of demythologizing is to be carried out not to make way for a philosophy of existence, but to set free the essential *kerygma* of the New Testament. This *kerygma* is totally different from a philosophy. The *kerygma* speaks to human existence, but it does not speak out of human existence. It is the proclamation of God's word addressed to man in his saving acts in Jesus Christ. 'The event of Christ', says Bultmann, 'is of a wholly different order from the cult-myths of Greek or Hellenistic religion'.[2] So the gospel record is not after all just the mythical presentation of a possibility of human existence. It refers to 'a concrete figure of history—Jesus of Nazareth', even if it customarily uses the language of myth to interpret his person and work. That concrete figure of history fulfilled a possibility of existence—he 'became obedient unto death, even death on a cross'.[3] Indeed, unless we were assured that someone had in actual fact fulfilled that possibility of existence which existential interpretation derives from the New Testament, how could we regard it as a genuine possibility for ourselves? It is of the nature of myth to soar into the regions of the fanciful and the extravagant. If a myth is to embody a possibility of human existence, and that possibility is to lie within the horizons of what is genuinely possible, then there must be some point of contact between the myth and actual historical existence. R. G. Collingwood, for whose work Bultmann has considerable admiration, put the point very forcibly in one of his earlier books. If Christ were a purely mythical figure, he maintained, then it would be as foolish to recommend his way of life to men as it would be to urge an athlete to emulate the feats of Herakles.[4] So too when Bultmann speaks of making Christ's cross our own or of a dying and rising with Christ, we can have confidence that he is speaking of genuine existential possibilities

---

[1] *Kerygma and Myth*, p. 23. [2] Ibid., p. 34. [3] Phil. 2.8.
[4] *Religion and Philosophy* (Macmillan, London, 1916), p. 53.

only if these belong to history as well as to myth. Bultmann is recognizing this when he differentiates between the event of Christ and those events which form the themes of Hellenistic myths. For him there is history as well as myth in the New Testament. He can speak of 'a transcendent God present and active in history', and it is not without significance that he ended his first and now famous essay on demythologizing with a quotation which is the antithesis to Gnosticism: 'The word became flesh'.[1]

The full range of Bultmann's affirmations will become clearer to us if we consider what he has to say about two constitutive elements of the *kerygma*—grace and revelation. These are terms which belong to theology rather than to philosophy. Admittedly they must be interpreted in relation to human existence, but in so far as they imply an activity of God towards man, their content is never exhausted in terms of existential analysis—that is to say, they resist complete demythologizing.

Grace, according to Bultmann, is an event.[2] More precisely, it is the event of Jesus Christ. It is God's decisive saving act in Christ. As a saving act, it is not merely a past event, but is present wherever the event of Christ is proclaimed in the *kerygma*. But grace is always God's act in Christ, and it is claimed that herein lies a radical difference from philosophy. The existentialist philosopher may speak of an authentic existence and he may describe it in terms which are very suggestive of the New Testament description of the Christian life. Of course, it is always worth remembering that our existentialist philosophers are working within the tradition of Christian culture and that whether it is acknowledged or not, the influence of the event of Christ and its interpretation can hardly fail to make itself felt in some way in their thought. But the important question, as Bultmann himself makes clear,[3] is not whether man's authentic existence is *conceivable* apart from Christ, but whether it is *realizable*. To the philosopher who brings forward a blueprint for an authentic existence, it might be replied in the famous words of Saint Anselm: 'You

---

[1] *Kerygma and Myth*, p. 44.
[2] *Theologie des Neuen Testaments* (J. C. B. Mohr, Tübingen, 1953), pp. 283ff (Trans. Kendrick Grobel, Vol. I, 1952, Vol. II, 1955).
[3] *Kerygma and Myth*, pp. 26-27.

have not yet considered the exceeding gravity of sin'.[1] The New Testament views man as disabled by sin so that he cannot of himself lay hold on his true life. Only God's gracious act can empower him to do that, and it is this gracious act that the *kerygma* proclaims. Here Bultmann ranges himself quite definitely on the side of the New Testament. Christian theology, he believes, must speak not only of a possibility of existence but also of God's gracious act in Christ which gives that possibility. And when it so speaks, it cannot pass over into philosophy, and a limit is set to demythologizing.

Bultmann's view of revelation is closely parallel to his view of grace. Revelation too is an event, and it is the same event, the saving event of Jesus Christ. Now, however, we are viewing the event in a different aspect. When viewed as grace, it is conceived as bringing to man his authentic existence. When viewed as revelation, it is conceived as giving some kind of understanding or knowledge. What is this understanding? According to Bultmann, it is the understanding of oneself in the new situation which the revelation discloses, and this new self-understanding is not accessible to man except as a gift.[2] Such understanding is attained not by philosophical reflection or analysis but through the encounter with God in Christ. Man misunderstands himself so long as he seeks to be self-sufficient. The true self-understanding comes when he sees himself in his relation to God, and it is God's saving act in Christ which enables him to do this. So Christian theology must find room for revelation as well as grace, and this indicates once more that for Bultmann theology is not going to be swallowed up in a philosophy of existence, and that there is a limit to demythologizing.

Bultmann strongly disparages the idea of a natural theology. Speaking of the revelation of God in nature and history, he says that its significance is this—'it constantly refers us to the revelation of the forgiving grace of God in Christ; it is only in doing this that it is revelation for us, and this means that, apart from Christ, it is not revelation for us'.[3] Yet at the same time he does not think of an absolute opposition between grace

---

[1] *Cur Deus Homo?*, I, 21.

[2] *Der Begriff der Offenbarung im Neuen Testament* (J. C. B. Mohr, Tübingen, 1929), p. 7.

[3] 'The Question of Natural Revelation' in *Essays*, trans. J. C. G. Greig (SCM Press, London, 1955), p. 118.

and man's natural aspiration towards his true life, or between revelation and man's natural self-understanding. The gift of grace can be appropriated only on the ground of an existential possibility, and the gift of revelation can be understood only on the ground of what he calls a pre-understanding (*Vorverständnis*). In both cases, however, the decisive importance belongs to God's saving act, for it is this alone which enables the latent potentialities to become realizable in men rendered powerless by sin.

Kerygma, grace, revelation; a word of God addressed to us, the decisive event of Jesus Christ, the saving act of God in Christ—these topics which we have just surveyed do not seem easy to reconcile with that radical demythologizing at which we looked at an earlier stage, yet they are just as essential to Bultmann's thought. He seems to speak with two voices. Sometimes one voice predominates, sometimes the other. At one time he seems to be moving inevitably in the direction of equating the New Testament teaching with a philosophy of man's existence, at another time he is strongly affirming the supreme importance of God's dealings with men in Christ. Our problem has become sharper even if we are no nearer to finding a solution for it.

4 *Paradox in Theology*

Hitherto we have spoken of a paradox in Bultmann's thought rather than of an inconsistency. By so speaking we have tried to avoid any prejudging of the question. If theology claims to be a genuine field of study worthy of respect, it cannot tolerate downright inconsistencies in its assertions. But it may well involve us in paradoxes. A paradox is usually defined as 'an apparent contradiction'. The appearance of contradiction arises because in a paradox we are trying to hold together two sides of a truth though we may understand only imperfectly how these two sides can be reconciled. The presence of paradox may well be a healthy sign in theology.

The word 'paradox' has become something of a favourite among contemporary theologians, and some of them use it in more or less specialized senses. We should therefore perhaps inform the reader that in this book it is being used only in its most general sense. We take it to mean any mode of expression which, on first sight, appears to involve self-contradiction, but which, on a closer examination, may turn out to be a legitimate way of expressing a complicated truth.

The late Professor D. M. Baillie has made some wise remarks on this subject.[1] Paradox, he maintains, is inevitable in all theology, because when we are theologizing we are seeking to conceptualize the living religious experience, and we can do so only by breaking it up and distorting it. It is as if we were transposing it into a different dimension, and he offers the very enlightening illustration of drawing a map of the world, which involves the projection of a curved surface on to a flat surface. This cannot be done without exaggerating some regions at the expense of others. Yet we must make maps, and we can avoid being misled by having two maps, each in a different projection. The two maps seem to contradict one another, yet in reality they correct one another and when taken together enable us to get a true picture. Just as we must make maps, so we must theologize (or at least, some people hold that we must). But this means that we must run into paradoxes. A theology without paradox would be suspect. The presence of paradox need not distress us if we bear in mind how it arises.

We are not, however, putting forward an apology for the unrestrained use of paradox or opening the door to a flood of unexplained inconsistencies. There are, it would appear, two wrong attitudes which may be taken up on this whole subject. On the one hand, we find some writers who are tempted to glory in paradox, so to speak. They rejoice in self-contradiction and seeming absurdity, and go out of their way to stress oppositions in their thought. The example which comes most readily to mind is that of Søren Kierkegaard with his contention that 'humanly speaking, the knight of faith is crazy, and cannot make himself intelligible to anyone'.[2] Doubtless Kierkegaard's paradoxes served a very useful purpose in their day as a protest against excessive rationalism in theology, but they are sometimes confusing and even irritating to the reader who rightly expects that the business of theology is to clarify rather than to mystify. It is not enough just to present the paradox and leave it. On the other hand, some writers are tempted to make the

---

[1] *God Was In Christ* (Faber & Faber, London, 1948), pp. 106ff.

[2] *Fear and Trembling*, trans. Walter Lowrie (Princeton University Press, Princeton, 1947), p. 115.

paradoxes of theology vanish altogether. But what happens in their case is that they generally ignore one side of the truth which they seek to express and exaggerate the other, with the result that they produce an unbalanced picture. That was the error of those whom Kierkegaard criticized—they had made Christianity something inoffensive but in doing so they had drifted away from the existential reality. In dealing with the paradox in Bultmann, we must try to avoid both of these ways, for in the first case we are offered an unintelligible picture and in the second case a distorted one.

Fortunately, however, we are not compelled to follow either of the ways described. There is a third possibility which we may call the vindicating of the paradox. Such a procedure would neither leave us with a blank unexplained opposition nor explain the opposition away by suppressing one side in the interests of consistency but would show how the opposition has its right. After all, paradoxes are encountered in other fields besides theology. The experts tell us that the modern physicist meets with a paradox when he deals with elementary units such as electrons. He finds that the electron has a dual character, so that he has to think of it as having both the nature of a particle and that of a wave. The physicist does not rest content with this apparently contradictory result, nor does he attempt to evade it by ignoring one set of findings in preference for another. Instead, he labours patiently to show how this paradoxical state of affairs can be so. He may give up the idea that we can ever picture the electron, but he will not give up the attempt to make the concept as intelligible as possible. The theologian must work in the same patient way with the paradoxes which arise in the course of his investigations. To vindicate a paradox means that he will have to show that both sides of it correspond to genuine elements in that living experience which theology seeks to conceptualize, and further that the two sides are not in flat contradiction to each other but rather constitute a polarity of opposites within a whole.

This is the end which we must keep in view in our approach to the paradox which arises in Bultmann's thought out of the limit set by him to demythologizing. It is not really surprising to find such a paradox in Bultmann when we recall what his theological development has been. When his name first became

known outside of Germany, it was as an adherent of the new
theological movement which was carrying out a revolt against
the liberal tradition in theology. Thus in introducing him
to the English-speaking theological public, the translators
of one of his early works described him as belonging 'to the
group often called "crisis theologians" who have worked in the
spirit of Barth'.[1] And although in the years which followed, his
path has diverged from that of Barth, the *kerygma* of the New
Testament has continued to have a central place in Bultmann's
thought. All his theological work has been closely tied to the
New Testament and there can be few if any scholars who have
a more exact and detailed knowledge of its teaching and background. Moreover, in this age of specialization, Bultmann has
kept himself abreast of some of the contemporary developments
in philosophy—a thing which scarcely any New Testament
scholars have succeeded in doing. With his background of
kerygmatic theology and New Testament studies as well as
philosophy, it is a misconception to look upon Bultmann as a
theologian on the extreme left wing. He objects to the older
liberal theologians precisely on the ground that although they
took the myth out of the New Testament, they took the
kerygma out of it at the same time.[2] It is nearer the truth to see
Bultmann in the middle of the road and to understand his
theology as an attempted synthesis of what is best in both
liberalism and kerygmatic theology. But to be in the middle of
the road means that one is able to get a more comprehensive
and balanced view than those who have veered out on one side
or the other. And to get this more comprehensive view on either
side leads in turn to paradox. The paradoxes in Bultmann have
drawn upon him attacks from both right and left, and he may
very well derive some satisfaction from this fact, for it would
seem to show that he cannot be very far off centre.

5 *Conflict among the Critics*

The misconception of Bultmann as a theologian of the
extreme left has been due to the fact that in the controversies
which have gone on round his theological work the emphasis
has been very largely on demythologizing, and we have heard
relatively little of the place of the *kerygma* in his thought.

[1] *Jesus and the Word*, Translators' Preface, p. v.   [2] *Kerygma and Myth*, p. 13.

Amid the storm of protests that has been raised against demythologizing, we are liable not to pay attention to the voices which have been raised well to the left of Bultmann, protesting against the place which he gives to the *kerygma* and suggesting that his demythologizing does not go nearly far enough. As we have pointed out, Bultmann is caught in a cross-fire from critics of both right and left.

In the course of the criticisms which have been made, Bultmann has been charged with many grievous errors. But the total result is bewildering in the extreme, not only because one set of critics regards as a virtue what the other set abhors as a vice, but also because it frequently happens that contradictory charges are made against Bultmann and he could not possibly be guilty on both counts at once. Since we shall be dealing with the critics in more detail at a later stage, we make here only a summary mention of some of the most noticeable conflicts between them. On the right, Helmut Thielicke, who attaches great importance to the character of once-for-all-ness in the Christ event, accuses Bultmann of *abandoning* this character; but on the left Fritz Buri, who thinks it is time that the Church forgot about once-for-all-ness, lays at Bultmann's door the precisely opposite charge of *retaining* this character. Again on the right, Karl Adam, who disapproves of radical theologians, accuses Bultmann of carrying the line of *liberal* theology to its very end; but here on the left Karl Jaspers, who equally disapproves of orthodox theologians, maintains that Bultmann is a most *illiberal* thinker. Emil Brunner comes to the curious conclusion that Bultmann's demythologizing *depersonalizes* the Christian gospel and he regards this as a strong argument against demythologizing; but H. P. Owen more plausibly maintains that Bultmann exaggerates the place of *personal encounter* to the exclusion of any other way of apprehending the gospel.

These instances are sufficient to illustrate the conflict among the critics. It might seem that the only point which is immediately clear is that they cannot all be right. Yet they could all be right if Bultmann has in fact put forward contradictory theses. To some extent, the confusion among the critics is a reflection of the paradox in Bultmann's own thought. Why should there be such confusion among them? Bultmann is often inclined to plead misunderstanding, but such careful scholars as those whom we have mentioned do not readily misunderstand what they read. The cause of the confusion must be attributed in part at least to a certain ambiguity and lack of lucidity in Bultmann himself. He speaks, as we have seen, with two voices, and he has not adequately shown how their seemingly diverse utterances are to be reconciled.

Karl Barth no doubt had his tongue in his cheek when he subtitled his little book on Bultmann 'an attempt to understand him'; for he says at the beginning: 'No living theological writer known to me speaks so much of understanding (as Bultmann does), and none seems to have so much occasion to complain that he himself gets misunderstood.'[1] Critics so diverse as L. Malevez and Fritz Buri likewise complain of a fundamental lack of clarity.

Bultmann may not indeed be so obscure as some of his critics make him out to be, yet it is true that he leaves us with many unresolved problems, and it is for the most part left to the reader to work out as best he can how the two sides in Bultmann's thinking are to be held together. It is only fair, however, to begin by assuming that Bultmann has good reasons for taking up his paradoxical position. It is not likely to be due just to logical inconsistency in one whose thinking is normally consistent. It is not likely to be due to squeamishness in face of the consequences of an unlimited demythologizing, as if he took fright when he saw where he was going. After all, Bultmann has shown himself ruthless enough in other matters, and it is not likely that he would have been deterred from following his method to the bitter end, had he thought that to be the proper course. He has reasons for adhering to the *kerygma* and setting the limit to demythologizing. We must try to elicit these reasons, and then see how far the paradox in Bultmann is capable of being vindicated.

Our brief glance at the critics suggests a method whereby we may seek to carry out our task. We shall begin by considering the criticisms of Bultmann which come from the right, in relation to a number of definite topics, and see how far Bultmann can stand up to them. Then in similar fashion we shall

[1] *Rudolf Bultmann—ein Versuch ihn zu Verstehen* (Evangelischer Verlag, Zürich, 1952), p. 3.

explore those criticisms which stem from the left. We may hope that by the time we have reached the end of this dialectical procedure, the paradox in Bultmann will have been sufficiently clarified to enable us to determine whether or not it can be vindicated.

The specific questions which we shall have to ask are, on the one side: How far is demythologizing a legitimate approach to the New Testament (Chapter II)? How far does demythologizing do justice to the historical element in Christianity (Chapter III)? What are the implications of demythologizing for Christian doctrine (Chapter IV)? And on the other side: Is demythologizing compatible with a *kerygma* (Chapter V)? Does demythologizing make any contribution towards a *rapprochement* between theology and philosophy (Chapter VI)? Does demythologizing contribute anything towards the problem of religious language (Chapter VII)? If we can get some light on any or all of these questions, we may be in a better position to return to the problem from which we have set out.

II

DEMYTHOLOGIZING AND EXEGESIS

6 *The Nature of Interpretation*

THE twentieth century has seen a remarkable change come over the work undertaken by the Christian apologist. Formerly he set out to demonstrate the *truth* of Christianity, and put forward arguments in support of Christian beliefs. Today his primary concern is to elucidate the *meaning* of Christianity, and to explore the nature of religious belief. This change of emphasis is to be welcomed, for the question of meaning is, of course, logically prior to the question of truth and has been too long neglected. The change has come about not simply because of the challenge of the logical positivists who claimed that statements about God are meaningless. More important than the influence of any particular philosophy in driving the apologist to consider the question of meaning has been the increasing remoteness of Christianity from the thinking of the ordinary man of today. The Christian religion is not so much rejected as merely disregarded. It does not seem to say anything which has meaning or relevance for contemporary life. Demythologizing represents one of the ways in which the Christian apologist seeks to respond to this situation. Bultmann's basic problem is one of translation. He is trying to elucidate the meaning of Christian teaching—especially the teaching of the New Testament—and to express that meaning in a way which will be intelligible today.

Demythologizing is therefore primarily concerned with the problems of interpretation and exegesis. This is well understood by such critics of Bultmann as Barth and Thielicke who, while attacking him for his views on history, on christology, and on various other topics, trace back all his alleged errors to what they regard as a mistaken method of exegesis. Bultmann himself

c

declares: 'Demythologizing is a hermeneutic method of interpretation and exegesis.'[1]

Anyone who sets himself up as an interpreter is of course
exposed to many dangers and temptations. Apart from the
difficulties which he may have in arriving at the meaning of the
text, he has to guard against reading into it what he would like
to find there. In ancient pseudepigrapha, it was a recognized
practice for authors to borrow authority for their writings by
attaching them to the names of famous personages. That
practice has long ceased, but nowadays we sometimes find a
writer in all innocence setting forth his own views in the course
of an alleged interpretation of a standard text. About John
Henry Newman's scholarly editions of the works of Saint
Athanasius, published last century, another great patrologist,
Archibald Robertson, remarked: 'The modern reader sits
down to study Saint Athanasius, and rises from his task filled
with Newman.' Some people think that the reader of today who
sits down to study the New Testament under the guidance of
Bultmann gets up filled with existentialist philosophizings.
We have to ask therefore whether Bultmann is really doing
what he professes to do. Does his method of exegesis set forth
the meaning of the New Testament, and can it withstand the
criticisms which have been made of it?

The ambiguities and obscurities of language are such that
scarcely anything can be said which does not need some kind
of interpretation if we are to be sure of what is meant. Legis-
lators know the difficulty of drawing up a law which shall have
no loopholes. Even a simple public notice like 'Halt at major
road ahead' may call for interpretation. When such notices
first appeared on our highways, a motorist charged with failing
to stop pleaded that 'to halt' means 'to proceed hesitantly or
limpingly'. When a statesman is reported as having made a rash
utterance, he can usually avoid the consequences by saying
that he was quoted out of context or that his meaning was
misunderstood. Thus even in our ordinary everyday language
we are constantly coming up against the need for interpretation
and for the more precise fixing of meanings.

In the case of a document like the Bible the need for interpretation is very much greater. We are separated by many

---

[1] *Jesus Christ and Mythology* (SCM Press, London, 1960; New York, 1958), p. 45.

centuries from the time when even the latest books of the Bible were composed. In many cases we cannot be exactly sure of what the authors wrote, and even when we can be reasonably sure of that, their language is not our language and many of their ideas are not our ideas. It is small wonder that many people today sit down to read the Bible and find that they can make very little of it. Like the Ethiopian struggling with the Hebrew prophet, they need help in the way of interpretation. Even those who maintain the verbal inerrancy of the Holy Scriptures presumably acknowledge that their meaning is not always obvious.

What is the function of interpretation in general? It is clear that there are at least two tasks which it must perform. The first is to grasp adequately the meaning of the text which is to be interpreted. The second is to convey that meaning intelligibly to those who are asking for the interpretation. The interpreter has a mediating function, and if he is to do his work properly, he must pay attention to both sides of his function. If someone is at a conference where the proceedings are in a language with which he is unacquainted, he will not be much helped by having at his side an interpreter who understands perfectly what is going on but who is unable to put it clearly into the visitor's own language. Similarly biblical scholarship is only one of the requisites for an interpretation of the Bible. However important such scholarship may be, it needs to be supplemented by an ability to discourse in the language of those to whom the interpretation is offered. Otherwise the whole enterprise is stultified.

If this statement of the function of interpretation is in any way correct, then we may immediately dispose of one of the criticisms which Barth directs against Bultmann. Barth asks: 'To whom is the exegete responsible? To the presuppositions of the thought of himself and his contemporaries, to a canon of understanding formed by these; or to the statements of the text which are to be understood, to the canon yielded by the spirit, content and intention of the text itself?'[1] One implication of this question is presumably that Bultmann makes himself responsible to the presuppositions of modern thought rather than to the statements of the New Testament. But another more

[1] *Ein Versuch*, p. 31.

important implication contained in the question is that the exegete is faced with a choice. It is suggested that *either* he must make himself responsible to the outlook of those to whom his interpretation is addressed *or* he must make himself responsible to the outlook of the text which is being interpreted. But this is not the case. We have contended that a genuine interpretation has a responsibility to *both sides at once*. This contention, of course, proceeds on the assumption that the text in question has something meaningful to say to us, and that the investigation into its meaning is not just a matter of antiquarian interest. But obviously Barth and Bultmann both agree that the Bible still has something to say which is relevant to us. It may indeed turn out that Bultmann has exaggerated his responsibility to his contemporaries at the expense of his responsibility to the New Testament—this will be a question for further discussion. For the present, however, it is enough to have shown that Barth's rhetorical question is a thoroughly misleading one and that the interpreter is responsible both to his text and to those for whom the interpretation is being provided.

We have noted that Barth and Bultmann are agreed that the biblical text has something to say to us today. They would both agree that exegesis is much more than a matter of historical and philological research, however important that may be. Barth is willing to concede that at least to some extent Bultmann is, like himself, oriented towards Reformation theology and its biblical emphasis.[1] As is well-known, Reformed exegesis had a threefold schema—*explicatio, meditatio, applicatio*. About the *explicatio* and the *applicatio* we shall have little to say, not because they are unimportant but because the chief theological interest lies in the intervening step, the *meditatio*. The *explicatio* has to do with that historical and philological research of which we spoke, and is vital if one is to have a responsible and intelligent relation to the text. The *applicatio* has to do with putting into practice in our situation the teaching of the text, and is equally vital if religion is to make a difference in life. But what is the *meditatio*, this hidden process at the heart of interpretation whereby the ancient text can become something meaningful on which someone can act here and now?

[1] Op. cit., p. 9.

It might of course be replied that this hidden process is indeed a mystery, and it is to be attributed to the 'inward testimony of the Holy Spirit' of which the Reformers spoke also. If we recall some of the illustrations of existential interpretation given in the first chapter—Saint Antony, Albert Schweitzer—then it might seem that the understanding of the text just 'comes to' people without any conscious inquiry or effort to understand on their part. The understanding which they gain seems to have a gift-like character, and this gift is conferred by the Holy Spirit.

This account of the matter, however, is scarcely adequate, and raises some serious difficulties. Why does understanding 'come to' some and not to others? We are driven to a doctrine of election and reprobation and must conclude that 'he has mercy upon whomever he wills, and he hardens the heart of whomever he wills'.[1] Understanding or the lack of it becomes an arbitrary matter. From our point of view we cannot say whether it is predestination or just chance, and in either case our responsibility in the matter is destroyed. Moreover, we have to remember that experiences of the kind which we have in mind can be given an alternative and very plausible explanation in terms of psychology without any reference to the supernatural operation of the Holy Spirit. It can be argued that understanding 'comes to' people in certain situations because their minds have already been preoccupied, perhaps at subconscious levels, with questions to which the words now heard or read supply an answer. They may be well acquainted with the words, but they never understood them in this way before. The suddenness with which the understanding comes makes them attribute it to an agency outside of themselves, but it may be just the result of their own concealed mental processes.

There is truth in the doctrine of the inward testimony of the Holy Spirit, and later we shall consider what that truth is. Our present criticism of the doctrine has been designed to show merely that we cannot invoke it in order to relieve ourselves of investigating the problem of right interpretation of the Bible. If we recall another of our illustrations, that of the Ethiopian, we shall remember that understanding of the text

[1] Rom. 9.18.

did not just 'come to' him. He needed guidance, and it was the
task of the Church, represented by Saint Philip, to supply that
guidance and to help elucidate the meaning for him. Even if
the understanding of the biblical message is always ultimately
of the nature of a *gift*, because it is the understanding of a
kerygma, interpretation is a *task* for the Church, whereby the
kerygma is set free and made accessible to understanding. Like
every other task, this one needs to be conducted on orderly
lines with sound guiding principles. The *meditatio* is not just a
matter of waiting for understanding to dawn and trusting that
it is the work of the Holy Spirit. It is a question of working out
hermeneutical principles which shall have regard to the two
conditions essential to any genuine interpretation—responsibility towards the text, and responsibility towards those for
whom the interpretation is being provided.

Bultmann has set forth his own views on hermeneutics at
considerable length.[1] If his exegesis is as perverse as some of his
opponents make out, the reason cannot be that he has neglected
to give serious thought to the subject. We do not propose to go
into all the details of Bultmann's treatment, but select three
important topics for discussion. The first topic (Section 7)
concerns the right formulation of the questions which we ask of
the text. Bultmann believes that before we bring forward any
answers, we must make sure that we have put our questions
properly. The second topic (Section 8) is that of the pre-understanding of the subject-matter of the text. Bultmann believes
that we must have such a pre-understanding if an interpretation
is to be possible. The third topic (Section 9) is the question of
existentialism and exegesis. Bultmann believes that philosophy
precedes exegesis and that the philosophy which best serves the
exegete is the philosophy of existence. If we consider each of
these topics in turn, along with the objections which have been
made to Bultmann's point of view, we should be in a position to
evaluate demythologizing as a method of exegesis.

7 *In Search of the Right Question*

It need hardly be said that many of the perplexities which
people have with the Bible arise from the fact that they are
asking the wrong questions. Much of the controversy between

[1] 'The Problem of Hermeneutics' in *Essays*, pp. 234ff.

scientists and theologians in the nineteenth century provides a lamentable illustration of this. It was supposed on both sides that the Bible might be expected to answer questions about the beginnings of the universe, the origins of man, and so on; and the answers which the Bible yielded to such questions were either upheld in the face of science, or condemned in the name of science, or else an attempt was made to harmonize them with scientific findings. Nowadays it is generally recognized that factual questions such as these lie wholly in the province of the sciences, and that the Bible supplies us with no information of the kind required. Yet the habit of asking factual questions of the Bible dies hard. We read a miracle story, and we ask, 'Did this really happen?' The question itself may be perfectly legitimate. But we may have to ask whether such a question can ever elicit the genuine meaning of the text. Any question carries with it certain presuppositions, and what is presupposed in the kind of questions which we have mentioned is that the Bible consists of statements of fact. No doubt the Bible does contain statements of fact, and there may be occasions when we wish to inquire about these facts. But surely the general intention of the Bible is not just to inform its readers of certain facts. It is an altogether different kind of book from, let us say, *Whitaker's Almanack.* To make sure that we ask the right questions is simply to fulfil that responsibility to the text which, as Barth reminded us and as we agreed, is one essential element in a genuine interpretation. We are bound to distort the meaning of a document or even to make it appear meaningless if we ask of it questions which it was not intended to answer.

But how are we to know the right question? Would we not first have to know with what intention the author wrote? And if he omitted to tell us his intention, could we have any confidence in saying what it was? Our questions may be carried further still. Was the writer always clear in his own mind about what he intended to say? Is there any consistent intention running through what he wrote, or may he not at one point intend to convey information on a point of fact, at another to communicate his reflections on the fact, at yet another to commend a course of action, and so on? At the best, it would seem that we could assure ourselves only of the *general* intention underlying any particular text.

A further complication arises when we remember the importance which has been shown by modern psychology to belong to the unconscious stratum of the human mind. The psychoanalyst will take an ancient legend like that of Oedipus or even a play of Shakespeare, and will proceed to interpret it in terms of the basic instincts and complexes of human nature. Someone may say to him, 'But surely the writer did not intend to convey the meaning which has been elicited by your interpretation!' But the psychoanalyst may reply with some plausibility that although the meaning which his interpretation has brought out was not consciously and explicitly present to the writer, it was latent in his unconscious mind, and the interpretation is therefore a valid one.

Any text provides us with a kind of matrix of meaning and we may place various interpretations upon it. But we would scarcely say that all of these interpretations are on exactly the same level. In each case, the interpretation will be in part determined by the interest of the interpreter, for his questions will be formulated in the light of that interest. But will there not be one case in which there is a correspondence between the interest of the interpreter and that of the writer—the case where the questions asked will be directed towards those matters with which it was the general intention of the writer to deal?

Let us suppose, for instance, that a number of persons are studying the writings of Jeremiah. One is a scientific historian, and he wishes to reconstruct a picture of social life in Judah at the beginning of the sixth century B.C. He will interpret the writings as historical documents, and will be specially interested in passages such as the prophet's graphic description of city life.[1] Another is a psychologist, and he wishes to find out what kind of person Jeremiah was. Here again the text lends itself to his purposes, for the prophet gives us many intimate glimpses of his own inward doubts and struggles.[2] Yet another is a person interested in literature, and for him the book is an aesthetic document, and its writer a poet with a very remarkable mastery of words and images.[3] Each of these ways of interpreting the book is valid in its way, for it does provide us incidentally with historical, psychological, and literary material. But it does so

---

[1] Jer. 5.1-5.   [2] E.g., Jer. 20.7-12.   [3] E.g., Jer. 4.23-6.

only incidentally. The writer's general intention is to speak his prophetic word, and we understand him only when our attention is directed to that. What is said here of the writings of Jeremiah is true of the Bible as a whole. Whatever else it may be, the Bible is primarily a religious book. Its general intention is a religious one. We are therefore fulfilling our responsibility to the text when, in seeking to interpret it, we ask religious questions of it.

What then is a religious question? Here a variety of answers might be given. For the present, however, we are interested in the answer which Bultmann gives. He says that 'the question which is appropriate to the Bible is the question about human existence—a question to which I am driven by the question which exercises me in an *existentiell* way, the question of my own existence'.[1] In other words, the question appropriate to the Bible is the existential question, and this gets its status by being derived from the basic *existentiell* question which each one asks about his own existence.

Before we go on to discuss the claim that the appropriate question is the existential one, a proviso should be entered at this point. It is that the existential question may not *always* be appropriate—and probably Bultmann would agree with this, though he does not explicitly say so. We have spoken of the *general* intention of the Biblical writers, and any particular kind of question can be only *generally* appropriate. To hold that the religious question (whether or not this is to be identified with the existential question) is always appropriate would be to maintain that the Bible is through and through a religious book and that the intention of its writers was consistently and unfailingly religious. This might be maintained by someone who held to a doctrine of plenary verbal inspiration. But it would be held in theory only, for there is no one who in practice does not regard some parts of the Bible as superior in value to others. The religious or existential question will not therefore be appropriate to those parts of the Bible which have no religious or existential truth to offer.

This proviso might seem unnecessary, were it not for the fact that in recent years there has been a recrudescence of the

1 'Zum Problem der Entmythologisierung' in *Kerygma und Mythos*, II (Evangelischer Verlag, Hamburg, 1952), p. 191.

idea that more or less profound theological meanings can be drawn even from the most unpromising parts of the Bible. It is well-known that when the fathers of the Church came upon an unedifying story in the Bible, they frequently exercised extraordinary ingenuity in giving to it a spiritual or theological interpretation. There is for instance a sordid story about the drunkenness of Noah.[1] Saint Augustine says: 'The planting of the vine by Noah, and his intoxication by its fruit, and his nakedness while he slept, and the other things done at that time, and recorded, are all of them pregnant with prophetic meanings, and veiled in mysteries.'[2] In another place, he tells us what these hidden meanings are: 'The sufferings of Christ from his own nation are evidently denoted by Noah's being drunk with the wine of the vineyard he planted, and his being uncovered in his tent. For the mortality of Christ's flesh was uncovered, to the Jews a stumbling-block, and to the Greeks foolishness; but to them that are called, both Jews and Greeks, both Shem and Japhet, the power of God and the wisdom of God. . . .'[3] Such allegorical interpretation is deficient in responsibility to the text. It goes on the assumption that every part of the Bible must be capable of yielding religious truth. It seems clear, however, that in the case of the passage chosen as an example, the intention of the writer was to cast a slur on the descendants of Ham, and this could hardly be called a religious intention even if it seemed such to an early Israelite. We must always remember that *meditatio* is preceded by *explicatio*—that a sound interpretation has regard to that critical work whereby a passage is placed in its historical context. Thus in claiming that the interpreter should address religious questions to the Bible we are not saying that he will always be in a position to do so, still less are we saying that recondite religious meaning should be read into every part of the Bible. We are merely saying that in general this will be the proper approach if we are to elicit the meaning of the Bible as primarily a religious book.

What we have called the religious question appears in Bultmann as the existential question. Can these two be identified? At first sight it might seem that the religious question would ask about God and angels and the beyond rather than

[1] Gen. 9.20-7.   [2] *Civitas Dei*, XVI, 2.   [3] *Contra Faustum*, XII, 23.

about human existence. But the religious question about God—as distinct, let us say, from the metaphysical question about God—is always the question of God in relation to the questioner's own existence. In his most recent book, Bultmann makes an assertion which is at first sight startling: 'The question of God and the question of myself are identical'. He explains this as meaning that 'man's life is moved by the search for God because it is always moved, consciously or unconsciously, by the question about his own personal existence'.[1] Bultmann's stark assertion, which might be misleading if taken in isolation, is seen in the light of its context to be a warning against a false antithesis. We are not compelled to make a disjunction, and to say that the religious question is *either* a question about God and the supersensible *or* a question about man. In religion God and man are together. The Bible tells us of God in his dealings with man and of man in his relation to God. Does not the very word 'religion', according to one view of its etymology, denote this 'bond' or 'relationship' between man and deity?[2] If religion always involves human existence, then a religious question must be at least in part an existential question. And since it would seem reasonable to approach any question from the side which is most accessible to us—in this case, our own existence—then a good case can be made out for the primacy of the existential question in our approach to the Bible or to any other religious document. We are not prejudging whether the existential question may need to be supplemented by other questions—such as factual questions or metaphysical questions—for an adequate interpretation of the religious content of the Bible. It is enough to claim that the existential question affords a legitimate starting-point, and to acknowledge that like any other principle of interpretation, it may have to be modified in the light of what it elicits.

We have maintained that Bultmann's insistence on the proper formulation of the question safeguards responsibility to the text—we do not ask inappropriate questions which would distort the meaning of the text. (This of course does not absolve us from asking *awkward* questions or running away from

---

[1] *Jesus Christ and Mythology*, p. 53.

[2] It is uncertain whether the word 'religion' is derived from *religare*, 'to bind', or from *relegere*, 'to gather up', 'to ponder over'.

difficulties.) But some of Bultmann's critics have maintained that it is precisely his way of formulating the question which distorts the whole biblical message. Thielicke writes: 'Bultmann does not reckon seriously with the possibility that the biblical text examines *me*; or, better expressed, that it throws all my orderly formulations of the question on to the dust-heap, and teaches me the right question—the counter-question of Jesus in the New Testament'.[1] Thielicke obviously has a point here. One could imagine a formulation of the question which would in advance put the text in a strait-jacket, so to speak, and allow it to say nothing except what we had already laid down for it to say. But it is not clear that his point touches Bultmann. The way of formulating the question which Bultmann suggests is surely broad enough to give the text plenty of scope—it offers the whole field of human existence! And it may well be that what the question elicits from the text will be not an answer in terms of human existence but a counter-question which points beyond existence. But could even such a counter-question be elicited without addressing the appropriate question to the text in the first place? We soon find Thielicke going on to concede: 'I cannot indeed get away from this examination of the text, because otherwise I renounce every hermeneutic criterion and am then in danger of being given over to a rigid doctrine of verbal inspiration. Such a doctrine would compel me to acccept everything in a lump as *verbum Dei*, as *kerygma*, for no other reason than that it "stands there" . . . It is indeed necessary to have certain critical principles of understanding'. He goes on to say that these principles are to be gathered from the text itself. But surely this is exactly what we do when we formulate the question *with regard to* the intention of the text. And surely also this procedure guards us against taking 'everything in a lump', as our illustration about the drunkenness of Noah has shown. Thielicke points out real dangers but he does not establish that Bultmann has fallen into them.

Barth's complaint is that Bultmann seems to know the answers before he begins on the New Testament.[2] Certainly one could scarcely formulate questions appropriate to any

---

[1] 'Reflections on Bultmann's Hermeneutic' in *The Expository Times*, LXVII, p. 157.

[2] Op. cit., p. 8.

particular text without having some prior notions about the text. Bultmann however would maintain that the formulation of the question does not prejudge the content of the answers to be elicited from the text but simply opens our eyes to them.[1] Without such a formulation of the question, the text would remain dumb. Yet at the same time he would concede that we do have in advance some understanding of the text. Barth's point deserves the most careful consideration. He once wrote: 'The Bible gives to every man and to every era such answers to their questions as they deserve . . . The question, "What is within the Bible?" has a mortifying way of converting itself into the opposing question, "Well, what are you looking for, and who are you, pray, who make bold to look?" '[2] And Barth rightly warns that it is all too easy to read the Bible with a view to finding confirmation for our own preconceived ideas, perhaps even with a view to representing God as the 'patron saint of our human righteousness, morality, state, civilization or religion'.[3] Is Bultmann, in spite of his disclaimer, really doing something of this sort? Has he really made up his mind on the answers before he begins to interpret the New Testament? These questions bring us to our next topic—that of the pre-understanding which is said to be involved in the interpretation of a text.

8 Pre-understanding

No matter how far we may be in time or in language or in outlook from any text, we could never enter into any understanding of it unless there were at least some minimum of common ground between ourselves and the text. If it is to mean anything to us, there must be some continuity between its subject-matter and what we already understand. If it were entirely 'out of another world' and did not link up at any point with our own experience, we could make nothing of it. Interpretation is made possible by a certain community of interest between the text and the person who is seeking to understand it. He already has certain categories of understanding under

[1] *K.u.M.*, II, p. 191.
[2] *The Word of God and the Word of Man*, translated by Douglas Horton (Hodder & Stoughton, London, 1929), p. 32.
[3] Op. cit., p. 22.

which the meaning of the text can be grasped, and these constitute the pre-understanding which he brings to the text. For
instance, if we read Saint Paul on sin, we can understand him
only if we already have from our own experience some understanding of what sin is. We shall not know in advance what
Saint Paul is going to say about sin, but we shall need some
prior understanding of the subject if we are to grasp what he is
talking about at all. Moreover, Bultmann thinks that the pre-
understanding which is relevant for interpreting the Bible is
the understanding which we have of our own existence. There
may be various senses in which the Bible comes, as it were,
'out of another world'. We may mean by that simply that the
Bible comes out of the ancient world which had an outlook
vastly different from that of the modern world; or we may be
claiming that the Bible contains a divine revelation of matters
not accessible to the this-worldly understanding. But at least
the Bible deals with human or existential situations in which
we can imaginatively participate. Here is the community of
interest which allows a point of entry so that we can come to
grips with the meaning.

Thus stated, the doctrine of a pre-understanding seems
plausible enough. According to Martin Heidegger, all understanding involves interpretation, and such interpretation is
characterized by what he calls the 'as'-structure and the 'pre'-
structure.[1] When confronted with anything, I understand it *as*
something, and in so doing refer it to some area of experience
of which I have a *prior* understanding. If I hear an unusual
noise out on the street, I may understand it *as* a car skidding.
If I see a dim shape by the roadside at night, I may understand
it *as* a bush. It is worth recalling that the New Testament
writers themselves, in seeking to interpret the person of Jesus
Christ, employed categories with which their readers would be
already familiar. Christ is represented *as* the Son of man, *as*
the divine Logos. Confronted with something which they
believed to be quite new or even unique, these writers nevertheless began the question towards understanding the novelty
by tying it in with concepts which they already had. Yet this is
not to say that they laid down in advance how the novelty
must be understood. As the interpretation developed, the

---

[1] *Sein und Zeit*, 6th Edition (Niemeyer, Tübingen, 1949), pp. 148ff.

categories developed as well. 'Son of man' took on a meaning of which the Jewish apocalyptic writers never dreamed, and 'Logos' acquired a signification which it did not have in Hellenistic speculation.

These last points should be borne in mind, for the charge is sometimes made that with Bultmann the pre-understanding acquires a normative status—that is to say, it has already determined just what the text may be allowed to say. Certainly, this is far from Bultmann's intention. The function of the pre-understanding is not normative but ancillary. It elicits the meaning of the text, and is indeed the necessary precondition for eliciting any meaning at all, but as the interpretation develops, the pre-understanding develops too. It could be normative only if it were rigid and immutable, and it is not so.

Here we have spoken of pre-understanding in general, but we must not lose sight of Bultmann's further point that the pre-understanding which is relevant for eliciting the meaning of the Bible is the understanding which we already have of our own existence. It was said that any interpretation has a twofold responsibility—on the one hand to the text, and on the other hand to those for whom the interpretation is being provided. In discussing the problem of formulating the right question, we said that what is involved there is responsibility to the text—we must ask the kind of questions which it is reasonable to believe the text is intended to answer. With pre-understanding, we come up against the other side of the interpreter's responsibility. His interpretation must be directed towards something which is already within the range of experience of those whom he is addressing. Whatever else in the Bible may be foreign to contemporary man, at least he can begin to understand what is being talked about when it is a question of human existence. Contemporary man is very much preoccupied with the meaning of his own existence. In the Western world to-day, are not Christianity's principal rivals, such as communism and humanism, alternative ways of understanding human existence? Christianity gets a new relevance as a genuine alternative to its streamlined rivals when it is presented not as something remote and other-worldly but as a way of understanding human existence itself. Of course,

Christianity speaks of more than merely human existence; but a pre-understanding of human existence is capable of developing into an understanding of human existence in its relation to God. The important point is that the interpreter should begin at the right end, and a good case can be made out that one enters into the understanding of the Bible on the ground of the pre-understanding of one's own existence.

Bultmann's conception of the pre-understanding and of the part which it plays in the interpretation of the Bible has been criticized chiefly by theologians like Barth and Thielicke who are anxious to maintain the unique revelatory character of biblical teaching and who deny that it can be made continuous with man's natural self-understanding. Thus, as Barth sees it, Bultmann identifies Christian existence with 'truly natural' existence. But Barth would question whether it is possible for us even to understand sin until we know what God has done about it.[1] In much the same way, Thielicke thinks that Bultmann is concerned to show 'the seamless join between revelation and natural understanding'.[2] Actually it is by no means clear that Bultmann allows so much to the natural understanding as these statements of Barth and Thielicke might suggest. Thus H.P. Owen takes the view that in Bultmann 'God comes to man in a wholly negative way; he comes to contradict nature, but not to fulfil it'.[3] We have already noted a certain ambiguity in Bultmann's thought[4] in so far as he rejects natural theology yet does not think of an absolute opposition between nature on the one hand and grace or revelation on the other. The natural theology which he rejects, however, seems to be natural theology in the narrow sense of an inference from the world of nature to God. In this matter, he holds that God is *present* in nature but not *revealed*.[5] If we understand natural theology in the wider sense as whatever man may learn about God by his natural understanding, then Bultmann would seem to be prepared to admit that from the understanding which he naturally has of his own existence man can grasp his own finitude and lostness; this gives rise to his quest for God, and in so far as he is seeking God, he already has some idea of God,

[1] *Ein Versuch*, pp. 14-5.   [2] Loc. cit., p. 157.
[3] *Revelation and Existence* (University of Wales Press, Cardiff, 1957), p. 105.
[4] See p. 25, above.
[5] *Marburger Predigten* (J. C. B. Mohr, Tübingen, 1956), p. 28.

however vague it may be. Owen would seem to be right in thinking that the concession which Bultmann makes to nature is a pretty meagre one, but apparently it is too generous for Barth and Thielicke.

These two theologians are rendered acutely unhappy by the thought that the natural self-understanding can serve as an introduction to the message of the Bible. In his earlier writings, Barth constantly comes back to the theme that 'within the Bible there is a strange new world'. We ask, *Qualiter?* and the answer is, *Totaliter aliter!* 'There are no transitions, intermixings or intermediate stages. There is only crisis, finality, new insight.'[1] But if the theme of the Bible is something altogether strange and new beyond the reach of any natural pre-understanding we may have, how can we get any glimmering of it at all? The reply would be that while it may be true that we need some kind of pre-understanding to interpret a secular document, the biblical revelation is peculiar. To understand it, we must 'learn in the school of the Holy Spirit'. Let Thielicke be the spokesman here: 'The final mystery of Bultmann's theology, or rather its final embarrassment . . . is that it possesses no teaching on the Holy Spirit. Only where this doctrine is properly worked out does it become necessary to move nearer to the thought that the Word does not ring a bell in a pre-understanding that is already given, but that the Word in which the Spirit works produces its own hearer, and that thus a new creation takes place.'[2] So once again we are brought to a doctrine of the inward testimony of the Holy Spirit. The 'wholly other' character of the biblical theme is preserved and we are allowed to dispense with the need for any pre-understanding because the Holy Spirit takes the place of such a pre-understanding and so informs the mind of the hearer that he can grasp something which would have been completely inaccessible to his natural understanding.

We have already briefly noted some of the difficulties into which such a doctrine brings us.[3] Now, in our discussion of the pre-understanding, we are in a position to see where these difficulties have come from. The problem is to show how a divine Word can be understood by a human hearer. The theory

---

[1] *The Word of God and the Word of Man*, pp. 33, 91.
[2] Loc. cit., p. 157.   [3] See p. 37, above.

of a pre-understanding proposes to solve the problem by assuming that there is already some affinity between the two so that what we already understand ties in with what the divine Word gives us to understand. Where such affinity is denied, one must suppose that an external agency—the Holy Spirit—takes over the mind of the hearer and in some mysterious way enables or compels him to understand. Obviously what has happened here is that a sharp distinction has been made between the God who addresses us and the Holy Spirit who enables his address to be understood. The Holy Spirit assumes the function of a mysterious *tertium quid*. But is not the Holy Spirit one and the same with God as he addresses us? Is the Holy Spirit not simply God as he comes to men?

The separation of the Holy Spirit from God as he addresses us arises from the confusions introduced by the 'person' language employed in trinitarian discourse. 'Person' comes to be understood as a 'centre of self-consciousness', although in the context of trinitarian language it means no more than a 'mode' or 'relation' of the divine being.[1] Saint Augustine recognized this point clearly when, in his treatise on trinitarian doctrine, he wrote: 'When the question is asked, What three? human language labours altogether under great poverty of speech. The answer, however, is given, Three persons, not that it might be spoken but that it might not be left unspoken.'[2] In a recent discussion of these topics which is distinguished for its clarity and sanity, Cyril C. Richardson would identify the Spirit with the Logos. However that may be, we would agree with him that 'the Spirit is not a "thing" over against God, but a way of expressing God in his relation to us'.[3] The truth in the doctrine of an inward testimony of the Holy Spirit is simply that sometimes we read or hear a word in human language and understand it as God's Word addressed to us. The Holy Spirit is the God who addresses us, not an intermediary between us. If we begin with an absolute discontinuity between God's Word and our natural understanding, then not even an infinite regress of intermediaries will be able to get that Word across to us if our understanding of it is to be anything other than the response of a

---

[1] Not, of course, in the sense of 'successive modes', as in the ancient modalist heresies.
[2] *De Trinitate*, V, 9.
[3] *The Doctrine of the Trinity* (Abingdon Press, New York, 1958), p. 53.

puppet when the appropriate string is pulled. We must begin
by supposing that the understanding which we already have of
our own existence affords a point of entry, however humble, into
the understanding of the divine Word.

In the foregoing discussion, we have considered an extreme
form of the opposition to the use of a pre-understanding in the
interpretation of the Bible, and we specifically cited one of
Barth's early writings. If, however, we look at some of his
later writings, we find that there is at least a slight modification
of his views. In a passage which discusses the function of the
meditatio as the middle step in the threefold scheme of exegesis,[1]
Barth acknowledges that we must make use of secular thought-
forms which we bring to the text. He is prepared to acknowledge
further that the use of such forms can be 'legitimate and fruitful', provided always that they are made subordinate to the
text and that they serve rather than dominate the work of
exegesis.[2] He lays down certain safeguards which ought to be
observed. Some of these offer no special problems. Thus Barth
thinks that the thought-forms which we bring to the text must
always have a tentative character; they must have no independent interest—for instance, they must not be seeking their
own confirmation from the text; and further, there is no one
pre-understanding which can be set up as a norm to which the
text must conform. Although Barth may think that Bultmann
offends against these principles, there is clearly nothing in his
hermeneutic method which compels him to do so.

Another of Barth's safeguards, however, has a more uncompromising character, and this one appears at the top of his
list. When the interpreter brings his own thought-forms to the
text, he must do so consciously, and he must be clear that they
are different in principle from those of the text itself; only the
Holy Spirit can enlighten us about the text. But if there is all
this difference between our human thoughts and those of the
text, if they are 'different in principle', then, if we recall our
earlier discussion, it is hard to see how we could bring our

---

[1] *Die Kirchliche Dogmatik*, I/2 (Evangelischer Verlag, Zürich, 1945), pp. 815-25.

[2] Op. cit., p. 823. The German word for 'meditation' is *Nachdenken*, literally a
'thinking after'. Barth exploits the etymology of this word when he writes that
our thought-forms can be fruitful 'if they are made really serviceable to thinking
after' (*wenn er eben wirklich dem Nach denken dienstbar gemacht wird*). That is to say, the
text itself must always lead the way.

human thought-forms to the text at all, or how they could serve in any way to unfold its meaning. Could the text even *contradict* a human point of view except on the basis of some affinity between them?

Yet even this seemingly intractable difference between Barth and Bultmann may be resoluble on the basis of a still more recent essay of Barth.[1] In discussing what he paradoxically calls the 'humanity' (*Menschlichkeit*) of God, Barth says that although in his early days it was necessary to stress the otherness of God, this was an exaggerated emphasis. We have also to recognize God's humanity. He has a manward side in so far as he relates himself to man. (Is not this just what we mean by the 'Holy Spirit'?) The 'wholly other' and the 'infinite qualitative difference' have been abandoned in their extreme form. But with this concession, the main obstacle in the way of recognizing the function of a pre-understanding in Bultmann's sense is removed.

We are far from suggesting that Barth has gradually come round towards Bultmann's position. So far we have looked at only a few of his criticisms, and he still remains deeply suspicious of Bultmann's whole enterprise. Yet there does seem to have been some narrowing of the gap between the two. In spite of his many uncompromising utterances, Barth has always tried to keep an open mind and to revise his thoughts where necessary. No one did more than he to overthrow the dominant theologies of the nineteenth century, yet in this very connection he tells us that the theologian of today must keep his ear open to the voices of that period for 'there is always the possibility that in some sense or other we may be in particular need of wholly unexpected voices, and that among them there may be voices which are at first wholly unwelcome'.[2] It may be in a similar spirit that he now writes, while expressing certain misgivings, that the value of Bultmann's theological existentialism remains to be seen.[3]

Barth's criticisms are valuable as a warning against excesses to which Bultmann's hermeneutic might lead. But provided that we recognize the dangers—as Bultmann presumably

---

[1] *Die Menschlichkeit Gottes* (Evangelischer Verlag, Zürich, 1957).
[2] *Die protestantische Theologie im neunzehnten Jahrhundert* (Evangelischer Verlag, Zürich, 1947), p. 3.
[3] *Die Menschlichkeit Gottes*, p. 19.

recognizes them also—we can acknowledge that our natural self-understanding functions as a pre-understanding in interpreting the biblical message; for that message treats of human existence, even if only to show us that such existence is rightly understood when it is seen in relation to something beyond itself.

9 *Exegesis and Philosophy*

To complete our survey of the relation of demythologizing to exegesis, we have still one topic to discuss—that of the place of philosophy in exegesis. We have to consider Bultmann's provocative claim that exegesis is in some sense dependent on philosophy—and of course the philosophy which Bultmann has in mind is that of existence.[1] To some extent the present topic has already been dealt with in the two preceding sections, for if it has been shown that the existential formulation of the question is a legitimate one in the approach to the Bible, and if it has been further shown that the understanding which we have of our own existence serves as a pre-understanding in interpreting the Bible, then it would seem to follow that if the interpretation is to be carried out in full consciousness of what it is doing we would need to have the clearest conception of human existence that we can get. It is the business of the philosophy of existence to provide us with such a conception.

Yet as soon as philosophy is dragged into the picture, suspicions are bound to be aroused. Karl Barth, for instance, reminding his readers of the dangers of applying a philosophy in scriptural exegesis, pictures the interpreter who brings with him an independent philosophy as standing over against the Word of God not as a man but as a 'second god', having authority to dispose of the Word of the first God who, therefore, cannot be the true God any more.[2] Barth's language may be rhetorical but his point is sound enough. There is no possibility of getting a fair and unprejudiced interpretation if we go to the text with some rigid preconceived pattern of thought to which it must submit.

Examples of such errors are not far to seek. It may be enough to recall the famous Tübingen school of New Testament critics who had to see in everything the pattern of the Hegelian

[1] *K.u.M.*, II, p. 192.   [2] *Die Kirchliche Dogmatik*, I/2, p. 821.

dialectic—thesis, antithesis, synthesis. Thus Acts is interpreted as a mediating document between a Petrine party and a Pauline party. Even if there was some truth in such speculations, one would never be likely to hear the authentic message of the New Testament if it is approached with such rigid schemata in mind.

It is understandable that Barth should have some fears about the direction in which Bultmann's theology has moved. For thirty years (and largely under Barth's leadership) theology was escaping from what he calls 'an Egyptian bondage in which a philosophy lays down what the Holy Spirit may say'. Now, as it seems to him, Bultmann has initiated a move back to Egypt and there is the danger that a new generation of theologians will find themselves in bondage again.[1]

On a superficial reading, Barth's detailed objections to Bultmann's use of the philosophy of existence are rhetorically impressive, but on closer examination they are found to have very little substance. In fact, they provide some remarkable examples of the fallacy of *ignoratio elenchi*. Barth impressively makes a point which looks as if it had a bearing on the matter in dispute but is really irrelevant.[2] Thus he tells us, 'Heidegger's philosophy has not come down from heaven'. Very true, but no one claims that it has. Barth is the one who deals in divine revelations. Perhaps he means that Bultmann pays excessive deference to Heidegger's philosophy. That may be the case, but we have still to be shown why Bultmann is wrong in doing so— if he does so! 'Heidegger has now passed the anthropological phase'. Again true up to a point—though Heidegger's aim has always been an ontological one, and even if he approached the problem of being from the side of man's existence, he did so in the explicit understanding that human existence itself can be properly understood only in the light of being as a whole. Barth seems to suggest that Bultmann has been left behind by

---

[1] *Ein Versuch*, pp. 52-3.

[2] A further difficulty in assessing Barth's criticisms is that he rarely expresses them directly, but usually puts them in the form of what he calls 'decisive questions'. These questions need to be carefully watched for they sometimes carry with them highly dubious implications—like the famous question with which King Charles II is said to have perplexed the Royal Society: 'Why does a live fish, when placed in a bowl full of water, not cause the water to overflow, whereas a dead fish does?' We met a sample of such a misleading question in Barth back on p. 35.

Heidegger. But for Bultmann the existential question leads into the question of God, and the real point at issue is whether this is a proper approach. 'Existentialism has not touched America and has been left behind in Russia'. Also true, but does this add up to anything so far as Bultmann is concerned? America has been relatively untouched by the radical questions of existentialism because, presumably, it has not known the radical overthrow of established ways which has been experienced on the European continent. The Russia of Dostoevsky has been replaced by that of Lenin and his successors because there was a communist revolution in 1917. If these facts have anything to do with Bultmann at all, they may mean that his presentation of the gospel is not likely to cut much ice in the United States or the Soviet Union. But in itself this is not necessarily a criterion of its worth. 'Schleiermacher and Biedermann tried the same thing (as Bultmann)—and who reads them now?'[1] Here the argument seems to have gone quite bankrupt. Bultmann can hardly complain that he is not read, even if he thinks he is misunderstood. He is probably not worrying whether he will still be read in fifty years time, if he can serve his own generation. But the whole point is that the value of any theology cannot be judged by the extent to which it is read at any given time. Barth has himself reminded us that voices which are silent for a long time may come alive again. What would he say of Kierkegaard, who was neglected for long enough before he began to enjoy his present vogue?

The mention of Schleiermacher and Biedermann is interesting. What these two religious thinkers had in common was their emphasis on self-consciousness. Barth betrays in more than one passage that he thinks Bultmann's emphasis is the same and that theology in his hands becomes a matter of describing man's inner religious life. But this is surely a misreading of existentialism. If one thing is clear in Heidegger, it is that he decisively rejects the thinking subject as the starting-point of philosophy. Existence is always the concrete situation of the self's involvement with the world and with other selves.

All that Bultmann would claim for existentialism is that it provides a conceptual structure which helps towards a clear and intelligible interpretation of the Christian faith for our

[1] These points will be found in *Ein Versuch*, pp. 38-9 and 28.

time. That is the only justification for its use in exegesis. Let an independent New Testament scholar speak. Erich Dinkler says: 'As far as I can see, Heidegger's analysis of human existence more than any other modern philosophy offers structures and defines terms fit for theologically clear speaking.'[1]

There need be nothing either normative or exclusive in such a claim—and indeed, there ought not to be. For instance, many people in the British Isles and the United States might think that Ian T. Ramsey's claim[2] that logical empiricism offers a useful tool for the clarification of theology has as much right to be heard as the claim on behalf of existentialism. Yet Bultmann shows no interest in logical empiricism.

Any approach to theology is limited in its insights and its usefulness, and this holds as much of demythologizing as of any other approach. But it is absurd to attack it for claiming to be normative and absolute if it makes no such claim. Theological movements are rather like the sputniks which are being sent up round the world nowadays. If they survive the hazards of launching, they get into orbit and continue to describe more or less eccentric paths for longer or shorter periods until eventually they burn out. They serve their purpose if they obtain the limited results expected of them, and each one makes a fresh contribution. Demythologizing is certainly not the last word on how the biblical message is to be interpreted today but it is one of the most promising approaches to the problem. It is not subservient to a philosophy, but it rightly recognizes that philosophical analysis is indispensable to theological transparency, and it makes use of such philosophical work as will contribute towards this.[3]

---

[1] 'Martin Heidegger' in *Christianity and the Existentialists*, edited Carl Michalson (Scribners, New York, 1956), p. 120.

[2] See his book, *Religious Language* (SCM Press, London, 1957).

[3] The problems discussed in this chapter are treated in an important book which Professor David Cairns has just completed—*A Gospel Without Myth?* (SCM Press, London, 1960). I am indebted to Professor Cairns for his kindness in permitting me to see the typescript of his book before it went to press. In a courteous criticism of some passages in my book, *An Existentialist Theology*, Professor Cairns concludes that in the matter of philosophy and exegesis, I have fallen into the error of 'taking Heidegger too seriously', though he thinks that I have been saved from the worst consequences of this by giving Heidegger a 'new look' and by bringing Christian apologetic into the existential analysis. Professor Cairns, on the other hand, wishes 'to have the right, on occasion, to snap his fingers at Heidegger's existential analysis, and to secure others in that right also'. There is, of course, sound common-sense in Professor Cairns' contention that the theological student

does not need to master Heidegger before he can start on the New Testament. I hope that I have made it abundantly clear in the present chapter that I would claim that the existential analytic has only a limited usefulness in the problems of biblical exegesis; and I doubt if Bultmann, in spite of some of his more extravagant utterances, would wish to claim more. Professor Cairns himself is 'ready guardedly to accept and apply Heidegger's insights individually'.

There is still, however, considerable disagreement between us. Whereas I have permitted myself to speak of demythologizing as 'one of the most promising approaches' to the interpretation of the Bible today, Professor Cairns describes the opening chapters of his book as 'a sustained attempt to refute' Bultmann's belief that Heidegger's concepts can have the value to theology which is claimed for them. The difference between us may be summed up by saying that whereas we both recognize a limit to demythologizing, Professor Cairns would set the limit much earlier than I would. Perhaps we would disagree further about where the limit comes in Bultmann.

It is among the many merits of Professor Cairns' book that he has pursued his theme into the practical field of preaching, and given critical analyses of sermons preached by Bultmann and his disciple Bartsch. As an appendix to his book, Professor Cairns has provided a translation of a sermon of Bartsch, taken from the collection *Die Anrede Gottes*, mentioned above on p. 18.

Reference may be made here also to a book by the Italian scholar, Giovanni Miegge, Professor in the Waldensian Faculty at Rome. Miegge's work appeared in Italian in 1956, and has now been made available to a wider public in a French translation by Hélène Naef: *L'Évangile et le Mythe dans la Pensée de Rudolf Bultmann* (Delachaux et Niestlé, Neuchâtel, 1958). At the time of writing, an English translation by Bishop Stephen Neill is in preparation (Lutterworth Press, London), and Miegge's book will be a valuable addition to the literature available in English.

Since Miegge—so far as I am aware—was introducing the subject of demythologizing to the Italian theological world, he naturally devotes a good deal of space to exposition and goes over the same ground as is covered in several other books. Miegge's views on the relation of existentialism to exegesis in Bultmann differ considerably from those of Barth and Thielicke. In general, Miegge shows himself more sympathetic towards Bultmann than the two German-speaking theologians mentioned.

Thus Miegge does not think of existentialism merely as an alien mould into which the New Testament teaching must be forced, but recognizes a certain affinity between existentialism and the thought of the New Testament. Further, he takes seriously Bultmann's own declaration that he does not propose to reduce Christianity to a philosophy of existence. In denying that Bultmann's approach must lead to a subjectivizing of the Christian message, Miegge ranges himself with the Jesuit scholar, Father Malevez, who distinguishes 'subjective' and 'objective' demythologizing, and believes that Bultmann's views are most fairly represented as the 'objective' type—see *The Christian Message and Myth*, pp. 67ff. Miegge is willing to acknowledge that by employing the existentialist categories in exegesis, Bultmann arrives at 'fruitful and interesting insights'.

While conceding these points in Bultmann's favour, Miegge makes an interesting observation. He suggests that sometimes in Bultmann it is not existentialism which helps to explain the New Testament message, but rather that it is the other way round: the concrete language of the gospel helps to clarify and give content to the rarefied conceptions of existentialism. If this is so, however, it would seem to be possible only on the basis of some kinship between the two (as Miegge himself recognizes) and we may add that this kind of two-way traffic between the hermeneutical key and the text which is to be opened up is entirely consonant with the views put forward above on pp. 46ff.

III

DEMYTHOLOGIZING AND HISTORY

10 *Christianity and History*

CHRISTIANITY, we often hear, is a historical religion, but precisely what is meant by this assertion is by no means obvious. Any religion is historical in the sense that it can be regarded as a historical phenomenon. It arises, flourishes, decays, revives and perhaps eventually passes away. But this cannot be what is meant when it is said that Christianity is a historical religion, for the adjective is used to point to one of the distinctive characteristics of Christianity, and not to say what it has in common with other religions. Perhaps it is meant that Christianity is founded upon certain historical events and that its life is dependent upon them. This may be true, but it is also the case that Buddhism is founded on the event of Gautama's enlightenment and that Islam dates its rise from Muhammad's flight to Medina. Yet these cases are not strictly parallel. If someone proved to adherents of these three religions that their faiths had originated in very different historical events from what has been traditionally believed, all three might be upset but the Christian would possibly be more upset than the other two. For the teaching of the Noble Eightfold Path and of the Koran might still claim to be valid, whatever their origin, but the peculiarity of the gospel is that it proclaims an event. The revelation is given in an event, and it is even claimed that the historical happenings out of which Christianity originated and which it now proclaims are in some way illuminating for all history.

The difficulty of knowing what is meant by the claim that Christianity is a historical religion points to the fact that the term 'history' is an extremely slippery one. Before we come to questions about the nature of history, we have to make up our minds about the areas of happening to which the name of history may be properly applied, for we find considerable diversity of usage. Most commonly, the term 'history' is used to cover the period for which records are available—at the most, about six thousand years, from the early river civilizations down to the present day. In this sense, history may be contrasted with prehistory, a very much longer period of possibly as much as a million years during which man has been on the earth. The archaeologist may find out something about prehistoric man, but at the best our knowledge of this long period can be only very fragmentary. But then we may find the geologist talking about the history of the rocks, or the astronomer talking about the history of the stars, or we may be told that radiotelescopy is going to throw new light on the history of the universe. The time-scale gets expanded to unimaginable dimensions, but still the word 'history' is used. This usage is, however, unfortunate. We would do better to restrict the word 'history' to that period of time in which man has been active and to use some such word as 'process' for those natural occurrences in which man has no part.

When we speak of a historian, we do in fact think of someone who has studied human affairs in time, not of someone who has studied the evolution of the stars or the formation of the earth's crust. John Macmurray has recently written: 'History is concerned with action, in the sense that the subject-matter of the historian's reflection is the doings of men in the world. Here the distinction between "action" and "process", between "what is done" and "what happens", is of primary significance. What merely happens lies outside the historian's province. He is concerned with natural events and organic processes only in so far as they enter into the activities of human beings and play their part in setting the field for human decisions'.[1] Thus history covers only a limited time. Its beginning is an indefinite ragged edge, so to speak, somewhere in the dim period which we call prehistory. Only in the past few millennia does history assume something like a definite and continuous shape.

The distinctions which have been made have much more than a merely academic value. They touch very closely upon the claims of Christianity as a historical religion. For these

[1] *The Self as Agent* (Faber & Faber, London, 1957), p. 205.

distinctions are all relatively recent discoveries. The biblical
writers did not know that man's recorded history had been
preceded by a very much longer prehistory, and still less
did they conceive that further back lay a vast period of cosmic
process. If they thought of a time before man had appeared on
the scene, then that time was just like another history, but a
mythical, unverifiable history. It was still a period of action in
which the agents were not men but beings analogous to men,
a period, for instance, in which 'war arose in heaven, Michael
and his angels fighting against the dragon'.[1] History, myth
and cosmic process were inextricably mixed up or, to speak
more strictly, they were not yet distinguished. The problem of
sorting them out had not yet arisen. Creation itself could be
reckoned as the first event in world-history for man too was
created at or near the beginning of the world. Then there
follows the familiar pattern of sacred history—the fall, the
flood, the call of Abraham, the destiny of the chosen people, the
event of Jesus Christ, the coming of the Holy Spirit, the life of
the Church, all moving towards the final consummation. On a
view which does not distinguish between history and cosmic
process and which regards these as roughly co-extensive in
time, the belief might be held with some plausibility that sacred
history supplies the clue to the meaning of the whole process.
This sacred history, which is a redemptive history centring in
the event of Jesus Christ, might thus be regarded as a kind of
basic framework which underlies the whole cosmic process and
imparts to it a redemptive character.

Whatever plausibility such a line of thought might have had
in biblical or even in medieval times, it is quite untenable in
the modern world. We now see that the sacred history is only
the merest fragment of human history as a whole. It would
surely be, to say the least of it, a most risky extrapolation if we
were to try to read off from this fragment the pattern of all
history. It is conceivable that we might be willing to take the
risk, and to argue that redemptive history, though only a
fragment, is nevertheless the core of history and can thus be
illuminating for the whole. It is, however, inconceivable that
we should go on from there to argue that it similarly illuminates
the whole cosmic process. For once the distinction between

[1] Rev. 12.7.

history and process has been made, we see that the two may have very little in common beyond the fact that they both take place in time. There is no reason to suppose that the structure of the one is analogous to the structure of the other. Indeed, they might seem at first glance to be entirely different. Thus whereas human history presumably had a beginning—or perhaps it had several beginnings before it got finally established—it may not be the case that the cosmic process ever had a beginning.[1] Again, even if history should appear to some people to be going somewhere and to have a 'straight line' pattern (whether this be interpreted in terms of redemption or of human progress or in some other way) it does not follow that the pattern discerned in history gives any clue to the pattern of the cosmic process. It might well be the case that the universe has produced and will continue to produce countless millions of 'straight line' histories analogous to human history without itself going anywhere or having any 'straight line' character. Its character would rather be cyclical, in so far as it kept on producing the same kind of thing over and over again in endless variations. To attempt to draw ultimate conclusions about God and the universe from a few episodes of the history which has been enacted on this planet would seem to be a most hazardous if not impossible proceeding.

The crux of the matter may be stated thus: the sacred history which the biblical writers were able to take as a frame of reference because they believed it to be co-extensive with all human history and with the cosmic process as a whole is now seen to be an episode of human history which is itself a fleeting episode within the cosmic process. Our understanding of history has been revolutionized since biblical times, and this revolution cannot fail to have profound consequences for the claims involved in the assertion that Christianity is a historical religion. If these claims can still be maintained, then it will be necessary to think out in a radically new way what the relation of Christianity to history is.

[1] The Christian doctrine of creation does not, of course, necessarily imply a beginning of the world in time. This doctrine teaches that the world is dependent on God, that it has a creaturely status, and this is quite compatible with there always having been a world. Whether the universe 'has no seasons' and has always been much as it is now, or whether there is 'continuous creation', or whether everything began with a big bang some billions of years ago, are questions for scientific cosmology, and theology can have nothing to say about them.

The foregoing remarks bring us into conflict with the view of sacred history which has been expounded by Oscar Cullmann[1] and which has rightly received considerable attention. If we regard Cullmann's book simply as an elucidation of the biblical understanding of such concepts as 'time', 'history', and so on, then it is a most valuable work. With great erudition, he works out in detail the kind of picture which we have sketched above. 'The work of Christ is primarily the mid-point of a special happening or process which *extends the length of the time-line*'. Compared with general history, sacred history 'forms a line which, *though not shorter*, is infinitely narrower'. 'Upon the basis of the slender Christ-line of the biblical history' it is claimed to be possible 'to render a *final judgment* even on the facts of general history'. There is a '*cosmic extension* of the historical line'. There is no interest in time as such; the word 'time' is used 'in concrete reference to the redemptive history'. Neither is there any distinction between history and myth, which Cullmann prefers to call 'prophetic history' as distinct from 'verifiable history'.[2] Thus Saint Michael, Adam, Abraham, Christ, Saint Paul are all on the same plane of action. All this is probably an accurate account of the biblical understanding of these matters and gives a general confirmation of our own summary statement of the biblical view of history. But we cannot follow Cullmann any longer when he claims that we must accept this biblical view ourselves. His polemic is mainly directed against Greek views of time, which he thinks have been a corrupting influence in theology, but the pure biblical understanding of time and history is just as incompatible with modern conceptions as with Greek ones. For instance, against the context of biblical ideas which Cullmann sets forth, it makes sense to talk about Christ as the mid-point of time, but can any sense be attached to the idea of a mid-point of time nowadays? We could accept Cullmann's views only if we were prepared to surrender the hard-won distinctions which thought has made among such concepts as 'time', 'process', 'history', 'myth', and to relapse into the confused undifferentiated thinking of two thousand years ago when these various ideas were still confounded and unseparated. But why should

---

[1] See his book, *Christ and Time*, trans. Floyd V. Filson (SCM Press, London, 1951).
[2] On these points, see op. cit., pp. 20, 21, 23, 49, 94.

we be asked to return to such an outlook? Is there any virtue in confusion? Can the historical claims of Christianity be made more plausible only by a 'willing suspension of disbelief' so that we can once again see history as a cosmic drama of redemption? It may be reasonable to ask for such a suspension of disbelief in literature, but surely not in religion.

Cullmann's aim is to set forth what is distinctive in the Christian proclamation, that 'which it does not have in common with philosophical or religious systems'.[1] He finds the required *differentia* in the biblical understanding of time. Since the whole argument proceeds on the assumption that the Bible contains an 'absolute divine revelation to men' and since the understanding of time is the 'specifically Christian element' in this revelation, we are asked to 'put aside completely' the question whether this biblical conception of time accords with any other conception which we may have. We should 'make an honest effort to renounce all standards derived from any other source than the most ancient Christian writings themselves'.[2] Hence, in an admittedly obscure passage, Cullmann seems to come close to drawing the astonishing conclusion that no one can be a Christian unless he accepts the biblical understanding of time and history.[3] It would appear therefore that on Cullmann's view anyone with a contemporary outlook is *ipso facto* banned from Christianity. It is doubtful if Leonard Hodgson is quite right in thinking that Cullmann finds the *differentia* of Christianity in 'some metaphysical conception which may be accepted as divinely revealed and must therefore be preserved free from adulteration by other views', for Cullmann expressly disavows that the biblical writers were interested in the problematic nature of time as such and the philosophical questions involved. But there is no doubt that Hodgson is right on the wicket when he goes on to say that 'to draw from this the conclusion that God wills us neither to raise these questions nor to seek to learn from those who have thought profoundly about them is ludicrously absurd. Why, in order to be a good Christian, should it be more important to have a Hebrew type of mind than to have a Hebrew cast of countenance?'[4] There is

---

[1] Op. cit., p. 12.   [2] On these points, see op. cit., pp. 12 and 23.
[3] Op cit., p. 29.
[4] *For Faith and Freedom*, I (Blackwell, Oxford, 1956), pp. 77-8.

robust common-sense in this last question. It is no solution to the problem of Christianity and history to recommend that we should return to an outmoded and naïve understanding of time and history. Cullmann cannot deliver us from the task of which we have spoken—that of rethinking the historical claims of Christianity in a radically new way.

So far, however, we have looked at only one half of our difficulties. We have asked ourselves how a series of historical events could possibly shed light on ultimate questions about God and the universe, but we have not asked about the trust-worthiness of the history itself. We did, indeed, note that the biblical writers make no distinction between history which is in principle verifiable and myth. But now we must remind our-selves that for a long time historical criticism has been eroding the sacred history itself. How much of it remains after critical analysis has done its work? Does it afford a firm enough founda-tion on which to rear the structure of Christian faith? On this side also, the historical claims of Christianity need to be re-examined.

Of Rudolf Bultmann, it can be said that at least he is acutely aware of the problems involved in Christianity's status as a historical religion, and he has tried to face them in a new way. This is the way of the existentialist approach to history, and what success it has, we shall have to judge. Cullmann thinks that Bultmann 'strips the Christian proclamation of its time-setting' and exhibits its meaning as 'nontemporal and non-historical'.[1] Bultmann however would deny this. No more than Cullmann does he deal in a timeless reality of which Christian history is the exemplification in time. He seeks to reinterpret the historical claims of Christianity in terms of a concept of history itself. His preoccupation with history is evident from the fact that he chose this theme for his Gifford Lectures, in which he starts off from the assertion that 'today history is our biggest problem'.[2] We must remember also that over against his existentialist approach to history, Bultmann is noted as a scientific historian who has done much work on Christian origins. It has been suggested by some critics that Bultmann turned to the existentialist view of history because the results of

[1] Op. cit., p. 30.
[2] *History and Eschatology* (University Press, Edinburgh, 1957), p. 1.

his scientific historical research were so negative. This, however, is not the case, for a glance at his early essays shows that the existentialist interest has been present in his thought for a long time. There is more justice in Thielicke's statement: 'Bultmann has been saying exactly the same things for decades. He has preserved a thoroughly rigid continuity of thought and even of terminology.'[1]

Confronted with the vast and complex field of problems which belong to history and historiography, we can do no more than examine a few selected topics which seem to bear most directly on Bultmann's treatment of history. These topics will be the scientific approach to history (Section 11); the metaphysical approach (Section 12); the existentialist approach (Section 13). When these topics have been surveyed, a reply will be made to some criticisms of the point of view which emerges (Section 14).

11 *The Scientific Approach to History*

Is history a science or an art, or is it somewhere in between? Many historians would claim that history is a science—or at least that the more scientific it can become, the better it is. It is undoubtedly true that history has advanced enormously since it availed itself of scientific methods and attitudes. However, the question which concerns us is not the more general one of whether history is or ought to be purely a science but the narrower one of whether history, in so far as it is scientific, can help either to confirm or destroy the historical claims of Christianity.

To provide ourselves with a concrete basis for discussing this question, we may set out from a consideration of the views of Ernst Troeltsch who stoutly maintained the scientific character of historical investigation. There are several reasons which make Troeltsch a good exemplar for our purpose. One reason is that his historical interest, like ours, was directed primarily upon Christianity—he was perhaps the most eminent representative of the so-called 'history of religion' school of theology. A second reason is that although he firmly believed that history is a

---

[1] Loc. cit., p. 154. The term 'demythologizing' is, of course, a later innovation. It is interesting to note that whereas Thielicke thinks this term has been a 'magic-laden catchword' which has helped to popularize Bultmann's thought, Barth regards 'demythologizing' as an 'uncommonly ugly' and repulsive word!

scientific study, Troeltsch was not an extremist in his views. He explicitly rejected a purely naturalistic approach to history. A third reason is that similarities have been alleged between Bultmann's approach to history and that of Troeltsch. Presumably what is in view here is Bultmann's work as a scientific historian of Christian origins—work which has led him to classify as myth or legend many of the New Testament narratives. Thus Thielicke asserts that Bultmann, without explicitly saying so, has taken over Troeltsch's criteria for discriminating historical events, and these criteria are listed as causality, immanence and analogy. According to Thielicke, Bultmann cannot ascribe historical factuality to some of the most decisive events in the New Testament record because of his tacit acceptance of these criteria.[1]

Troeltsch's starting-point is in striking contrast to that of Cullman. In Troeltsch's view, the only people in the ancient world to get a true glimmering of history were the Greeks, and anything which they had accomplished was speedily extinguished by Christianity. Although itself historical, Christianity did not produce historical reflection, but revived the mythological way of looking at history. The course of history was divided up into various stages in the cosmic drama, and 'the mythology of redemption now takes the place of historical reflection'. Rational inquiry was suspect; 'the desire to explain came to be regarded as the mark of a profane mind'. Only in modern times, from the Renaissance onwards, does a genuine historical interest re-emerge, and history begins to take shape as a science. We pass over the details of this development to the consideration of Troeltsch's own view of the historian's task.

[1] Loc. cit., p. 176. Incidentally, it may be noted that different writers vary among themselves in assessing the fundamental principles of Troeltsch's work. H. Thielicke, as we have seen, speaks of three 'criteria'—causality, immanence, analogy. H. R. Mackintosh mentions three 'laws of inquiry' and he lists them as criticism, relativity and analogy. See his book, *Types of Modern Theology* (Nisbet, London, 1937), pp. 197ff. Mackintosh refers to a passage in an essay of Troeltsch published in 1898—'Ueber historische und dogmatische Methode in der Theologie', reprinted in *Gesammelte Schriften*, II (J. C. B. Mohr, Tübingen, 1922), pp. 729ff. But in this passage, curiously enough, we find yet another formulation. Troeltsch speaks of 'principles' or 'basic concepts' (*Grundbegriffe*) and the three which he mentions are criticism, analogy and correlation! However, no simple schema does justice to Troeltsch's complex and eclectic thought. The summary of his views given below relies primarily on his own article 'Historiography' in *Encyclopaedia of Religion and Ethics*, ed. James Hastings (T. & T. Clark, Edinburgh, 1913), VI, pp. 716ff., supplemented by the early essay mentioned and the relevant passages in his later book, *Der Historismus und seine Probleme* (*Gesammelte Schriften*, III).

Modern historical reflection, he claims, takes a 'purely scientific attitude to facts'. History as a theoretical science has to be distinguished from history as an element in literature, politics and the like. Historians may often have varied interests, and sometimes it may be their non-historical interests which make their books readable. Someone, for instance, may write history in order to illustrate a political theory. Nevertheless, it should always be possible to separate the purely historical element from other elements, and this will be done the more easily if it has been conscientiously dealt with. 'The sole task of history in its specifically theoretical aspect is to explain every movement, process, state and nexus of things by reference to the web of its causal relations'.

One consequence of this approach to history is that it can yield results which are only probable. This is the so-called 'law of criticism' in Troeltsch. The price which history pays for becoming a science is that its findings, like those of every other science, are always open to correction and revision. Every tradition and every generally received interpretation of history must be sifted by criticism, and this work is never finished. It may be that in some cases the degree of probability will be high, in other cases low, but it will always fall short of certainty. Fresh facts may come to light or a more stringent criticism may overthrow earlier results. For the Christian, this means that scientific historical research can establish at most only the probability of the events recorded in the New Testament. Some may have a fairly high degree of probability, others may have little probability. In any case, he must keep his mind open for the possibility that some day an Arab boy may stumble upon a *cache* of ancient documents which will throw an entirely new light on the matter.

Troeltsch, as we have seen, attaches great importance to the notion of causality. He interprets this notion in a peculiar way, as we shall see in a moment. But however it is interpreted, it asserts an 'integral continuity' in history. Every event is correlated with other events in the same series. Some events may indeed be highly distinctive in their significance but none are of a different order from the others. All have to be considered as immanent in an 'unspeakably complex yet altogether coherent whole'. Since everything is to be understood in terms of factors which are immanent in the process, there can be no divine irruptions or interventions. God may indeed be at work in the process, and may even be revealing himself in it, but if so his activity would be continuous and immanent, not the special or sporadic interventions of a transcendent deity. Nor could any event be regarded as final or absolute. Everything is relative and must be understood with respect to its setting within the continuous series. For the Christian, this means that 'biblical research is to be brought within the general political, social and spiritual history of antiquity and that finally the investigation and assessment of Christianity is to find its place within the framework of religious and cultural history'. The implication is that the Christian must give up the belief that God has spoken once for all in Jesus Christ. The event of Christ may indeed be the culmination so far of a process of divine revelation, but on Troeltsch's view it cannot be final.

The principle of analogy is to some extent bound up with the notion of continuity. 'We discern the same process of phenomena in operation in the past as in the present. . . . On the analogy of the events known to us we seek by conjecture and sympathetic understanding to explain and reconstruct the past.' Thus the events recorded in a tradition which are analogous to events in our own experience will be regarded as probable, events which exhibit no such analogous character will appear improbable. However, there is something more than this to the principle of analogy. We get a clue from the words 'sympathetic understanding' in the quotation just given. Troeltsch set his face against a purely naturalistic view of history. It is true that he could write: 'The history of mankind merges in the purely evolutionary history of the earth's surface.' This would seem to indicate that he had not properly distinguished natural process and historical action. But he goes on to make a sharp distinction between historical causality and natural causality. The distinction is so sharp—'historical causation is something *entirely* different'—that one wonders why the same word should be used for both sets of events. What is the difference? Troeltsch thinks of natural causation as a matter of the transformation and conservation of energy—a continual reshuffling of patterns, as it were. Historical causation, on the other hand, is 'almost exclusively a matter of psychological

motivation'. It is not completely so, because natural causes—
earthquakes, famines and so on—can be historical causes as
well. Psychological motivation, on Troeltsch's view, is not just
a quantitative matter but involves a qualitative element. For
this reason, it is said to be able to produce novelty in a way
which is not possible where transformations of energy are
concerned.

How do we understand this historical causality? It is here
that we begin to see the full implications of the principle of
analogy. Troeltsch points out that whereas natural science
seeks to find general laws, history selects 'individual causes
from the flux of phenomena'. It seeks 'by means of the individual causality proper to history to make an event as
intelligible as if it were part of our own experience'. Even if we
could grasp the entire history of mankind we would not,
Troeltsch thinks, understand it as an instance of the operation
of general laws, but as a particular historical concatenation.
Thus it is only on the analogy of our own experience that
historical understanding is possible at all. We can understand
a natural process from the outside, as it were, but the factors
which operate in history are understood by the fact that we
ourselves have analogous experiences—that we ourselves are
historical. Here Troeltsch is clearly approaching Bultmann's
view of the place of self-understanding in historical investigation. And that is not to be wondered at, since both acknowledge
their debt to Wilhelm Dilthey as one of the first to distinguish
between natural science and historical science. Troeltsch's
kinship with Bultmann comes out still more clearly when he
declares that history 'enables man to comprehend himself so
far as a causal comprehension of himself is possible or necessary.
It is, in fact, only on the basis of such causal self-comprehension
that our own historical work can be clearly and circumspectly
extended'.

If we now ask whether these tendencies in Troeltsch's
thought do not conflict with his view of history as a 'pure
theoretical science', we find that he himself does not think
that there is any conflict. He acknowledges that subjective
factors come in, and that because of the richness or the limitations of their own experiences, different investigators will
attach varying degrees of importance to certain facets of

historical happening. 'Historical investigation is, in practice, always subjectively conditioned by the fulness, depth and range of the personal experiences of the investigators themselves, and is thus always marked by irreducible differences in their starting-points.' But Troeltsch thinks that these interests of the investigators provide only a heuristic principle. They give way before historical reality and we need not, because of them, surrender the scientific claims of history.

There are some criticisms which might be made at this point. It might be agreed that the claim to scientific status on the part of history is not necessarily upset by differences in the experiences and interests of the investigators for the same would be true in all fields of investigation. There would seem, however, to be an essential difference between the natural scientist who can observe with the detachment of a spectator and the historian who must employ sympathetic understanding and analogous participation. Troeltsch's claim, we must remember, is that history is a 'pure *theoretical* science'. But does not his distinction between natural and historical causality demolish this claim? For, to use Macmurray's language, the starting-point for understanding historical causality is not 'I think' but 'I do'. Such understanding is not a purely theoretical matter. In saying that history is a science but not at all like a natural science, Troeltsch may well have surrendered the claim that it is a science at all. It may be that history is a reflective discipline with a peculiar status—as Macmurray says, 'neither an art nor a science, though it has certain affinities with both'.[1]

These questions, however, need not detain us. Whether or not history can become a pure science, it has a scientific element. We have seen in the work of Troeltsch the kind of results which emerge when the scientific approach is applied to biblical history. We have now to ask about the implications of these results for theology. We come back to our question whether scientific historical research can either confirm or destroy the claims of Christianity as a historical religion.

Can it confirm these claims? It would seem that it cannot. For historical research must view Christianity as a historical phenomenon on a level with other historical phenomena. It

[1] Op. cit., p. 207.

must seek to give its explanations in terms of factors immanent in history. For this reason, the principal 'events' of which the New Testament speaks—for instance, incarnation, atonement, resurrection—cannot be recognized by historical research as historical events at all. Such research might confirm the birth of a child in a particular year under particular circumstances; but it could not possibly confirm the appearance of God in the flesh. It might confirm a particular crucifixion under Pontius Pilate; but it could not possibly tell us whether that crucifixion provided a way for man to be reconciled with God. The resurrection is in a slightly different category. Historical research might even show the probability that the victim of the crucifixion had been seen alive by certain people after three days. But it would have to leave this as an unexplained event. Or if it sought for an explanation, it would try to find one in natural terms. It might conjecture, for instance, that the victim was not quite dead after the crucifixion. It could not possibly explain the happening on the ground that after three days God raised him up, though if it decided that the event was inexplicable, the door would be open for extra-scientific explanations. In a sentence, because it deals with phenomena, scientific historical research could show only that at a certain time some people had come to believe that God had acted in a special way among them, but it could not show that God had in fact so acted.

Nor should we blame the scientific historian for taking up the attitude that he does. The desire to explain events in terms of factors immanent in the process within which the events occur is one which historical research shares with other sciences, and it is surely one which has brought great advantages and delivered mankind from many follies and superstitions. If men had never looked for such immanent explanations, we might still think that Iris traces out the rainbow in the sky. More seriously, when there is an outbreak of plague, we might still think that the appropriate procedure is to offer sacrifices to Apollo rather than take action against the bacillus responsible. There is nothing impious in the determination of the scientific historian to stick to verifiable phenomena. He is simply trying to follow a path which has been tried with success in other fields.

Commenting on Troeltsch's principles of historical investigation, H. R. Mackintosh remarked: 'It is always depressing to
be told in advance how much we are going to be permitted to
believe'.[1] This remark, however, could bear at least two
interpretations. Mackintosh may mean that it is wrong to lay
down in advance principles which would from the outset rule
out the possibility of our discovering certain facts, and if this
is what he means, then he is surely right. This is certainly what
he does mean in a later passage where he says: 'The possibilities
have been fixed in advance; the facts are compelled to fit the
method by which they are to be treated; just as, though an
automatic machine when opened may disgorge nothing but
unbent pennies, this is not because the outer world is made up
of unbent pennies and nothing else, but because the selective
mechanism at work will accept no other sort'.[2] The scientific
historian, for instance, should not decide in advance that a
resurrection is impossible. The more scientific he is, the more
open he will be to consider the evidence for any alleged fact,
however improbable it may seem at first glance.[3] But Mackintosh's remark might be taken in another way, which ought to be
distinguished from the one just considered. Mackintosh may be
complaining, not that the facts are prejudged, but that the way
of explaining them has been laid down in advance. If this is
what is meant, then it is more difficult to agree. We have seen
already that the scientific historian has a right and even a duty
to try to explain any event in terms of the factors which are
ordinarily immanent in history. Thus even if he were persuaded
of the fact of a resurrection, his first move would be to look for
an explanation in natural terms, such as that death was only
apparent. Suppose, however, that no explanation in natural
terms seemed to be adequate, then the scientific historian
would have to leave the fact as inexplicable, and such an
inexplicable fact might lead him to modify his hypothesis that
all historical happenings are of the same order. But clearly the
evidence for such an inexplicable fact would need to be very
strong indeed before the hypothesis was abandoned. It is
unrealistic to suggest, as Thielicke does, that the historian

---

[1] Op. cit., p. 197.   [2] Op. cit., p. 203.
[3] Cf. my criticism of Bultmann for apparently ruling out in advance the very
possibility of a resurrection: *An Existentialist Theology*, pp. 185-6.

should reverse his order and, instead of beginning from the hypothesis that historical phenomena are explicable in terms of other phenomena of the same order, 'furnish from these events (the events from Christmas to Whitsunday) the concept of what history in the strict and *authentic* sense is'.[1] It would also be scant comfort to the Christian if his belief that God has acted depended on the inexplicability by ordinary means of certain events, for such gaps in explanation have a way of getting filled up, and what cannot be explained now may well be explained later.

We must therefore conclude that scientific historical research cannot confirm the claims made on behalf of the sacred history. For such research is, by the very principles on which it is based, directed upon the phenomena which are immanent in historical happening and has nothing to say about the kind of explanations of certain events which Christian theology might give. Even if research were able to establish a high degree of probability for all the major events recorded in the New Testament, this would still come far short of a confirmation of the historical claims of Christianity.

Can historical research, on the other hand, destroy these claims? If by its very nature it cannot confirm them, we might expect that it cannot destroy them either. But suppose that research were to show that a very low degree of probability attached to the events recounted in the New Testament— presumably it could not altogether disprove them, for again by its very nature it deals in probabilities—then would that not come close to destroying the historical claims of Christianity? But however improbable historical research might make the record seem, the Christian might not unreasonably continue to hold that some events had indeed taken place. For surely there are some things which we may reasonably believe about the past apart from historical research altogether. For instance, historians and literary critics have argued for a long time about whether there ever was a poet called Homer. Some say that the author of the *Iliad* was different from the author of the *Odyssey*; and some claim that several hands went into the making of one or even both of these poems. Whatever the present state of the controversy may be, I can still read and enjoy my *Iliad*. On the

1 Loc. cit., p. 176.

basis of this present experience in my reading, and quite independently of what Homeric scholars may be saying at the moment, I can surely infer with reasonable confidence that there was at least one epic poet of outstanding genius in ancient Greece. About the details, I may be quite uncertain, but that there was at least one literary giant I cannot reasonably doubt when I have his work lying before me. The controversy between the historical critics takes place within certain limits and there is a certain minimal core of historical factuality which cannot be affected by the results of that controversy. In an analogous way, is it not possible to hold and to seek to practise the Christian religion without continually looking over one's shoulder at the latest (and probably conflicting) theories of New Testament scholars about Christian origins or the latest (and even more conflicting) speculations on the significance of the Dead Sea Scrolls? For on the basis of one's present experience of the gospel, it is reasonable to believe that it originated with at least one person of quite extraordinary stature—a person who gave rise to the Christian Church which still bears its continuing witness to him.[1] What would be the minimum which one would be entitled to believe in this way, and why one should wish to believe anything about the past at all are questions to which we must return when we have a clearer view of what is involved in the nature of Christianity as a historical religion. For the present, however, we merely note that the controversy over Christian origins, like the Homeric controversy, moves within certain limits. There are some basic facts there, even if they can never be properly disentangled. It may be that Christianity, as a historical religion, is more liable to be modified by historical research than a religion whose essence consisted in timeless truths, but even the most destructive results of historical criticism would not reach far enough to overthrow it.

But we must not linger too long over extreme and unlikely possibilities. It is much more likely to be the case that historical research will continue to present an ambiguous picture, conferring a reasonably high degree of probability upon some of

---

[1] Perhaps it is an excess of caution to write 'at least one person' in this sentence for Christian origins, obscure though they may be, are at least not so obscure as the origins of the Homeric poems.

the events of which the New Testament speaks, leaving others much more doubtful, and saying nothing about those 'events' such as the incarnation which are not recognized as historical events at all by the scientific historian. We do not wish in any way to disparage the patient and careful work of such research. Its findings may be both interesting and instructive. More important still, it is our bulwark against relapsing once more into mythology and superstition. Nevertheless, our discussion has made it clear that scientific historical research can never be decisive either one way or the other for the claims of Christianity as a historical religion.

Historical reflection involves a scientific element, and the use of the scientific approach to history has brought great gains. But in our discussion of Troeltsch we have seen reason to believe that history is not exclusively scientific in its nature. History is more than a science or—perhaps we should say—is different from a pure science. Is there some other approach to history which would be more successful than the one we have tried in coming to grips with that peculiar kind of history on which Christianity is said to be founded?

12 *The Metaphysical Approach to History*

By the metaphysical approach to history, we mean the attempt to exhibit history in relation to the total scheme of things and, in the light of such a synoptic view, to set forth the pattern and meaning of history as a whole. Saint Augustine, for instance, considers that all history is subject to God's providential control, and the grand pattern of world-history is set forth in terms of the interaction between the heavenly city and the earthly city. Hegel, on the other hand, considers history to be the field in which Spirit realizes itself and the pattern is that of the dialectic whereby the clash between thesis and antithesis is resolved in synthesis. It might be thought that we need some such bold speculative approach to history if we are to do justice to the claims of Christianity as a historical religion, and indeed the exponents of such views have often been concerned to uphold these claims. But we are bound to pause when we remember that such comprehensive interpretations of history are by no means popular at the present time. The contemporary historian is usually more modest in his aims and often he tells us outright that he can discern no overall pattern in history at all.

Arnold Toynbee mentions four ways in which the pattern of history has been pictured.[1] Two of these offer fundamental alternatives. One is the cyclic view (or Indo-Hellenic view, as Toynbee calls it) which understands history on the analogy of the recurring rhythms of nature—the alternation of day and night, summer and winter and so on. On this view, history keeps coming back to its starting-point—it moves in circles. The other fundamental view (Toynbee calls it the Judaeo-Zoroastrian, rightly recognizing the influence of Persian thought) sees history as non-repetitive. The analogy is that of a drama which moves from a definite beginning through various crises to a definite outcome—history moves in a straight line. Of the two subsidiary views, one (the Chinese) thinks of history on the analogy of a theme with variations, and has certain affinities with both the cyclic and the non-repetitive views. The other (Toynbee says that it has been 'the prevalent view of one school of Western historians in a post-Christian age of Western history') sees only 'a chaotic, disorderly, fortuitous flux, in which there is no rhythm or pattern of any kind to be discerned'. Of course, if one is to be able to make anything of history at all, presumably some patterns must be recognized. Toynbee is right in saying that when the historian speaks of 'Europe' or 'the Orient' he is admitting a pattern of sorts. But it may be doubted if Toynbee is being quite fair to the kind of historians whom he has in mind. A historian might recognize various fragmentary patterns and yet not be convinced that there is any overall pattern; or he might be unable to see any such overall pattern, and suspend his judgment as to whether there is one. Toynbee says that this view of history 'stands convicted of failing to go to the root of the question that all historians ought to be trying to answer' and he gives this question as: 'What is the nature of the universe?' But it is by no means obvious that historians ought to be asking such a question. Many of them may believe quite conscientiously that their concern is with much less imposing questions. It may be that in the long run and in spite of positivist bans we are all

---

[1] *An Historian's Approach to Religion* (Oxford University Press, London, 1956), pp. 8ff.

driven to ultimate questions, just because 'all men by nature desire to know'.[1] But we must be fair to the anti-metaphysical temper of our time. Has not that temper arisen partly because in times past men have rushed in too precipitately with answers to the question about the nature of the universe? If a modern historian asserts, 'There is no overall pattern', then of course he has become the champion of a rival metaphysic. But if he is simply saying, 'I see no pattern of this sort', then he may be merely exercising a commendable caution.

Confronted with these different views of the pattern of history, we find that there arise many bewildering questions. Are these views all mutually exclusive, or do several of them glimpse aspects of the complex course of history? How do we choose between them or how do we reconcile them? Where do we get them from? Do we derive them from history itself? Or do we import them into history from an extra-historical source —for instance, would a prior belief in impersonal law as the governing force in the universe predispose us in the direction of a cyclical interpretation of history, whereas a prior belief in a personal God would lead us to see history as a non-repetitive drama?

To begin with the last of these questions, it would seem unreasonable to base our pattern on some extra-historical consideration. Sometimes this is done, but it may distort the nature of history altogether. A rigidly mechanical idea of history imported from physical science or a rigidly providential idea imported from a type of theology in which God is conceived as a despotic 'Louis XIV of the heavens' really destroys history as the story of human action in the world. History is reduced to a process the course of which is predetermined at all points. Men's decisions are only apparently decisions, for in reality everything that they do has been laid down in advance —whether they are conceived as the playthings of blind natural forces or whether it is thought that 'they do nothing save at the secret instigation of God, and do not discuss or deliberate anything but what he has previously decreed with himself, and brings to pass by his secret direction'.[2] Yet apart from such extreme points of view, it has been increasingly recognized

---

[1] Aristotle, *Metaphysica*, I, 980a.
[2] Calvin, *Institutes of the Christian Religion*, I, xviii, 1.

that we cannot pronounce on history from some extra-historical standpoint for the very good reason that we ourselves are always within history. This seems to be recognized by modern historians of very diverse types. We have noted how the principle of analogy in Troeltsch's scientific approach to history implies that we can understand history only through our own participation in it. Toynbee points out that the historian is always to some extent the 'prisoner of his own time and place'.[1] And the existentialist historians, to whom we shall be turning shortly, insist that the study of history is possible only on the basis of man's own historicity. Bultmann affirms that 'the historian cannot see history from a neutral standpoint outside history. His seeing of history is itself a historical event.'[2] Thus if we are to reach any comprehensive understanding of history, we must begin from within history itself. And this of course accords with Christian teaching, for if the revelation is given in history we must proceed from history to the understanding of God; we may not proceed from a preconceived idea of God to an interpretation of history in the light of it.[3]

If then it is agreed that we must begin the quest for an overall interpretation of history from within history itself, we may recall Thielicke's proposal, quoted above,[4] that we should take the events from Christmas to Whitsunday and furnish from them 'the concept of what history in the strict and authentic sense is'. But when this proposal was quoted, it was described as 'unrealistic'. It is so for two reasons. In the first place, Thielicke assumes that the events which he wishes to make the criterion for all history were not just ordinary historical events. They were what the theologian variously calls 'supra-historical' or 'meta-historical' events. But the trouble with words like 'supra-historical' and 'meta-historical' is that although they seem to mean something, it is very hard to determine what their meaning is. They get plausibility from their incorporation of the word 'historical' to which we can attach at least an approximate meaning, but this meaning is so

[1] Op. cit., p. 6.   [2] *History and Eschatology*, p. 143.
[3] This procedure is not always observed. The criticism of the extreme Calvinist view to which we have alluded above is precisely that it reverses the procedure. Thus the *Westminster Confession* speaks of 'God's eternal decree' which was made 'before the foundation of the world' and only subsequently goes on to speak of his covenant with men and of the incarnation.
[4] See p. 72.

modified by the prefixes that the only thing which is immediately clear is that the 'supra-historical' and the 'metahistorical' are not straightforwardly historical. How, for instance, could an 'irruption into history' be itself historical? And how could something which is at most only in part historical provide the clue to 'what history in the strict and authentic sense is'? In the second place, Thielicke is working on a very narrow front in laying all the stress on the first thirty years or so of our era. We might agree that these years are the most important that the human race has lived through, and the very fact that we date our calendar as we do tends to confirm this. Though it is only fair to notice that not everyone would agree with Thielicke's selection—the historian of science might think that the most decisive period in the world's history was when Thales and others around 600 B.C. began to look for rational explanations of things, while others have attached chief importance to man's spiritual awakening about the same time, with the emergence of the Hebrew prophets and other great religious and moral teachers throughout the world. But even granting the primacy of the first thirty years of our era, are we entitled to read off from them the character of all history?

It is true, as we have already noted, that the historian selects individual events. Even if all historical events are of the same order, they are not all of the same importance or significance—just as someone's marriage is a much more important event in his life than the haircut he had last week. But if we are seeking a comprehensive view of history, we ought to start off from the widest data that we can get. For this reason, Cullmann's approach is more promising than Thielicke's, for Cullmann keeps in view the sacred history as a whole and sees the culminating event of Jesus Christ as set in a series of events which extends both before and after. Although we rejected the view that the sacred history is co-extensive with the time-line, and although we must cut out the beginning and the end (creation and eschatology) as not historical events at all, we are left with a series of events which is roughly co-extensive with recorded history. This series of events—the call of Abraham, the experiences of Israel, the coming of Christ, the birth of the Church, and so on—has undoubtedly been of the highest importance and significance in the recorded history of mankind. It would be reasonable enough for someone to claim that this series of events has the primary significance in recorded history and even to interpret it as God's redemptive activity in history. He might say that the great illuminating power in this history is self-sacrificing love.

But we should notice immediately that this point of view can claim to be reasonable precisely because it is saying something much more tentative and limited than the kind of things which Thielicke and Cullmann are wanting to say. It is simply maintaining that within the very limited period of history accessible to us, the events of which the sacred history speaks are events of decisive significance which may be illuminating for that whole period. But since it is recognized that there are vast periods of prehistory behind us about which we know little and perhaps vaster periods of future history in front of us about which we know nothing, there is no talk of a 'mid-point of time', of 'once-for-all' happenings, of events which are final, unique, cosmic, exclusive, or whatever word may be used. There is, in short, no attempt to set up an ultimate metaphysical explanation. Toynbee remarks: 'The acceptance of a belief that there have been, and of an expectation that there will continue to be, decisive new departures does not require the acceptance of a belief that any one of these new departures has been, or will be, not only decisive but unique or final. The two beliefs are, indeed, incompatible'.[1]

The results of our inquiry may seem to be meagre enough. If we agree that no one can stand outside of history so as to grasp it as a whole and that all of us within history see only a very limited area from our own particular perspective (to say nothing of the fact that we do not know whether the universe gives birth to millions of such histories) then we shall not rush forward to make pronouncements about all time and all existence on the slender basis of the events known to us. But we need not be unduly depressed by the failure of those bold attempts to grasp the story of the universe as a whole. After all, it is only with a limited area of history that we have to do. In it we have to make our decisions and our own history. It is surely important if in it we can discern some events which seem to us significant and from which we get light for our tasks.

[1] Op. cit., p. 140.

13 *The Existentialist Approach to History*

Neither the scientific approach to history nor the metaphysical one has taken us very far in our attempt to elucidate what the historical claims of Christianity can mean in terms of a post-mythological outlook. They have however indicated that these claims, if they can still be maintained, need to be very drastically restated. Bultmann offers us such a restatement in terms of the existentialist approach to history, and at this we must now look. But we may say in advance that while we shall find that he has some remarkable successes, there is a limit to the applicability of this method, and we shall still be left with some problems on our hands.

What is this 'existentialist' approach to history? The designation is a very loose one. The three thinkers who seem to have had the greatest influence on Bultmann's view of history, Wilhelm Dilthey, Martin Heidegger, and R. G. Collingwood, are very diverse; the existentialist label is not applicable *simpliciter* to any one of them, not even to Heidegger. We can only say that they show a certain affinity in their several approaches to the problems of history, and since this affinity centres on the relating of history to the historical existence of the historian himself, we find it convenient to speak of an 'existentialist' approach to history. But as well as affinity there is difference among the three thinkers mentioned; and as well as differences among themselves, different interpretations can be given of the thought of any one of them.[1] For the purpose of the present discussion, it will not be necessary to go into all these complexities of detail. Instead, we shall try to formulate the essence of the point of view which we have in mind by setting down four basic propositions; always remembering that not all of the philosophers who stand behind Bultmann would necessarily assent to each of these propositions.

The first proposition is: Historical reflection has for its subject-matter human existence in the world. We have indeed worked on this assumption since we distinguished 'history' and

---

[1] For a discussion of the differences between Dilthey and Collingwood, see H. A. Hodges' book, *The Philosophy of Wilhelm Dilthey* (Routledge & Kegan Paul, London, 1952), pp. 315ff., and for a criticism of the 'received interpretation' of Collingwood, see Alan Donagan's article, 'The Verification of Historical Theses' in *The Philosophical Quarterly*, VI, pp. 193ff.

'process',[1] but now its implications must be brought out more clearly. This point of view is common to all the thinkers whom we have taken to illustrate the 'existentialist' approach to history. We have already noted how Troeltsch ascribes to Dilthey a clear understanding of the distinction between natural science and historical science.[2] Heidegger asserts that it is man who is 'primarily historical'.[3] Collingwood is also quite explicit on this point: 'History is not the same thing as change. . . . All history properly so called is the history of human affairs'.[4]

Our first proposition needs some qualification and explanation. It is not meant to deny that a natural event can be a historical event—and surely such a denial would be absurd. But a natural event is also a historical event only in so far as it touches on human existence. The Lisbon earthquake of 1755, for instance, was a historical event because it affected a great many people and also had considerable consequences for European thought in the eighteenth century. But the much more spectacular earthquakes of which the geologists find evidence would not be regarded as historical events since at that time there were no human beings to be affected by them.[5] On the other side, since our proposition speaks of 'human existence in the world', it cuts out from the category of history those pseudo-histories which tell of actions before the world began (like the war of the angels) or after the world has run its course (eschatological myths) or of events 'in heaven' which run parallel with events on earth (as in the drama of Job). If we are to discern the divine activity in history, we must look for it not in 'histories' of a peculiar sort but in man's historical existence in the world.

The consequence of the first proposition is that we must seek to understand history in ways and with categories which are appropriate to the understanding of human existence in

---

[1] See above, pp. 59ff.   [2] See above p. 69.   [3] Op. cit., p. 381.

[4] *The Idea of History* (Oxford University Press, London, 1946), p. 212.

[5] Of course, it might be said that in so far as human beings have discovered such primeval happenings and thought about them, then in some way these happenings have also entered into the sphere of the historical. On the relation of nature to history, the reader may be referred to another work of R. G. Collingwood— *The Idea of Nature* (Oxford University Press, London, 1945). There he concludes that 'no one can answer the question what nature is unless he knows what history is' (p. 177).

general. In this sense, the approach must be an 'existential'
one. Here we may recall the function of pre-understanding in
exegesis. If history always has to do with human existence,
then in order to understand history we must already have
some understanding of what human existence is and we do
have such a preliminary understanding because we are ourselves human existents. This consideration leads into our next
proposition.

The second proposition is: In historical reflection, the reflecting subject participates in a peculiar way in the object of his
reflection. Here we get some very clear statements from
Collingwood. He says: 'The historian, investigating any event
in the past, makes a distinction between what may be called
the "outside" and the "inside" of an event. By the "outside"
of the event I mean everything belonging to it which can be
described in terms of bodies and their movements. . . . By the
"inside" of the event I mean that in it which can only be described in terms of thought. . . . The historian is never concerned with either of these to the exclusion of the other. His
work may begin by discovering the outside of an event, but it
can never end there; he must always remember that the event
was an action, and that his main task is to think himself into
this action, to discern the thought of its agent.'[1] Although in
this passage Collingwood stresses thought, the thought of which
he is speaking is the kind which goes with action. Thus to
think oneself into an action is to re-enact it in one's own mind,
and in such a way that it is criticized and evaluated.[2]

Our second proposition calls for further comment and elucidation. We have used deliberately vague language in speaking
of 'a peculiar way' in which the historian, as the reflecting
subject, participates in the object of his reflection. Gogarten
speaks more definitely of 'overcoming' the subject-object
relationship, but it is by no means clear what he puts in its
place and he acknowledges that his view 'involves lines of
thought which have not yet been fully explored'.[3] What does
seem quite clear is that there is a great difference between the
way in which someone understands a chemical reaction (which

[1] *The Idea of History*, p. 213.   [2] Op. cit., p. 215.
[3] Op. cit., p. 48ff. Dr James Brown has taken for his Croall Lectures the difficult
theme, *Subject and Object in Modern Theology* (SCM Press, London, 1955).

he can observe with a maximum of detachment or get instruments to observe for him) and the way in which someone understands a historical event (into the action of which he must think himself). Of course, one *may* look upon historical events as one looks on chemical reactions, for historical events have their outside as well as their inside. But simply to exhibit such events as so many brute facts or series of brute facts which occurred in the past is something less than history as the study of past *action*. In this sense, history demands an 'existential' relation between the historian and the events which he tries to understand.

If we turn now to the special problem of the sacred history, our second proposition seems to have permitted us a certain advance. Considered objectively, from the outside, how could a past event, such as the crucifixion of Jesus, be regarded as also an atonement which is still efficacious today? Presumably the solution would have to be along the lines of regarding the event as a 'supra-historical' or 'meta-historical' event, and we have noted already the difficulties which arise when such dubious conceptions are introduced. But if we seek to understand this event from the inside—by thinking ourselves into it, by participation, or however we care to express it—then its character as an atonement becomes clear. For is it not the case that the Christian who gets inside this event—by being 'crucified with Christ', by 'taking up his cross and following Christ'[1] —experiences the event as the attaining of wholeness, as an atonement? This account of the matter seems at least to make sense. The atoning character of the event is exhibited *within history itself*, when the historical event is understood in relation to the historical existence of whoever is trying to understand it.

Karl Barth objects that on this view the gospel is reduced to an *imitatio Christi*.[2] The cross does not become significant only when someone understands it from the inside and accepts its challenge. It is 'significant in itself'. What happens in men is only a consequence of what has been done outside of them, without them, and even against them. The event of the cross does not just inaugurate a process but has finished it. Barth regards the cross as an atoning event, but he wishes to see its atoning character in the event itself apart from any existential

---

[1] Cf. Gal. 2.20; Mark 8.34.   [2] *Ein Versuch*, pp. 19ff.

relation to that event. Presumably we meet here once again the conception of a 'meta-historical' event. But when we proceed to examine Barth's statements, it is difficult to make sense of them.

We need not linger over the charge that the gospel is reduced to an *imitatio Christi*, for this ignores the stress which Bultmann lays on the function of grace in the Christian life. But we may ask how atonement could be effected 'outside of' men? Or how it could be 'already' finished before they know anything about it? In a sense, these questions raise the old theological issue of an 'objective' theory of atonement. We do not, however, need to choose as an alternative a 'subjective' theory—indeed, the proposition which we are at present discussing insists that in any event of this kind 'subject' and 'object' are inseparably bound up with each other. Supposing it were a case of rescuing a herd of cattle from a forest fire which threatened to envelop them, then the rescue operations might be carried out quite independently of the cattle—they might not know that they had been rescued or even that they had ever been in danger. But the kind of salvation which the gospel offers is quite different. It offers an atonement, a healing of the estrangement which belongs to man's sinful condition. That means that it touches directly on the existence which is always man's own and for which he is responsible. Atonement, as salvation of this kind, cannot be 'outside of' man nor can it have 'already' happened without anyone knowing about it. It is realized only as it is accepted, only as there is participation in the event which makes it possible. Again, what can be meant by saying that the cross is an 'event significant in itself'? For anything to be 'significant', surely it must be *significant to someone*. One could imagine an event which no one knows about at present, but which will prove to be significant when it does come to be known. But it would be better to call such an event 'potentially significant' rather than 'significant in itself'. And the significance of such an event would be only potential until it became significant to someone. But an event which is 'significant in itself' and need never be 'significant to someone' would seem to be no different from an event which is without significance at all.

Similar remarks might be made about the resurrection. As

understood existentially, the resurrection is the 'new life' which is experienced upon acceptance of the cross. But Barth wants to know what Bultmann has to say about the resurrection of Jesus himself.[1] Has the event been transferred from Jesus to his disciples, so that it happens in them? One might reply that if it happened outside of them and not in them, it would not be a 'saving' event but only a historical curiosity. But Barth presses his question further. Are we not retreating into talk 'about the inner life of man' and so cutting the connection with history altogether? Here it might be replied that the existentialist approach rejects the 'bare subject' as much as it does the 'bare object', and that existence consists in the inter-action of the self with its world. But we would still be far from having answered the problems which Barth raises. What constitutes that pole of the resurrection event which lies in the world and not in the self? Can we point to anything as ob-jectively factual as is the cross? We must remember that the earliest account of the resurrection which we have is Saint Paul's.[2] He makes no mention of an objectively verifiable event, such as an empty tomb, but speaks of the appearance of the risen Christ to him, and apparently regards this appearance as on a par with earlier appearances to other believers. It is not unreasonable to suppose that it is also on a par with the encounters which subsequent believers may have had with the risen Christ. In all this, it is difficult to pin down anything more objective than psychical events in the minds of believers. Bultmann's solution is to regard the resurrection as a myth, and the function of such a myth is to bring to expression the significance of Christ for the existence of the believer. But we cannot escape the question whether in the long run the existen-tial approach to history does not drive its adherents, in spite of their protestations, into a radical subjectivizing. This question, however, can be deferred until we have examined the two remaining propositions.

The third proposition is: The function of historical reflection is to provide a self-understanding. Collingwood asks the question, 'What is history for?' It should be noted that he answers his own question in modest terms. He says he will 'suggest an answer', and though he thinks that no historian

---

[1] See *Kirchliche Dogmatik*, III/2, pp. 531ff.   [2] I Cor. 15.3-8.

will reject it, he agrees that it gives rise to many difficult problems. The answer is that 'history is for human self-knowledge'. And this self-knowledge is explained to include: 'knowing, first, what it is to be a man; secondly, knowing what it is to be the kind of man you are; and thirdly, knowing what it is to be the man *you* are and nobody else is'.[1]

Following our usual procedure, we shall first comment briefly on the meaning of the third proposition. Collingwood is to be commended for the modesty with which he replies to his own question. It is clear that history may have more than one function. It is quite conceivable that someone might study a particular period of history very carefully simply in order to satisfy his curiosity about what did happen in that period. Such an aim, though a legitimate one, would fall short of Collingwood's. On the other hand Toynbee, as we have noted,[2] thinks that the business of history is to throw light on the nature of the universe. This aim is of more doubtful legitimacy and obviously goes beyond Collingwood's. When we recall that history has to do with human action, the view that the function of history is to lead to self-understanding is a reasonable one, provided that we do not deny that historical reflection may have other possible aims or functions.

A further point which calls for elucidation is this. We are now saying that the purpose of history is to provide an understanding of our own human existence, but we have said earlier[3] that it is the prior understanding of our own existence which makes the study of history possible. Is there not a contradiction here? There is not a contradiction, but the two statements draw attention to a circle which is inevitable in any kind of interpretation. We can only interpret if we already have some idea of the subject-matter; yet this prior understanding of the subject-matter is always held in a tentative and heuristic way and may be increased or modified or transformed as a result of the interpretation. Thus, on the one hand, the historian's understanding of history may be limited by his own lack of experience; but on the other hand, his study of history may disclose to him new possibilities of experience. It is in some such way that Bultmann understands the manner in which men come to grasp the message of the gospel. Their point of entry is

---

[1] Op. cit., p. 10.   [2] See above, p. 76.   [3] See above, p. 83.

afforded by the understanding of themselves as not at one with themselves—an understanding which they already have. This self-understanding is sharpened and corrected by the gospel message so that men find themselves called to a new self-understanding.

Thus the function of the sacred history is conceived to be that of awakening a new self-understanding. The events of that history are re-enacted or re-presented in the historical existence of the individual in such a way that there takes place the transition from one kind of self to a new kind of self. Moreover, since the function of myth is, in Bultmann's view, to express a self-understanding, the mythical elements which are inextricably bound up with the sacred history also play their part in bringing about the new self-understanding. The story of creation teaches the finitude and creatureliness of human existence, while eschatology is not only realized but individualized when the coming end is seen to be one's own death. Yet Bultmann would say that there is nothing new in all this, except that it is now being made explicit. He maintains that Saint Paul interpreted the sacred history on the basis of his anthropology. This, he says, 'is indicated by the fact that Paul can present the course of history from Adam, by way of the law, to Christ, in the form of an autobiographical "I" '.[1] The past events are taken into a present autobiography and are experienced as saving events—but all this takes place within the sphere of the historical.

The fourth proposition is: Historical reflection is concerned primarily with possibility. This may seem a very paradoxical assertion to make if we are accustomed to think of the historian as one who is primarily concerned with facts. It will certainly call for considerable elucidation and qualification. Yet it is a proposition towards which we are driven by the first three propositions, and it is saying something very close to what was said in the third proposition. For an explicit statement of this fourth proposition, we must go to Heidegger.[2] Historical reflection, he thinks, takes as its theme the possible, and is therefore oriented to the future. It is interesting to note that in

[1] *History and Eschatology*, p. 41. The passage which Bultmann has in mind is Rom. 7.7-25.
[2] Op. cit., pp. 394ff.

his Gifford Lectures Bultmann makes only one passing reference to Heidegger's teaching on history, but devotes considerable space to Collingwood, and even declares with enthusiasm that 'the best that is said about the problems of history is, in my view, contained in the book of R. G. Collingwood'.[1] However, he criticizes Collingwood for not making it sufficiently clear that 'self-knowledge is consciousness of responsibility over against the future'.[2] It would seem that the major influence with Bultmann is still that of Heidegger.

Our fourth proposition requires to be qualified first by noting that Heidegger uses the words 'possible' and 'possibility' in a quite specific sense. For him, 'possibility' always means a possible way of existing for which an existent can decide. It does not mean a possibility in the wider sense of an event which may possibly happen. Clearly if one took the word in this wider and more usual meaning, it would be absurd to say that historical reflection is directed towards the possible or oriented to the future. If 'possibility' is understood in this way, then Collingwood is right in saying that 'the historian's business is to know the past, not to know the future'.[3] But if we understand 'possibility' in the first of the two senses, then to assert that historical reflection is concerned with possibility is simply a corollary of the assertion that its function is to provide self-understanding. A second point to note is that the possibilities which Heidegger has in mind are what he calls 'factical' possibilities, that is to say, the possibilities which are open in a situation that is 'factical' in the sense that it has arisen out of what has been. It is not being asserted that the historian should be concerned with any and every free-floating possibility of human existence, or that he should confound history with fiction and legend. What is meant is rather that 'the only clue to what man can do is what man has done'.[4] The stress on possibility and futurity by no means implies a severing of the link with factuality and pastness.

So far as the interpretation of the sacred history is concerned, we have now arrived at our destination. By means of demythologizing and existential interpretation, the sacred history can be exhibited in terms of a way of life, a possibility

---

[1] *History and Eschatology*, p. 130.   [2] Ibid., p. 136.
[3] *The Idea of History*, p. 54.   [4] Collingwood, op. cit., p. 10.

of human existence. No doubt this is a great gain, for it enables us to understand how the events recounted in that history can be events with a present significance—how the cross, for instance, can be an atonement—and this has been done without going outside of history itself. But it would be foolish to pretend that we are anywhere near to having attained our goal of restating the claims of Christianity as a historical religion. We are still faced with many unsolved problems. Have we been so concerned with the 'inside' of events that we have forgotten that they also have an 'outside' and that we agreed that the historian can never be concerned with the one to the exclusion of the other? Can we sit back and applaud when the existential content of the sacred history emerges, and shrug our shoulders when it is a question about the past events themselves, although we have asserted that the link with factuality is not being severed? Is it not rather the case that although we have seen the gain which demythologizing brings, we have seen also that there is a limit to it, in the sense that there is still something more to be said?

Gnosticism has always had its attractions, and not the least of them is that it provides an easy solution to the kind of problem which confronts us here. Once you grasp the '*gnosis*' (in the present case, the existential significance) you can be indifferent to the story which embodies it. But the Church rejected Gnosticism, and rightly so. For how can we know that it is a *genuine* possibility that is being set before us, unless it can be pointed out in history? How can we know what can be done except on the basis of what has been done? Bultmann himself recognizes this when he sharply differentiates the Christian story from Hellenistic myths. We recall that Collingwood insisted on the reality of the historical Jesus[1] and no account of his historical theories would be complete if it omitted his explicit affirmation that the 'prime duty' of the historian is 'a willingness to bestow infinite pains on discovering what actually happened'.[2] For that matter, neither Collingwood nor Bultmann is pontificating about history from an armchair—each has bestowed 'infinite pains' on the labours of research, the one on Roman Britain and the other on Christian origins.

[1] See above, p. 23.   [2] Op. cit., p. 55.

What we have to do is to try to show how demythologizing can be supplemented in such a way that it does not result in a complete subjectivizing of the sacred history and therefore in a complete uncertainty as to whether the possibility of existence which it exhibits is a genuine one or not. Gogarten, for instance, so stresses the difference between objective history and existential history that all contact between the two seems to be lost. Bultmann too sometimes speaks as if historical factuality were quite irrelevant, and for this reason Barth is able to make one of his keenest attacks, when he asks whether Bultmann does not make the *kerygma* something quite independent of the events which it proclaims, with Christ pushed out on the edge. The present writer has elsewhere ventured to criticize Bultmann on the grounds that he sets up a 'Christ of faith' whose relation to the 'Jesus of history' is, to say the least, exceedingly tenuous. And it is interesting to note that some of Bultmann's younger continental disciples, such as Ernst Käsemann, have raised much the same questions—whether the 'exalted Lord' of the Church stands in continuity with 'Jesus of Nazareth', and whether Bultmann's views do not ultimately commit us to the worship of a purely mythological figure.[1] Bultmann usually replies to such criticisms by saying that the critics are confusing two distinct matters—the *facts* which are accessible to historical research and the existential *possibilities* which are the province of theology. But surely it is not just a case of confusing these two, but rather of raising the real problem of whether and how they are related.

[1] On these points, see K. Barth, *Ein Versuch*, pp. 17-8; J. Macquarrie, *An Existentialist Theology*, pp. 22-3 and pp. 177-80; E. Käsemann, 'Das Problem des historischen Jesus' in *Zeitschrift für Theologie und Kirche*, LI, 1954, pp. 125-53. There has newly appeared a brief but scholarly examination of these issues, to which the reader should be referred: *A New Quest of the Historical Jesus*, by James M. Robinson (SCM Press, London, 1959). Professor Robinson takes the view that the older quest of the historical Jesus criticized by Albert Schweitzer—the nineteenth-century researches into the 'facts' about Jesus—was both impossible and illegitimate. It was impossible because the Gospels, as kerygmatic documents, do not supply the kind of data required by such research, and it was illegitimate— so he maintains—because this research worked with an inadequate conception of history. But fearing that contemporary theology may be driven into a realm of pure mythology, Professor Robinson adumbrates the possibility of a new quest. The purpose of such a quest, he tells us, would be 'to test the validity of the *kerygma's* identification of *its* understanding of existence with *Jesus*' existence'— op. cit., p. 94. In its essence, this view is perhaps not very far removed from the one put forward in the following pages, that the existential interpretation of the *kerygma* needs to be supplemented by pointing to an actual instance within history of the kind of life which the *kerygma* proclaims.

We have already rejected the idea that faith can be made to depend on historical research. The results of such research keep changing like the patterns of a kaleidoscope. To build a theology upon them would be like building a house on quicksands. There is scarcely an incident or a saying in the New Testament which does not get challenged at one time or another. But if we refuse to make theology dependent on historical research, are we not giving up historical factuality altogether? By no means; nor is anything new being claimed here.

Away back in David Friedrich Strauss, who was a pioneer in these matters, we find on the one hand the rejection of the idea that Christianity depends on historical research. 'It is', he says, 'impossible that the happiness of man, or, to speak more intelligibly, the possibility of fulfilling his destiny . . . can depend on his recognition of facts into which scarcely one man in a thousand is in a position to institute a thorough investigation, and, supposing him to have done so, then to arrive at a satisfactory result'.[1] Yet on the other hand he denies that 'the ideal Christ might have been present within us as much as it is now if a historic Christ had never lived or worked'.[2] Against a different background of ideas, Kierkegaard denies that the disciple who was contemporary with Jesus and had every opportunity for amassing biographical details has any advantage over the disciple of eighteen centuries later.[3] Yet he supposed that some information would need to have been left. 'If the contemporary generation had left nothing behind them but these words: "We have believed that in such and such a year God appeared among us in the humble figure of a servant, that he lived and taught in our community, and finally died", it would be more than enough.'[4] Whether it would indeed have been enough, we do not pause to inquire. These statements from such diverse figures as Strauss and Kierkegaard have been quoted simply to show that to claim that Christianity is not dependent on the variable results of historical research does not imply that one

---

[1] *A New Life of Jesus*, authorized translation (Williams & Norgate, London, 1879), II, p. 435. Nowadays it would probably be nearer the truth to say 'one man in a hundred thousand'!

[2] Ibid., p. 436.

[3] *Philosophical Fragments*, translated David F. Swenson (Princeton University Press, Princeton, 1936), pp. 44ff.

[4] Ibid., p. 87.

must therefore throw out the objective-historical altogether.

On the contrary, we have already seen that historical research into the New Testament always moves within certain limits.[1] Whatever its changing verdicts on this incident or that saying, there is here a minimal core of historical factuality which cannot be reasonably doubted, for just as our present experience of the *Iliad* testifies to the fact that there was an epic poet of genius in ancient Greece, so our present experience of the Church and the New Testament bears witness to an altogether outstanding person of about two thouand years ago. What is the minimum which we would need to infer? Simply that there was someone who once exhibited in history the possibility of existence which the *kerygma* proclaims. We may of course believe more than that. But that alone would be strictly necessary if we are to be assured that the existential possibility proclaimed in the *kerygma* is a genuine possibility and not just a moral or psychological fantasy. Talk of 'following Christ' might be just as ridiculous as talk of emulating the feats of Herakles if there were no assurance that the possibility of Christian existence has been fulfilled by someone under the conditions of 'real' life. And we can have reasonable assurance on this point, whatever historical criticism may be saying about the details of the Christian story at any given time. Put into theological language, the minimal assertion is that 'the Word became flesh and dwelt among us',[2] in one possible sense of this pregnant saying. And we may recollect that it was with precisely this quotation that Bultmann ended his essay on demythologizing.[3]

Of course, someone may ask whether the sceptical historian would admit even this minimum of historical factuality—that is to say, a real someone who exhibited in history the kind of existence which the *kerygma* proclaims. We come back to our assertion that historical research into the New Testament moves within certain limits. The limiting cases are, on the one hand, literal acceptance of everything in the New Testament as the veridical record of what happened, and, on the other, some form of Christ-myth theory which denies that there ever was a Jesus. But neither of these extreme positions stands up to scrutiny. Just as literalism has declined among educated

---

[1] See above, p. 74.   [2] John 1.14.   [3] *Kerygma and Myth*, p. 44.

Christians, so the Christ-myth theories are left with hardly an advocate—except perhaps in the Soviet-occupied area of Germany, where the Marxist views of Kalthoff and Kautsky (according to whom the figure of Jesus was the purely mythical creation of the Roman proletariat) have been revived for political ends. The research of scholars today lies between the extremes, and starts from the assumptions (*a*) that there was a Jesus and (*b*) that the accounts of him will embody legendary and mythical material. A few paragraphs back we referred to David Strauss as the pioneer in such research. Strauss was attacked not only by the orthodox for casting doubt on the literal truth of the record, but also at a later date by the advocates of the Christ-myth theories for not making it clear whether Jesus created the Church or the Church created Jesus. Surely the true judgment on Strauss—which agrees with the position which is being maintained here—is that which has been well expressed by H. G. Wood: 'Strauss showed his continued hold on the realities of history when he recognized that the Christian Church cannot be explained at all without the existence and influence of a creative personality, and when he assumed that the founder of a religious movement would be enshrined in an idealizing tradition'.[1]

Thus the picture which has emerged from our inquiry into the historical nature of Christianity is by no means a simple one. There is no straightforward solution to the problem. The existentialist approach has proved enlightening, but it leaves questions unanswered and demands supplementation. While we may accept Bultmann's statement that 'Christianity agrees with Gnosticism in placing the eschatological event in the present',[2] we have also to notice the other point (to which he almost immediately draws attention) that the Gnostic stories belong to a mythical age before history began, whereas the Christian story alludes to events which were quite recent for the early Christians. Again, while much of the New Testament history readily lends itself to existential interpretation and ought to be so interpreted, there is some of it which can hardly be taken as anything but plain factual assertion about the past.

---

[1] *Did Christ Really Live?* (SCM Press, London, 1938), pp. 21-2.
[2] *Primitive Christianity in its Contemporary Setting*, translated R. H. Fuller (Thames & Hudson, London, 1956), p. 200.

For instance, when we read that 'in the fifteenth year of the reign of Tiberius Caesar, Pontius Pilate being governor of Judea, and Herod being tetrarch of Galilee, and his brother Philip tetrarch of the region of Ituraea and Trachonitis, and Lysanias tetrarch of Abilene, in the high-priesthood of Annas and Caiaphas . . .'[1] we can only conclude that the writer's intention was to fix certain past events as accurately as he could in the framework of world-history.

Here we come up against what Bultmann himself recognizes as 'the paradox of Christ as the historical Jesus and the ever-present Lord. . . . For although the advent of Christ is an historical event which happened "once" in the past, it is, at the same time, an eternal event which occurs again and again in the soul of any Christian in whom Christ is born, suffers, dies, and is raised up to eternal life.'[2] But this is to acknowledge a limit to demythologizing, for in some sense the present event depends on the past event. Because human existence is not pure possibility but always possibility conditioned by facticity, we need some empirical anchor if we are to recognize any possibility as a genuine one and be assured that we are not being invited to chase after a chimera. Hence demythologizing needs to be supplemented with the assertion that there really was this kind of person, that this possible way of life has actually been exhibited in history.

14 *A Reply to Critics*

The conclusions which we have reached in the foregoing discussion may seem paradoxical enough, yet we have seen that nothing simpler will do justice to the very complex problem with which we were confronted. Three points which emerged were: a refusal to make theology dependent on historical research; a qualified approval of the existentialist approach to history; and an insistence that talk of possibilities must not be allowed to wander away from actualities. Much the same three points were made by the present writer in an earlier discussion of these topics along somewhat different lines.[3] Since the point of view expressed on that occasion has been subjected to some

---

[1] Luke 3.1-2. [2] *History and Eschatology*, pp. 152-3.
[3] *An Existentialist Theology*, pp. 159ff.

criticism, I should perhaps explain why I still impenitently adhere to the main features of it. Certainly, it is not that I have ignored the criticisms offered. On the contrary, I hope that I have sufficiently profited from them to have been able to present the case more clearly and more carefully than last time. Some of the criticisms have been taken into account in the preceding pages. There are, however, some specific points which call for further discussion.

Professor Ian T. Ramsey[1] acknowledges that the existentialist approach to the sacred history has some value, but he complains that the 'existential-historical is only related to the objective-historical problematically' and that the whole existentialist approach 'compromises, and may even exclude any reasonable account of' the objective-historical. His complaint is justified if the existential-historical and the objective-historical are set forth as if they were in flat opposition to each other, as if the 'outside' of a historical event and the 'inside' could get along independently of each other. But I have tried to show that no such divorce is necessary, and that indeed we must strenuously guard ourselves against it. The Christian way of life is not something which the Church has just made up out of her imagination, but something which she has learned from an actual instance of that kind of life to which her own continued existence testifies. Yet once the Church had grasped the significant structures of this way of life—in terms of love, self-giving, atonement, new life and so on—the details of the actual instance of the life become unimportant, and such incidents as may have been remembered become symbols illustrative of the kind of life itself. For this reason Bultmann can say that 'the historical person of Jesus was very soon turned into a myth in primitive Christianity'.[2] For this reason also theology is free from dependence on historical research, for what the Church preserves in her tradition is not the detailed portrait of a particular life, but her symbolic presentation of the way of life which that particular life first manifested. Is not Ramsey

---

[1] *Religious Language*, pp. 104ff.

[2] *Primitive Christianity*, p. 200. See also *Jesus Christ and Mythology*, p. 80: 'It is precisely the mythological description of Jesus Christ in the New Testament which makes it clear that the figure and the work of Jesus Christ must be understood in a manner which is beyond the categories by which the objective historian understands world-history.'

himself recognizing something of the sort when he says that 'the "facts" of the Gospels are never facts for which science or history is appropriate currency'? And even more when he points out that 'at the moment when the "risen Christ" is known in the village house in Emmaus, he ceases to be "seen" in a perceptual sense'?[1] The objective fact which is of importance is that around nineteen hundred years ago this kind of life was concretely manifested and shown to be a genuine possibility of historical human existence. But this need not be compromised by an existentialist approach to history. Rather, it needs to be asserted if we are not to lose ourselves in what we have loosely called 'gnostic' speculation.

Professor David Cairns has also criticized my views on the relation of Christian faith to history.[2] He himself holds a rather unusual view on the relation of faith to historical research—a view which would perhaps be difficult to defend. For though he does not think that faith can be confirmed by the positive findings of such research, he does believe that faith is vulnerable to negative findings. Referring to a passage in which I maintained that faith is independent of historical research, he asks frankly what the position would be if someone were to show that Jesus never lived.

I should have to reply first of all that, for reasons which have already been given, I cannot visualize that such a situation could ever arise. I have tried to show that historical research can neither confirm nor deny the claims of Christianity because, *inter alia*, such research deals only in probabilities and could never produce *conclusive* evidence. Moreover, I have also tried to show that antecedent to all research there is a minimal core of historical factuality attested by the existence before my eyes of the Christian Church and the New Testament—namely, the overwhelming probability that Christianity originated from a life of the kind which it proclaims. This means that I do not take Christ-myth theories seriously. If we examine the handful of scholars who have advocated such theories, we find that they never arrived at them through historical research but because of some presuppositions of one kind or another having nothing to do with history—presuppositions which may have been

---

[1] *Religious Language*, pp. 106, 129; cf. Luke 24.31.
[2] See *A Gospel Without Myth?* (1960), Part II, Chapter IV.

Marxist (K. Kautzsky) or pantheistic (A. Drews) or rationalist (J. M. Robertson) or psychological (P.-L. Couchoud).

For the sake of argument, however, let us suppose that someone had vindicated one or other of the Christ-myth theories. Obviously for some Christians this would make no difference at all—for instance, those who share the views of Braithwaite and Buri, whom we shall be discussing later. But from the point of view from which this book is written, it would make a serious difference. It would mean a grave impoverishment of the Christian religion if its central figure was not a real person but only the fictitious product of some starry-eyed dreamers. For then the Christian way of life would not be a way that had been opened up for us, but only a remote ideal which has never been manifested in the world and on which no one could embark with any confidence. It is for this reason that I have insisted that a purely existential interpretation of the sacred history needs supplementation if it is not to lead to a gnostic view. I have therefore stressed the importance of what I call 'the minimal core of historical factuality'—a core which, as I have tried to show, may reasonably be assumed to be constant and unshakable through all the shifting patterns of research.

Dr Ronald W. Hepburn has recently published a book in which he weighs the work of contemporary Christian apologists in the balance of logical analysis, and finds it wanting.[1] His criticisms deserve the careful attention of all theologians who are alive to the need for clear and coherent thinking about religious faith. I should like to discuss here some of the points which he raises in the course of a criticism of my exposition of the existential-historical approach to the New Testament.

After characterizing Gogarten's treatment of history as an audacious flight into subjectivity, Dr Hepburn laments that such continental aberrations appear to be spreading to the British Isles, traditionally the home of 'concreteness and empiricism'.[2] The biblical critics, it is said, have left us with so little 'pure history' on which to maintain a historical religion that even in this country the Bultmann line is winning adherents. It is true that some resistance is offered to a thoroughgoing subjectivizing. Dr Hepburn applauds my statement that

[1] *Christianity and Paradox* (Watts, London, 1958).   [2] Op. cit., pp. 109ff.

there could only be saving events if there had been certain objective events. 'We have', he says, 'touched down in the sanity of objective history.' But this blink of sanity is short-lived, for he finds the Bultmann influence supervening so that I am prompted to deny that theology can be dependent on historical research. I hope that in the present chapter I have made it clearer in what sense one can be reasonably sure of something in the past even when there are all kinds of conflicting theories about it. To give yet another example: if I am driving through an Irish valley and come upon a large boulder by the roadside, I can be reasonably sure on the evidence of what I see that at one time the boulder was set down there. Later I may inquire how it got there. Local legend tells me that Finn MacCoull tossed it over the hill from the next valley, but the guidebook tells me that it was deposited by a glacier. Here I have no difficulty in deciding which explanation is correct. Any explanation, however, would go on the assumption that the boulder had been set down. In the case of the origins of Christianity or of the Homeric poems, it is and probably will continue to be practically impossible to decide between the competing explanations. But here also there is a minimum which cannot reasonably be doubted—in the case of Christianity, a life of the kind which is set forth in the New Testament. We may well believe more, but I think that theology can get along quite well with this minimum of factuality, which it needs in order to assure itself that the way of life which it commends is a possibility in 'real' life.

I think that Dr Hepburn has misunderstood my remarks on the resurrection, though I acknowledge that they could have been more clearly stated. But I do not know on what grounds he can possibly impute to me the view that from 'the way the world looks to Christians today' or from 'the way they feel', one must conclude that 'the resurrection of Jesus occurred'. I suppose that to Christians as to other people the world sometimes looks cheerful, sometimes bleak, that their feelings may vary accordingly, and that if in some sense they believe in the resurrection, their belief rests on quite different grounds. Nor do I understand why Dr Hepburn should rebuke me for failing to bring psychology into the picture and confining myself to theology. The fact that I did so was not due to any lack of respect for the psychology of religion, but because I have always thought that theology and psychology work on different levels of explanation and do not, as Dr Hepburn seems to suggest, offer 'alternative explanations' between which we have to choose. Every belief, whether religious or irreligious, has its psychological history, but the question of its truth is another matter, even if its history is not entirely irrelevant to its truth. For instance, R. H. Thouless mentions the case of a man who became a convinced atheist and believed that he had done so as a result of long and careful study. Psychological analysis revealed that his fiancée had eloped with one of his fellow Sunday school teachers. The reaction to this event was the repudiation of the beliefs which had formerly bound them together.[1] It would be absurd to conclude from this that no one can be an atheist on intellectual grounds or that any argued defence of atheism is mere rationalization. Equally so with Christianity.

After Dr Hepburn has so stoutly championed objectivity, it is somewhat surprising to find him telling us that 'in so far as a story or parable delineates a way of life that we judge to be valuable, it is not of paramount importance whether or not the story or parable is historically true. It can do its job equally well if fictitious; sometimes better'.[2] It is even more surprising when he goes on to say that some of the existentialist historians come near to looking on the Bible in this way but they would not be easy in their mind if told that the biblical story is entirely fictitious. Here Dr Hepburn seems to be blaming these people for wanting to hold on to some objectivity, though formerly he was blaming them for running away from it! It is true, as he says, that the purely 'gnostic' view is 'immensely attractive'. But I would certainly want to hold on to some objectivity to persuade me that the way of life which is delineated is a possible one within the conditions of historical existence, and I should have thought that Dr Hepburn, as a good empiricist, would wish to do the same. For much of our fiction wanders far from fact and it is surely not being suggested that we should derive our way of life from a dream-world. The kind of fiction which would serve Dr Hepburn's purpose best

---

[1] *An Introduction to the Psychology of Religion* (Cambridge University Press, Cambridge, 1950), p. 82.
[2] Op. cit., p. 192.

would be the kind which attends most accurately to the possibilities and the limitations of human life—that is to say, the kind which comes nearest to actual historical existence. The existentialist historian would agree with Dr Hepburn that the Bible is to be interpreted primarily as the delineation of a way of life. But for my own part I would like some assurance that in a world which seems so inhospitable to it there *has been* a life of this kind—that the Word has become flesh.[1]

---

[1] Dr Hepburn thinks that for the Christian 'human ideals, strivings, aims must admit of ultimate realization'.—Op. cit., p. 151. The point which I wish to make here, however, is not that any ideal or way of life must be *realizable* but that it must be *realistic* if it is to engage our serious endeavour.

IV

DEMYTHOLOGIZING AND DOGMA

15 *Roman Catholic Interest in Demythologizing*

PROFESSOR BULTMANN'S advocacy of demythologizing has attracted quite considerable attention from Roman Catholic theologians. Two admirable full-length studies of his views have come from the pens of Jesuit scholars; a volume of essays in which Roman Catholic theologians consider various aspects of demythologizing has appeared in Germany; and in many recent books on general theology, Roman Catholic authors have devoted some space to a discussion of the subject.[1] As one may anticipate, Bultmann's views do not find acceptance. But nevertheless the examination of his teaching by these Roman Catholic scholars is fair-minded, patient and thorough; there is some sympathy with his aims, even when his methods are rejected; and there is frequently a more genuine appreciation of the fundamental issues than one finds in certain superficial criticisms which have come from other quarters.

Some of the Roman Catholic criticisms of Bultmann reiterate points which are made also by Protestant writers. There is, for instance, dissatisfaction with Bultmann's attitude toward the historical status of the events recorded in the New Testament. In particular, Bultmann's views on the resurrection have been attacked by Professor Karl Adam who wishes to maintain that 'the Easter events were a question of real history' and who thinks that Bultmann's analysis excludes such 'real' historicity.[2] Again, Roman Catholics join with Protestants in expressing

---

[1] See L. Malevez, S. J., *The Christian Message and Myth*, trans. Olive Wyon (SCM Press, 1958); René Marle, S. J., *Bultmann et l'Interprétation du Nouveau Testament* (Aubier, Paris, 1956); and *Kerygma und Mythos*, V, 'Die Diskussion innerhalb der katholischen Theologie' (Evangelischer Verlag, Hamburg, 1955).

[2] *The Christ of Faith*, translated Joyce Crick (Burns Oates, London, 1957), p. 351. Cf. his essay, 'Das Problem der Entmythologisierung und die Auferstehung des Christus' in *Kerygma und Mythos*, V, pp. 101ff.

dissatisfaction with Bultmann's approach to the problems of exegesis. In particular, his attempt to elucidate the New Testament teaching in terms of a self-understanding is criticized by Father Malevez who says that 'the Bible is not primarily a treatise on anthropology; its whole aim is the knowledge of God and the contemplation of God'.[1]

Yet these criticisms are made with a difference. It is interesting to note that both Bultmann and the Roman Catholics come under fire from Protestant critics on the ground that they surrender the 'once-for-all' character of the saving events of the New Testament. It may be that these attacks rest partly on misunderstanding and partly on the fact that some Protestants tend to make a fetish of the idea of 'once-for-all-ness'. But they point to something which Bultmann and the Roman Catholics have in common over against traditional Protestantism. This is the idea of a 'making present' or 're-presenting' (*repraesentatio*) of the past event in such a way that in some sense it is re-enacted now. The Council of Trent taught that Christ instituted the eucharist so that in it 'that bloody sacrifice which was once offered on the cross should be made present'.[2] Bultmann teaches that the cross becomes a present event not only in the sacraments but in every proclaiming and hearing of the Word. No doubt some of the underlying ideas about the nature of this 're-presenting' may be very different, but in each case there is the recognition that a saving event must be a present event rather than a bare fact of past history.

On the question of exegesis also, we find Father Malevez, in the course of an essay[3] in which he compares Bultmann and Barth in their approaches to the Bible, awarding more marks to Bultmann than to Barth. For from the Catholic point of view, there is more truth in Bultmann's opinion that the understanding which we already have of our own existence serves as a pre-understanding for the interpretation of the gospel than in Barth's contention that the content of the gospel is quite discontinuous with our natural self-understanding.

[1] Op. cit., p. 157.

[2] The conciliar and pontifical documents quoted in this chapter may be found in the standard work of H. Denzinger: *Enchiridion Symbolorum*, thirty-first edition, ed. K. Rahner (Herder, Freiburg, 1957).

[3] Reprinted as 'Appendix II' to the English edition of *The Christian Message and Myth*.

Although Catholic criticisms of Bultmann have thus partly coincided with Protestant criticisms, albeit with certain differences, we may also discern a distinctive field in which Catholic criticism has been especially active. This field is the relation of demythologizing to dogma. In the various Catholic writers who have discussed Bultmann, we find ourselves coming again and again to the question of what demythologizing implies for the traditional doctrines of the Christian faith. It is contended that 'nothing remains of the doctrine of the Trinity'; that the 'christological question, in the sense of the two-nature doctrine, is for Bultmann as impossible as it is unnecessary'; that, in short, Bultmann 'cannot escape the charge of having made an attack on the very substance of Christianity'.[1] It is indeed acknowledged that Bultmann's motives may be praiseworthy, for as one writer says, he has 'a pastoral and missionary concern', 'he is worried over the estrangement of our time and of the man of our time from God's Word and from the Christian faith';[2] and of course the Roman Catholic has exactly the same concern and worry. Yet it is believed that Bultmann has come to terms with contemporary thought only through an almost complete sell-out of the body of revealed Christian truths.

We can now appreciate more clearly why Bultmann's work has attracted so much attention among Catholic theologians, and why it should have been received with a mixture of sympathy and censure. For Bultmann's motives are not far removed from the motives of many Catholics who are concerned to advance the claims of the Christian faith in the modern secularized world, and who might well be attracted by some features of Bultmann's approach. But the results of Bultmann's work are at some points so much at variance with official Catholic teaching that it must be rejected, and a warning given of the danger to those Catholics who might be attracted. The present trends in Catholic theology seem to be quite definitely away from the direction in which Bultmann is moving.

After the Second World War, there was in the Roman Catholic Church a certain stirring of the theological waters. Large masses of the people had drifted away from any effective

---

[1] On these points, see Malevez, op. cit., pp. 125, 156; and H. Fries in *K.u.M.*, V, p. 32.
[2] Heinrich Fries, loc. cit., p. 31.

contact with the Church. It was felt—just as Bultmann felt—
that new language and new formulations were needed if the
gospel was to mean anything in the modern world. How could it
make any impact upon the people of today if it remained
tied to its expression in terms of an outmoded philosophy? For
any Roman Catholics who were thinking along these lines,
demythologizing might have had some attraction. But such
tendencies in Roman Catholic theology have not been en-
couraged, but rather the contrary. The official trend is in a
different direction. This official trend is towards strengthening
the position of Thomism, thus continuing the policy inaugurated by Pope Leo XIII's encyclical letter, *Aeterni Patris*,
of 1879, which recommended the study and development of
Thomism as a kind of perennial philosophy of Catholicism.
The present trend also stresses the teaching authority of the
Church, so that the area of free theological discussion is cut
down. And further, the trend is in the direction of doctrinal
developments—such as the interest in mariological doctrine—
which seem to make wider rather than narrower the gap
between Catholic dogma and contemporary thought.

The present official policy in Catholic theology has been
clearly laid down in the encyclical letter of Pope Pius XII,
Humani Generis, issued in 1950. A study of this encyclical will
help to throw light on some of the factors which determine
the Roman Catholic assessment of demythologizing.

First of all we must ask against whom this encyclical was
directed, and what were the errors into which they had fallen.
No theologians or groups of theologians are specifically indicated by the Pope. But it is made clear that some theologians
within the Catholic Church are following dangerous courses
and that their errors 'have already borne their deadly fruit in
almost all branches of theology'. What these errors are is stated
clearly enough. We may classify them under four headings.

1. Negatively, there is an alleged contempt for traditional
Catholic philosophy. We are told that the 'philosophy, received
and honoured by the Church, is scorned by some, who shame-
lessly call it outmoded in form and rationalistic, as they say, in
its method of thought. They say that this philosophy upholds
the erroneous notion that there can be a metaphysic which is
absolutely true. . . . Our traditional philosophy, with its clear

exposition and solution of questions, its accurate definitions of terms, its clear distinctions, can, they concede, be a useful preparation for studying scholastic theology which was in accord with the medieval mentality; but it hardly offers a way of philosophizing suited to the needs of modern culture. . . . While scorning our philosophy, they extol other philosophies of all kinds, ancient and modern, oriental and occidental, by which they seem to imply that any kind of philosophy or theory, with a few additions and corrections if need be, can be reconciled with Catholic dogma'. Three types of modern philosophy which the encyclical specifically mentions as having found favour with the innovators are immanentism, idealism and existentialism.

2. A further charge is that the theologians in question are lacking in proper respect for the teaching authority of the Church. This accusation follows from the first one. For if the Church has officially commended a certain philosophy, then to regard that philosophy as no longer adequate to the needs of the times is to disregard the teaching of the Church in this matter. The theologians who are being criticized may be on the way to subverting the teaching office of the Church and to claiming that matters on which the Church has already pronounced its mind should be open for free discussion. In this connection it may be noted that one of Bultmann's Catholic critics has maintained that in the controversies over demythologizing in the German Lutheran Church, that church has abdicated its teaching office and substituted for it discussion among theologians.[1]

3. A further accusation is that the innovators wish to bring dogma into line with modern thinking. They think of dogma as changing and evolving, at least in the manner in which it is expressed. 'Some', the encyclical says, 'wish to reduce to a minimum the meaning of dogmas, and to free dogma itself from a terminology long established in the Church and from philosophical concepts held by Catholic teachers.' Their motives may indeed be good—they are trying to 'satisfy modern needs' and to arrive at 'a more efficacious propagation of the kingdom of Christ'. But the effects are disastrous. If dogma, instead of adhering to traditional definitions, adapts

[1] Adam Fechter in *K.u.M.*, V, p. 71.

itself to new and perhaps ephemeral philosophies, it ceases to be something stable. It is replaced by 'conjectures and certain fluid and vague expressions of new philosophies'. Such conjectures are like the flowers of the field—they flourish today and tomorrow they are withered away. 'Dogma', says the encyclical, 'will become a reed shaken by the wind.' Among matters which the innovators are said to have called in question are whether God's existence can be proved by reason, whether creation had a beginning, whether angels are persons, the notion of original sin, the satisfaction made by Christ, the necessity of belonging to the true Church in order to be saved.

4. Finally, we notice some charges which give us a more positive indication of the nature of the views which are being censured. Apparently the innovators lay stress on the place of doing, willing, and deciding in religion. They distrust any purely intellectual approach to religious questions. Thus the encyclical claims that there is 'a denial of the validity of reason in the field of metaphysics'. Along with this denial, the innovators allege 'that our perennial philosophy is only a philosophy of immutable essences, while the contemporary mind must look to the existence of things, and to life, which is ever in flux. . . . They reproach this philosophy taught in our schools for regarding only the intellect in the process of cognition while neglecting the function of the will and the emotions.'

As over against these errors, the Pope gives guidance for Catholic theology. He maintains the ability of the human mind to attain to metaphysical knowledge. He upholds the place of traditional Catholic philosophy—'a patrimony handed down by earlier Christian ages' in which the 'method, doctrine and principles of the Angelic Doctor' have a special place of honour. It would be wrong to discard this philosophy, for it represents a point of view 'which has been formulated and perfected through many centuries of effort by men of no common genius and sanctity under the vigilance of the teaching Church, and not without the light and inspiration of the Holy Spirit'. Moreover, the teaching authority of the Church has weighed the principles of this traditional philosophy and given approval. Thus something like an intrinsic connection has grown up between the divinely revealed truths and the formulae in which they are expressed. All theological work must have regard to the teaching of the Church on these matters. It is acknowledged that theological language can be improved and perfected, that theologians must return to the sources of doctrine, and that false theories should be studied because even in them 'a certain amount of truth is concealed'. But all this must be subject to the pronouncements which the Church has made, and the encyclical is careful to lay stress on the Church's teaching office. It states that 'together with the source of positive theology, God has given to his Church a living teaching authority to elucidate and explain what is contained in the deposit of faith only obscurely and implicitly. This deposit of faith our divine Redeemer has given for authentic interpretation not to each of the faithful, not even to the theologians, but only to the teaching authority of the Church.'

When we look at this document, we cannot fail to notice the resemblance between the views of the Catholic theologians here censured and those of Rudolf Bultmann. There is the same dissatisfaction with traditional formulations, the same desire to find new theological expressions which will make an impact on contemporary thought. There is moreover the same tendency to turn away from rational metaphysics to the practice of the Christian life, from immutable essences to the flux of actual existence as willing and doing. But one cannot fail to notice either that the views criticized in the encyclical echo in certain respects the views of the Catholic modernists who were condemned some forty years earlier. It is easy to see that Bultmann's views might have an attraction for Catholics who have thought along similar lines. But it is easy to see also that these views are bound to come into collision with the official trend in Catholic theology.

The censures contained in *Humani Generis* are, however, very moderate, compared with the severity which was shown towards the modernists at the beginning of the century. Commenting on the encyclical, Dr Patrick J. Hamell says: 'The Holy Father's authoritative analysis and treatment of the errors and dangers inherent in such a new orientation of theology is at once enlightened, paternal and firm. He does not condemn indiscriminately, nor does he confine himself to condemnation. He does not deny that the aims and methods in question spring from motives in part praiseworthy, that there is a real problem to be faced, and that these new theories can provoke discussion ultimately to the good of theology. He affirms that our theology, philosophy and apologetics can and should be improved. But, nevertheless, these views contain grave errors and serious dangers, and the Sovereign Pontiff would be failing in his duty if he did not take cognizance of them, and he states openly and plainly that these dangerous opinions are being held and disseminated by some, a minority indeed of Catholic teachers, but a minority that can command a large audience.'[1] Dr Hamell's remarks are just. But some real problems remain here. Can we ascertain more precisely just where the difference lies between the official Catholic theology and those tendencies which it censures, while at the same time acknowledging that they have something commendable in them? Is it even possible that there may be some way of reconciling the two points of view?

In order to explore this problem, we must first direct our attention more closely to the Catholic conception of dogma (Section 16). Then we shall compare Bultmann's views with modernist tendencies within the Roman Catholic Church itself, and see how much they have in common (Section 17). This will bring into view two distinctive interpretations of Christianity (Section 18) and we shall be able to come to grips with the problem of how these two interpretations are related and whether they can be reconciled (Section 19).

16 The Catholic Conception of Dogma

The word 'dogma' has had an unfortunate history, so that today it has become almost a term of reproach. For long it has been used especially to designate the principles laid down by the Church in matters of faith. But in common usage it is now applied indiscriminately to any tenaciously held opinion, as when we speak of a political dogma or even of a scientific dogma; and usually the word carries with it the implication that the opinion is held not only tenaciously but on very insufficient grounds. We must try to put aside these misleading connotations which have gathered round the word if we are to

---

[1] See his paper, '*Humani Generis*: its Significance and Teaching' (Leinster Leader, Naas, 1956), pp. 6-7.

appreciate what it signifies in the very exact meaning assigned to it in the Catholic Church.

Dr Ludwig Ott says: 'By dogma in the strict sense is understood a truth immediately revealed by God which has been proposed by the teaching authority of the Church to be believed as such.'[1] This definition calls for some comment and amplification. Clearly it recognizes two distinct factors in dogma.

On the one hand, there is revelation. To say that a dogma is immediately revealed means that it is to be found in the sources of revelation which, from the Catholic point of view, include both the Holy Scriptures and the tradition of the Church. Thus a dogma is quite literally a God-given truth. It is not, for instance, an interpretation of religious experience or a symbolical way of expressing some element in the religious consciousness. It may, of course, be implicit rather than explicit in the sources. But in any case, it is held to be the expression of an *objective* truth.

On the other hand, there is the teaching authority of the Church. A dogma is not only revealed, but is proposed for belief by the Church, and this may be done either through a specific decision or else through the universal and authoritative teaching of the Church. Since the Church may from time to time promulgate a dogma, it might be supposed that there takes place a gradual change or evolution of dogmas. But it is denied that there can be any change in the content of dogmas such as was envisaged by Adolf von Harnack, for instance, in his conception of the history of dogma. 'The truth of the Lord endures for ever.'[2] When the Church promulgates a dogma for the first time, what happens is that something which has always been implicitly believed is now explicitly proposed for belief, or, as it is sometimes expressed, that a material dogma (which is not yet a dogma in the strict sense) is raised to the status of a formal dogma. Thus it is held that dogma is the expression of *immutable* truth.

These points may be illustrated from a recent example— the dogma of the assumption, promulgated in 1950 by the apostolic constitution, *Munificentissimus Deus*. It was pronounced

---

[1] *Fundamentals of Catholic Dogma*, trans. Patrick Lynch (Mercier Press, Cork, 1957), pp. 4ff.
[2] Ps. 117.2.

that 'Mary, the immaculate perpetually virgin mother of God, when the course of her earthly life was completed, was assumed body and soul into heavenly glory'. Here there is no direct scriptural evidence. But by deduction from various passages in the Bible together with ancient traditions of the Church, it is maintained that this dogma is divinely revealed and is contained in the sources of revelation. And further, although the bodily assumption of Mary into heaven has only recently been proposed for belief as a dogma, it is held that the Church has always believed in it. Thus there is claimed for even a recently promulgated dogma exactly the same objective and immutable truth as may be claimed for a dogma which is expressly set forth in the sources of revelation and has always been regarded as a dogma.

Objectivity and immutability are ideas which seem hard to reconcile with the kind of approach to Christian theology which we find in Bultmann and in those Roman Catholic innovators who might be expected to have some sympathy with his views. For either an existential interpretation of the Christian faith or one which tends to stress the will and emotions as over against the intellect would seem to have abandoned a pure objectivity, though it would be rash to say that they necessarily lead to subjectivity. But the opposition may not be so sharp as it seems at first sight. We may find that the choice is not between a pure objectivity on the one hand and a sheer subjectivizing on the other, but that religious truths are of a peculiar kind in which both subjective and objective factors are involved. Again, it would seem that movements like demythologizing or Catholic modernism clash with the idea of the immutability of dogma, in so far as they try to restate the beliefs of the Christian religion in terms of contemporary thought. But even here there need not be a head-on collision. It may be that in every formulation of a belief, there is something which is of permanent value and something which is merely accidental, arising from the circumstances under which the belief is formulated. To assert that Christian doctrines need to be brought up to date is not incompatible with the belief that there may be a 'faith which was once for all delivered to the saints'.[1] Bultmann in particular is very eager to maintain that his way of interpreting

[1] Jude 3.

Christianity is closely akin to what we find in the New Testament itself.

A more serious difficulty arises when we consider an aspect of dogma which has not so far been explicitly mentioned—its obligatory or binding character. According to Dr Ott, the promulgation of a truth by the teaching authority of the Church 'implies the obligation on the part of the faithful of believing the truth'.[1] In what sense can one ever be said to be obliged or bound to believe in the truth of anything? If I believe that all men are mortal, and that Socrates is a man, then it may be said that I am bound or obliged to believe that Socrates is mortal. Here the bindingness is logical in its nature and it would make sense to say that anyone is bound or obliged to believe whatever is logically implied by other beliefs which he holds. But clearly this is not what is meant when it is said that a dogma is obligatory for the faithful. For it might be the case that one of the faithful, after very careful study, was not convinced of the truth of a particular belief, let us say, the assumption of the Blessed Virgin. Let us suppose that this belief is now promulgated as a dogma. Then he becomes obliged to believe it, but the bindingness of this obligation is not logical. It is an obligation to obedience, and such obligation pertains to conduct rather than to belief. It is an axiom of ethics that one can be obliged to do only what is within one's power to do, and surely it is not within one's power to believe a statement at will, especially if there appear to be good reasons for withholding belief. One may even have a 'will to believe' and yet be reluctantly compelled to disbelief. The only way out of the difficulty would be to acknowledge that a dogma, in so far as it is obligatory, involves some practical element which can command obedience. But to acknowledge this is to abandon the idea that the content of a dogma is purely an objective truth of fact.

What about the teaching authority of the Church, which bulks so largely in any discussion of Roman Catholic theology? Is not this idea quite incompatible with the existentialist insistence on individual responsibility? On the one hand, it has to be said that individualism can run riot, and that it would be a rash and foolish man who never paid any attention to the collective wisdom and experience of the Church. On the other

[1] Op. cit., p. 4.

hand, it must be pointed out that the teaching authority of the Church is not so rigid as is sometimes supposed. Since the concept of the Church's teaching authority was already employed in the definition of dogma from which we set out, it would seem that belief in such an authority is not itself a dogma but rather a presupposition of all dogma. It is true that the nature of this authority may be clarified in a dogma, for instance, in respect of its infallibility. But not all the assertions of the teaching authority of the Church are held to be infallible or irrevocable, though naturally they would command respect.[1] The usual form of papal pronouncements in encyclical letters and the like is not, of course, held to be infallible. Thus, in a book which bears the *imprimatur*, Dom Illtyd Trethowan criticizes some aspects of Thomism, and writes concerning the encyclical *Humani Generis*: 'This encyclical certainly makes large claims for the philosophy of Saint Thomas Aquinas, but it does not impose belief in Saint Thomas's philosophical doctrines. What it does is to ordain that Saint Thomas's system must be taught in ecclesiastical establishments as a solid basis for Christian thought. There is no obligation to hold it all as true, but it must be expounded.'[2] Too much should not be read into this sentence, of course, for as its author rightly says, his book is an attack not upon Thomism but upon atheism. Nevertheless, we seem to find confirmation of the point made above —that one may have an obligation to do what is in one's power, in this case, to teach a certain philosophy, but hardly an obligation to do what may not be in one's power, in this case, to give intellectual assent to everything in that philosophy. That is to say, the recognition of a teaching authority need not mean the abrogation of the individual's responsibility, even if in fact it sometimes means as much.

We must now turn to the question of how the Catholic modernists interpreted dogma, and of how far Bultmann represents a point of view similar to theirs.

17 *Bultmann and the Catholic Modernists*

The most notable representative of Catholic modernism in the British Isles, Father George Tyrrell, defined a modernist

[1] See Ott, op. cit., pp. 10 and 287.
[2] *An Essay in Christian Philosophy* (Longmans, London, 1954), pp. 16-7.

H

as 'a churchman of any sort who believes in the possibility of a synthesis between the essential truth of his religion and the essential truth of modernity'.[1] The definition is a very wide one, but so was the movement itself. In a famous phrase, Pope Pius X called it the 'compendium of all heresies', and this phrase was expanded in the encyclical *Pascendi Gregis* of 1907, which, in its condemnation of the movement, said: 'Undoubtedly, if anyone were to attempt the task of collecting together all the errors that have been broached against the faith and to concentrate into one the sap and substance of them all, he could not succeed in doing so better than the modernists have done.'

Tyrrell and others maintained that the encyclical had travestied their views. But at least it is right in pointing to the eclectic nature of the movement. The modernists included men who were primarily biblical scholars, like Alfred Loisy, and who had come to very sceptical conclusions about the factual historical content of the New Testament, just as Bultmann has done.[2] On the other hand, the movement included men like Maurice Blondel, Lucien Laberthonnière and Edouard Le Roy, whose interest was rather in the philosophy of religion. It is in these philosophical views and in particular the conception of dogma to which they lead that we shall concentrate our interest, for we shall find here some kinship with Bultmann's view. And although modernism was proscribed by the Church it seems clear from the encyclical *Humani Generis* that similar views are still to be found in the Roman Catholic Church, even if they do not find favour with the authorities.

The two philosophical movements which had the chief influence on modernist thinking were the activism of Henri Bergson and the pragmatism of William James. But these two movements are fairly close to each other. According to one historian of philosophy, 'the difference between Bergson and James is the difference between a psychological biology and a biological psychology'.[3] These philosophies, with their stress upon living and doing, seemed to the modernists to offer a way

---

[1] *Christianity at the Crossroads* (Longmans, London, 1909), p. 5. See also A. R. Vidler, *The Modernist Movement in the Roman Church* (C.U.P., 1934).

[2] For an instructive comparison of Bultmann and the modernists, see B. M. G. Reardon's article, 'Demythologizing and Catholic Modernism' in *Theology*, LIX, pp. 445ff.

[3] Ralph B. Perry, *Philosophy of the Recent Past* (Scribners, New York, 1926), p. 186.

whereby the desired synthesis between religious faith and modern thought might be achieved. They were impelled towards this type of philosophy not just because the devastating results of historical criticism called for a re-interpretation of the Christian faith, but also because the traditional conception of faith in the Roman Catholic Church seemed inadequate in other ways. As it seemed to the modernists, too much stress had been laid on the idea of faith as an intellectual assent. Vitalism and pragmatism had stressed that the concrete reality of human life involves will and emotion as well as cognition, and faith is correspondingly conceived as the response of the total personality to the divine action. Faith has indeed its intellectual element, but this is thought of as derivative from action. Similarly, revelation is not to be regarded as an imperfectible deposit of objective truth. One could give assent to such truth without holding what could properly be called a religious belief. Revelation has to be lived in order to be apprehended. The dogmas of the Church are the partial and imperfect translation into intellectual terms of the living experience which man has of God.

It is clear enough that the views summarized here have much in common with Bultmann's existential interpretation of the Christian faith. There are, of course, differences as well. It may be that the modernist emphasis on religious experience leads to a more subjective view of faith than does existentialism which is as much opposed to a bare subjectivity as it is to a bare objectivity.[1] It may also be the case that Bultmann, having lived through the Barthian revolution in theology, has a more positive conception of revelation than the modernists who tended to think of it in evolutionary terms as man's developing awareness of God. But there is common ground in the view that religious beliefs get their meaning as they are lived out in human existence.

The modernist conception of dogma was expressed in an extreme form by Le Roy who, after the controversy was over, succeeded Bergson at the Collège de France. On this view, the

---

[1] It may be noted, however, that in another sense the modernists were more 'objective' than Bultmann. B. M. G. Reardon rightly points out that 'the experience to which appeal is made (by the modernists) is not merely individual but corporate and has therefore an "objectivity" which the former notably lacks' (loc. cit., p. 450).

dogmas of Christianity are not statements of objective truth but are to be regarded as symbols which function as rules of action. Thus the statement, 'God is a person', is interpreted not as an assertion about the nature of ultimate reality but as a command: 'Treat personal values as absolute.' The doctrine of Christ's resurrection becomes the injunction to live as if you were a contemporary of Christ. The principle may easily be extended to the dogma of the assumption. This dogma becomes a symbol which enjoins a proper reverence for the Blessed Virgin. When dogma is interpreted along these lines, then, of course, mariology presents no more intellectual difficulty than christology does. For in both cases the dogmatic formulations are regarded not as factual assertions but as symbols which commend a particular kind of conduct. Moreover, the theory explains how a dogma can have an obligatory character. The obligation is to lead a way of life, not to assent to propositions.

Le Roy was probably more radical than Bultmann. But there is obviously a fairly close tie-up between their respective points of view. There is not much difference, for instance, between saying that the resurrection is a symbol which enjoins a particular kind of conduct, and saying that it is a myth which is to be understood in its existential significance.

The extent to which Bultmann is in agreement with the modernists may perhaps be best illustrated by considering his treatment of a particular doctrine. For this purpose we may select a doctrine which is central to the Christian faith—the doctrine of the person of Christ. Bultmann's treatment of this doctrine has been especially criticized by Roman Catholic theologians. In his view, christology is subsequent to soteriology. That is to say, one does not begin with the idea of a pre-existent Son who becomes incarnate and atones by his blood for the sins of men.[1] It is rather that when one experiences atonement through hearing and responding to the Word, through following in the way of the cross and resurrection,[2] one recognizes Christ as the Word of God. This is made very explicit by Bultmann in one of his essays. He asks: 'How far is a christological pronouncement about Christ also a

---

[1] See above, p. 22. See Ian Henderson, 'Christology and History', in *The Expository Times*, LXV, p. 367ff.
[2] See above, p. 84.

pronouncement about oneself? Does he help me because he is God's Son, or is he the Son of God because he helps me?—so that the sentence, "And we have believed and have come to know that you are the Holy One of God", would be quite simply just a confession of significance for the "moment" in which it was uttered, and not a dogmatic pronouncement.'[1] Of course, as everyone knows, the ancient Church was concerned to define the metaphysical status of the person of Christ, and is often thought to have done so in a final form. But Bultmann points out quite correctly, just as the Catholic modernists had done, that assent to such formulae need not be an act of religious faith. 'Even the demons believe—and shudder'.[2] Bultmann's own contention is that in the New Testament 'the pronouncements about Jesus' divinity are not, in fact, pronouncements about his nature but seek to give expression to his significance'. Quite bluntly he declares: 'The formula "Christ is God" is false in every sense in which God is understood as an entity which can be objectivized, whether it is understood in an Arian or Nicene, an orthodox or a liberal sense. It is correct if "God" is understood here as the event of God's acting.'[3]

Of course, Bultmann is not saying anything very novel here. In the nineteenth century Albrecht Ritschl was saying something similar when he taught that a christological pronouncement is a value-judgment and 'not a judgment which belongs to the sphere of disinterested scientific knowledge'.[4] Long before that, Philip Melanchthon had taught that 'to know Christ is to know his benefits, not . . . to contemplate his natures'.[5] However, it has to be remembered that, in the hands of his more radical disciples, Ritschl's christology was reduced to the assertion of the unique importance of Jesus as a religious teacher; and that Melanchthon omitted his famous utterance from later editions of his writings. The question is not whether there is some truth in the pragmatic approach to christology, but whether such an approach is adequate.

[1] 'The Christological Confession of the World Council of Churches', in *Essays*, p. 280. Cf. John 6.69.

[2] James 2.19.   [3] Loc. cit., p. 287.

[4] *Justification and Reconciliation*, trans. H. R. Mackintosh and A. B. Macaulay (T. & T. Clark, Edinburgh, 1900), p. 398.

[5] *Loci Communes*, 1521, quoted by Ritschl, op. cit., p. 396.

That there is truth in the point of view under consideration is plain enough when we ask what was meant by the primitive confession of the Church that 'Jesus Christ is Lord'.[1] Here we are not asking the historical or philological question about what the word κύριος meant in the Hellenistic cults or in the Septuagint, whether, for instance, it implied divinity, as it presumably did. We are asking a purely logical question about the semantic function of the word 'lord' and its synonyms in other languages. And that question is easily answered. The word 'lord' is basically a rank-word, that is to say, it indicates a place on a scale. To say that Jesus Christ is Lord is to declare a commitment rather than to make a statement of fact, or, as Bultmann would express it, the sentence speaks not of Christ's nature but of his significance for faith. And indeed it is a commitment to a way of life which is involved. The sentence asserts the Christian paradox that the servant is Lord, that worldly valuations need to be reversed, that it is the man who loses his life who will find it.

But is the content of dogma exhausted when we have perceived its pragmatic sense? Is christology nothing more than the explication of Christ's significance for human existence? It is on such points as these that the Roman Catholic theologians who have written about Bultmann find it most difficult to come to terms with him. In particular, Father Malevez returns again and again to the criticism of Bultmann's christology. Malevez maintains that 'in the traditional interpretation, christology, without being separated from soteriology and remaining in close and vital connection with it, did in some way or another precede it, and was indeed its founder'.[2] He is asking, in other words, whether there could be a soteriology without a christology as its presupposition. In Bultmann, he finds that 'we are no longer confronted either by the ontological reality or the spiritual presence of the ever-living Christ. . . . All that concerns us is the message of which he is the instrument. The essence of faith is the confession of Jesus as Lord.'[3] In yet another passage, Malevez points out that traditional christology 'predicates a kind of external objectivity of the union of God and man, entirely independent of the faith which man professes'; but in Bultmann's theology everything is referred to 'the *existentiell*

[1] Phil. 2.11.   [2] Op. cit., p. 78.   [3] Ibid., p. 124.

hic et nunc of actual faith'.[1] Malevez thinks that Bultmann's approach means a grave impoverishment of the Christian faith, for he believes that it makes our Lord's own status an ambiguous one. Aptly quoting the words of Saint Mary Magdalene in the garden, he asks: 'How can the Christian reader of Bultmann help exclaiming in his surprise, "They have taken away my Lord, and I do not know where they have laid him." '[2]

18 *Two Views of Christianity*

At this point we seem to have come to an *impasse*. On the one hand there is the view of dogma as the expression of objective supernatural truths; on the other hand, there is the view of dogma as the more or less mythical expression of a way of life. The first view is maintained by official Catholic teaching, and, of course, by much Protestant orthodoxy besides; the second view is put forward by Bultmann and by those more or less heterodox elements in the Catholic Church which emphasize willing and doing. The contrast is brought very sharply into focus if we consider what a distinguished Roman Catholic scholar has recently said about the New Testament. Jean Daniélou sees the essence of the New Testament revelation in the doctrine of the Holy Trinity. 'Without doubt', he says, 'the master-key to Christian theology is contained in the statement that the Trinity of Persons constitutes the structure of Being. . . . The whole history of salvation may be considered as a gradual unveiling of the ineffable Trinity.'[3] The language here is unmistakably 'transcendent' and metaphysical. Bultmann's approach to the New Testament is, on the other hand, frankly anthropological, and for him the history of salvation is the unveiling of a possibility of human existence. These two points of view seem to be separated by an unbridgeable gulf.

Yet it may be the case that these two views of Christianity are both as old as Christianity itself. There have always been those who thought of Christianity primarily as a revelation of supernatural truth and those who thought of it primarily as a way of life. And we may take some encouragement from the fact that even when one of these views has assumed an extreme form, it never seems to have been able quite to do without the other

---

[1] Ibid., p. 144.   [2] Ibid., p. 117. Cf. John 20.13.
[3] *God and Us*, trans. Walter Roberts (Mowbray, London, 1957), pp. 118-9.

one. Like transcendence and immanence, subjectivity and objectivity, and many other pairs of opposites, it may be that these two views imply one another, and that each needs to be supplemented by the other.

This point may become clearer if we consider briefly two fairly extreme manifestations of the opposing points of view in the nineteenth century—at the one extreme, Cardinal Newman, and at the other, Matthew Arnold. Newman may be taken to stand for the dogmatic interpretation of Christianity, and Arnold for the pragmatic interpretation.

Newman's attitude to religion is strongly intellectualist. 'First', he says, 'was the principle of dogma. . . . From the age of fifteen dogma has been the fundamental principle of my religion; I know no other religion; I cannot enter into the idea of any other sort of religion; religion, as a mere sentiment, is to me a dream and a mockery.'[1] Whether a religion is necessarily 'mere sentiment' because it is not dogmatic is, of course, questionable. But for Newman, the language of dogma is exact scientific language. Theology is a science which describes, for instance, the being and attributes of God with the same precision and objectivity as geology describes the strata of the earth's crust. Even Newman's hymns are dogma—'Firmly I believe, and truly, God is three and God is one'.

Matthew Arnold, on the other hand, says: 'When we are asked, "What is the object of religion?"—let us reply, "Conduct" '.[2] As he sees it, the chief concern of religion is to produce a certain kind of life. He denies that the language of religion is scientific. It is on the contrary literary language—perhaps we would now say 'mythical' language—which, as he says, is 'thrown out at a not fully grasped object of the speaker's consciousness'. Metaphysics, he thinks, has nothing to do with religion. Salvation cannot depend upon having correct metaphysical opinions about the personal nature of God, about the consubstantiality of the Son with the Father, and so on. Arnold is never tired of hitting at those who profess to have this exact knowledge of the mysteries of God. 'To think they know what passed in the council of the Trinity is not hard to them,' he writes; 'they could easily think they even knew what were

---

[1] *Apologia Pro Vita Sua* (Longmans, London, 1864), p. 120.
[2] *Literature and Dogma* (Smith Elder, London, 1873), p. 18.

the hangings of the Trinity's council chamber.'[1] Arnold himself speaks of God in vague terms as the 'Power not ourselves which makes for righteousness'. He tells us that doctrine is 'practical and experimental'; it has no meaning 'except in positive application to conduct, but in this application is inexhaustible'. A greater contrast from Newman could hardly be conceived, but this view of religion is certainly not 'mere sentiment'.

However, we are able to recognize both Newman and Arnold as Christians because neither of them really pushed his point of view beyond a certain limit. For if anyone carried the dogmatic point of view to its conclusion, Christianity would become a system of metaphysical truths about God and the universe to which one might give an intellectual assent without becoming involved in anything of the nature of a religious commitment. And if one carried the other view to its conclusion, then Christianity would become an ethic with, once again, nothing distinctively religious left in it. One point of view or the other may be pushed pretty far, but so long as we remain within the ambit of what is still recognizable as a form of Christianity, it would seem that each needs to be supplemented by the other. But if this is so, then the gulf between them cannot be entirely unbridgeable.

With this in mind, let us now return to the opposition between official Roman Catholic theology and those points of view, including Bultmann's, which interpret doctrine in terms of what it means for our human existence. By the decree, *Lamentabili Exitu*, of 1907, the Roman Catholic authorities condemned sixty-five propositions. The sources of these propositions were not specified, but in general they may be taken to represent positions imputed to the modernist movement. A good many of the propositions are concerned with matters of biblical criticism, and clearly some of the condemnations would strike at Bultmann's work as a biblical scholar. But it seems to be the case that in practice the Catholic Church now allows a reasonable amount of freedom to the biblical critic. Again, some condemnations which apply to certain ideas of the nature of revelation might be escaped by Bultmann, for, as we have noted, he probably has a more positive conception of revelation than had some of the Catholic modernists. The crucial

[1] Op. cit., p. 322.

point so far as Bultmann is concerned may well be the condemnation of Proposition 26, which reads: 'The dogmas of faith
are to be held only according to their practical sense, that is,
as a preceptive norm of action, not as a norm of belief.' But
even in this proposition there is a saving word, and that is,
of course, the word 'only' (*tantummodo*). Although the essence
of demythologizing is existential interpretation, it is not clear
that Bultmann holds that the doctrines of the Christian faith
are 'only' a way of commending a possible kind of human
existence. The two ways of looking at Christianity which we
have contrasted are, for all their opposition, not mutually
exclusive. Both have their origin and their right within the
nature of religion itself, and though either may be exaggerated
at the expense of the other, the theological problem is to find a
proper balance between them. To the further consideration of
this problem we must now turn.

19 *The Possibility of Reconciling the Two Views*

The question confronting us is that of the nature of dogmatic
language. Does dogma, as it seems to do, make an assertion
about 'reality'? Or does it express a self-understanding, or
disclose a possibility of existence, or commend a way of life, or
however we may wish to put it? Or—as we have already seen
some reason to believe—does it in some obscure way combine
these functions? Modern linguistic analysis has made it plain
that forms of language may often mean something different
from what they appear to say—that their grammatical form is
not necessarily a guide to their logical function.

We may go to the heart of the matter by considering the
key-word of all Christian theology—the word 'God'. What
does the word 'God' mean? We are not of course asking about
the nature and attributes of God in the Christian idea of God.
Prior to such questions is the question of how the word 'God'
functions in sentences in which we use it. Consideration will
show that the word has a dual meaning, and seems to perform
two distinguishable semantic functions.

Let us begin with Martin Luther's understanding of the
meaning of the word 'God'. He thought that 'God' means the
best that one can know. In his catechism, he taught that a
man's 'God' is what he sets his heart upon and trusts to.

Luther's way of describing God was actually the result of a mistaken etymology. He thought that the word 'God' (*Gott*) is cognate with the word 'good' (*gut*). Philologists tell us that this is not the case, but nevertheless what is bad etymology might happen to be good theology. It is clear enough that on this view 'God' functions chiefly as a value-word. Indeed, it denotes a supreme value. One could quote many instances in which the word is plainly used in this way. When Saint Paul says of certain people that 'their god is the belly', he immediately goes on to explain his meaning by adding that they have 'minds set on earthly things'.[1]

To ascribe a supreme value to anything is, however, to express one's own attitude towards it. We may recall Bultmann's view that a christological pronouncement about Christ is also a pronouncement about oneself. So it is, if the sentence, 'Christ is God', means 'Christ is the best that we can know'. In this sense, it is what Ritschl called a value-judgment. It expresses what Bultmann calls a self-understanding. What it brings to words is a commitment rather than an objective statement of fact. In the use of 'God' as a value-word, we find the source of existential and pragmatic interpretations of dogma. Clearly, however, this axiological sense, if we may call it such, is fundamental to the word 'God'.

It need not therefore surprise us that Luther's colleague, Melanchthon, could say that 'to know Christ is to know his benefits'. Nor does it surprise us to find that Matthew Arnold quotes with approval Luther's definition of 'God'—though Arnold knew more about the etymology than Luther did.[2] And finally, it does not surprise us to find Karl Barth, in a critical passage, asking how he is to classify Bultmann. Is he a rationalist, or an apologist, or a disinterested historian? Or is he a philosopher or a theologian? Barth concludes that the best description is to say that Bultmann is simply a Lutheran, with Herrmann, Ritschl, Melanchthon and Luther himself behind him.[3]

If the word 'God' were used *purely* as a value word, then there would not, of course, be involved any assertion of the reality of God. The ultimate conclusion, if the value interpretation of God were pushed to its extreme, would be either

---

[1] Phil. 3.19.   [2] *Literature and Dogma*, pp. 12-3.   [3] *Ein Versuch*, pp. 41-7.

an ethic or a religious atheism. That 'religious atheism' is not a contradiction in terms may be seen from an essay of Professor J. N. Findlay which has received a good deal of attention. Findlay disbelieves in the existence of God, but he thinks that religion is still possible. The place of God is taken by what he calls an 'imaginary focus'[1] of ideals which demand the same 'unquestioning reverence' as does the God of theism. Now, one of the reasons which Findlay gives for preferring an atheistic to a theistic religion may seem at first sight very surprising. He says: 'I am by temperament a Protestant, and I tend towards atheism as the purest form of Protestantism.'[2] These words would probably horrify Luther, if he could read them, yet they might well be claimed to follow from ascribing a *purely* axiological meaning to the word 'God'.

Findlay thinks that to identify ideals with anything existent may easily lead to idolatry. But would it not rather be the case that to set up one's own ideals as the object of a religious reverence would even more easily conduce to idolatry? Findlay seems to think, mistakenly, that Christianity identifies God with the historical Jesus, for he says that in Christianity 'the divine is *identified* with a particular historical person who existed in no analogical manner but precisely as you and I do'.[3] It is indeed true that some of the Ritschlians came near to making such an identification, but the charge made against them was precisely the one which Findlay makes: idolatry.[4] Since orthodox Christian theology thinks of Christ as one of the 'persons' of the Trinity, the proposition, 'Christ is God', is not convertible. The Christian, on the other hand, might think that it was idolatrous to identify 'God' with one's own subjective aspirations. For however exalted these aspirations might be, they would have arisen from one's own creaturely and imperfect nature. Can we speak of a truly religious and unquestioning reverence unless it is directed to something

---

[1] 'Can God's Existence Be Disproved?' in *New Essays in Philosophical Theology* (SCM Press, London, 1955), pp. 47ff. See especially p. 56 and pp. 73-5.

[2] Even Findlay, however, does not seem to carry this point of view to its uttermost length, for he is willing to speak, albeit tentatively, of what he calls a 'godward trend in things' (loc. cit., p. 74).

[3] Loc. cit., p. 75.

[4] Cf. Sydney Cave, *The Doctrine of the Person of Christ* (Duckworth, London, 1925), pp. 196ff.

which stands over against ourselves, before which we recognize ourselves to be 'but dust and ashes',[1] and to which we ascribe a 'reality' of its own? We may recall Saint Augustine's quest for truth which led him to find 'the unchangeable and true eternity of truth, above my changeable mind'.[2] This truth he identifies with God. But the demand which this truth makes upon him he experiences as coming from beyond himself. In a rather similar way, Bultmann thinks of the kerygmatic word addressing us as a word of God—a word which has about it an absolute quality, differentiating it from any merely human word. It is not simply that we set a supreme value on something and call it 'God'. The very fact that we regard some gods as idols implies that there is a 'true God'. And the true God is the God who is experienced as standing over against us and demanding that we set value on him. He is independent of us in not being just a subjective ideal or an imaginary focus.

This brings us to the second strand of meaning in the word 'God'—what we may call its ontological sense. Saint Thomas Aquinas has an entirely different approach to the meaning of 'God' from the one which we found in Luther. And curiously enough, like Luther, he bases his interpretation on a very doubtful piece of etymology which connects the name of Yahweh with the Hebrew verb signifying 'to be'. Once again, however, doubtful etymology may lead to sound theology. Saint Thomas has in mind the scriptural passage in which God reveals his name to Moses. 'I AM WHO I AM. Say this to the people of Israel, "I AM has sent me to you."'[3] Saint Thomas asks whether this name, which he renders HE WHO IS, is the most proper name of God, and he replies that it is, because, among other things, 'it does not signify some form, but being itself. Hence, since the being of God is his very essence (which can be said of no other being) it is clear that among other names this one most properly names God; for everything is named according to its essence'.[4] This ontological sense of the word 'God' is just as primordial as the axiological sense. The ontological sense makes it possible for religion to be conceived as a doctrine, just as the other sense makes possible the interpretation of religion as a way of life. It would seem that we cannot dispense with either sense

---

[1] Gen. 18.27.   [2] *Confessions*, VII, 23.   [3] Ex. 3.14.
[4] *Summa Theologica*, I, q. 13, art. 11.

without losing something that is fundamental to the meaning of the word 'God'.

In a recent essay, R. M. Hare remarks: 'If we take religious language as a whole, it is too factual to be called specifically moral, and yet too closely bound up with our conduct to be called in the ordinary sense factual'.[1] In the current jargon, such language is both descriptive and prescriptive. We are suggesting that religious language gets this paradoxical character from the dual function of its key-word, 'God'.

The contemporary theologian who has perhaps most clearly grasped the ambivalent character of the word 'God' is Paul Tillich. He has two characteristic ways of talking about God. The first way is in terms of 'ultimate concern', which corresponds to the existential or axiological sense of the word 'God'. The second way is in terms of the 'ground of being' or 'being-itself', which corresponds to the ontological sense.[2] Tillich has the further merit of having sought to clarify the ontological sense of the word 'God'. When used as a noun, the word 'being' has two distinct senses, which some other languages are able to distinguish better than English does. 'Being' may mean 'that which is', 'entities', τά ὄντα, das Seiende. It may also mean 'is-hood', the character in virtue of which entities 'are', τὸ εἶναι, das Sein. If we use 'entity' for the first of these two senses, and reserve 'being' for the second sense, then we must admit that traditional theology has wobbled between them, sometimes speaking of God as if he were an entity, sometimes speaking of him as if he were pure being. Clearly, however, he cannot be both. Tillich appears to think of God as being,[3] and for this reason one cannot properly say that he 'is'; attempts to prove his 'existence' are bound to fail, and yet one must ascribe to him more 'reality' than to anything else.

Someone may object that being, in the sense in which we have spoken of it here, 'is' just a ghost in the machine. But what

[1] 'Religion and Morals' in *Faith and Logic*, ed. Basil Mitchell (Allen & Unwin London, 1957), p. 189.

[2] See his *Systematic Theology*, I (Nisbet, London, 1953), pp. 14-5, 173, 259, etc.

[3] Even Tillich is not quite clear in his use of the word 'being'. To say that God is the 'ground of being' and to say that he is 'being-itself' involves a double sense in the word 'being'. For as an ultimate, 'being-itself' cannot have a 'ground'. The 'ground of being' must mean the 'ground of entities'. 'Being-itself' 'is' the 'ground of entities' in the sense that it is through participation in 'being' that anything 'is'.

makes a machine as distinct from a collection of wheels, nuts, bolts, and so on, is precisely its 'machine-hood', the unity which gives it the kind of being belonging to machines, and this is not another wheel or cog or anything of the sort. It is not another thing, and yet it is more important than anything in the machine. To say that God is being rather than that he is an entity is not to detract from his reality, but rather to assert for him a 'reality' beyond that of any possible entity.

Now Tillich's criticism of Bultmann is that while they both share an existential approach to theology, Bultmann gives an ethical interpretation while Tillich claims that his own interpretation is ontological. But this is really the point behind the Roman Catholic criticisms of Bultmann. Dogma has an ontological sense as well as an existential or pragmatic sense. In some way, it illuminates being-itself as well as existence, or man's being. Father Malevez may be exaggerating, but he has some grounds for saying that Bultmann's theology 'is absolutely silent about the God whom it urges us to worship; there is nothing about his nature or attributes'.[1]

It has to be admitted that Bultmann sometimes speaks as if the doctrines of Christianity could be reduced entirely to statements about possibilities of human existence. Yet it is only fair to recognize that it is certainly not his intention that all 'transcendent' reference should be eliminated from dogma, and he explicitly says so.[2] As a disciple of Heidegger, he is well aware of the connection between the existential and the ontological. The approach to the problem of being is by way of existence, because man, as existent, is the entity which not only is but has some understanding of its own being; yet that understanding which he has of his own being can be clarified only in the light of an understanding of being as a whole. Bultmann lays the stress on the attainment by man of his own authentic being. But to attain such being would at the same time be to penetrate into the mystery of being-itself. In the long run, the existential and ontological senses of dogma cannot be divorced.

This does not mean that any particular dogma has two meanings, and that it has to be interpreted both as a statement of fact and as an illustration of an existential possibility. The meaning is rather that the body of Christian doctrine as a whole

[1] Op. cit., p. 156.   [2] See pp. 22ff.

has a twofold function—it sets forth a way of life, an authentic existence for man, and yet at the same time it sheds light on the problem of being as a whole. The value of the Roman Catholic criticisms of Bultmann is that they bring out very clearly the second of these two functions. When one has asked all the questions that can be asked about this human existence of ours, one has still to go on to ask the questions about that wider being within which 'we live and move and have our being'.[1] It is certainly the function of religion to shed some light on these wider questions. Heidegger is right in regarding existential analysis as preparatory to the problem of being as such, and the Catholic Church is right in condemning the proposition that dogmas are to be understood *only* according to their practical sense. This means, however, that in the field of doctrine, as in the fields of exegesis and history, we strike upon a limit to demythologizing, understood as a purely existential interpretation. The existential interpretation needs to be supplemented by an ontological interpretation. But that Bultmann himself is well aware of the limit will become clear when we turn, as we must now do, to those strictures which have been passed on his theology by his critics on the left wing.

[1] Acts 17.28.

V

DEMYTHOLOGIZING AND KERYGMA

20 *From Demythologizing to Dekerygmatizing*

WE have now reached a turning-point in our inquiry. Up
to this point, we have examined some of the discussions which have taken place between Bultmann and
those of his critics whom we have described as belonging to the
right wing—men like Barth, Cullmann, Thielicke, Malevez
and others whose theological outlook is in general more
conservative and traditional than Bultmann's is. Now we must
turn to critics of the left wing—to those theologians and
philosophers in whose eyes Bultmann himself appears too
conservative. This means that we shall have to submit ourselves
to a mental readjustment. We must now expect that those
features of Bultmann's theology which were condemned as
vices by the critics so far considered will be hailed as virtues by
the critics to whom we are about to turn; and we must expect
equally that the few virtues which the right-wing critics were
able to find in Bultmann will now be condemned as remnants of
superstition and dogmatism from which Bultmann has failed to
purge his thought. Some of the problems we shall consider will
be much the same as those we have met already, only we shall be
seeing them from the other side. Thus they may appear very
different, just as a range of mountains may present very different
aspects, depending on whether one sees it from the east or from
the west.

We have now to ask what lies beyond the limit which Bultmann sets to demythologizing, and see what happens when the
method is followed out to its end. If we recall the tableau from
which we set out on our inquiry,[1] what is now demanded of us
is that we should make the perilous descent down the cliff

---
[1] See above, p. 11.

before which Bultmann himself turned aside, and explore the
country which lies down there. It will be remembered that
Dante in his pilgrimage had the good fortune to meet with
Vergil, and that the latter offered to be his guide and instructor
on a visit to the underworld.[1] We too are fortunate in finding a
guide who is willing to conduct us through that region which we
desire to visit. He is Professor Fritz Buri, who has made a
preliminary survey of the territory which lies beyond Bultmann's limit to demythologizing, and who has brought back
glowing reports of what he has found there. These reports
suggest that Buri has discovered a promised land for theology,
where she may dwell in peace, no longer harassed by sceptical
philosophies. Before we embrace these reports too enthusiastic-
ally, however, we must make sure that the desirable state of
affairs which they describe has not been achieved by banishing
theology to a limbo where she enjoys peace only because she
has been reduced to a shade. The present writer once mentioned
some grave dangers which he believed to be inherent in
Bultmann's theological method, and suggested that there might
appear 'some disciple of his, with more consistency and less
insight than his master', who would run straight into such
dangers.[2] These words might well be applied to Buri—at
least, as far as the greater consistency is concerned, though
whether he shows greater or less insight than Bultmann can be
judged only after we have examined what he has to say.

It must, however, be conceded at the outset that, as a
thinker, Buri is not lacking either in courage or in originality.
Having once chosen his path, he is prepared to follow wherever
it may lead. It is likely that we shall hear more of him in
the years to come, for in one of those multi-volumed dogmatics,
beloved of continental theologians, he is working out a distinctive type of theology, streamlined (in thought if not in
bulk) to the needs of the contemporary age. It was announced
by the publishers as 'the first liberal dogmatics in thirty years',
and certainly to read Buri's work is like getting a breath of clean
fresh air after the stuffiness of the Barthian period. However,
this is liberalism with a difference. Buri may be fairly classed as
an existentialist theologian. As Bultmann stands to Heidegger,
so Buri appears to stand to Jaspers. They are colleagues at

[1] *Inferno,* Canto I.   [2] *An Existentialist Theology,* p. 243.

Basel, just as Bultmann and Heidegger once were at Marburg. Strangely enough, however, although Jaspers is commonly supposed to teach a philosophy which stands closer to Christianity than Heidegger's does, Buri's theology turns out to be more radical than Bultmann's.[1]

Karl Barth has described Buri's work as 'an uninhibited radicalizing of Bultmann's radicalism', and that is quite a good description.[2] In his relation to Bultmann, Buri is at once a disciple and a critic. He embraces with enthusiasm the method of demythologizing. Our task is to interpret the Christian faith in terms of existence. 'The mythological expression for the success of this undertaking', he says, 'is the testimony of the Holy Spirit which, for existence, is neither a magical nor a rational force, but the actualization of the mythical symbol in a concrete historical situation'.[3] Here we seem to get all the demythologizing that anyone could demand. Buri acknowledges that Bultmann is a master in demythologizing. All this side of Bultmann's theological enterprise is for Buri clear and convincing. Unlike the critics whom we have so far considered, Buri has no doubt that demythologizing is a proper path for Christian theology to follow. But when Bultmann goes on to speak of the *kerygma* and of God's decisive act in Jesus Christ, Buri can no longer applaud his work. If we once set out upon the road of demythologizing, then, according to Buri, we ought to stick to that road. He cannot see how the kerygmatic element in Bultmann's thought can be combined with the principles of demythologizing at all. Thus Buri's criticisms are directed not upon demythologizing but upon the place which Bultmann wishes to give to the *kerygma* in theology. It seems to Buri that Bultmann, after starting off in the right direction, has turned aside and lost the way. He has allowed himself to be deflected from his task when he was only halfway through with it. A work which in its beginnings seemed so clear and promising

---

[1] The account of Buri's thought given in the present chapter is based on the following works, published by Paul Haupt, Bern: *Die Reformation geht weiter* (four popular lectures), 1949; *Theologie der Existenz* (an outline of systematic theology), 1954; *Dogmatik als Selbstverständnis des christlichen Glaubens*, Band I, 1956; three further volumes of the *Dogmatik* are projected. Buri's criticisms of Bultmann are to be found in the two essays, 'Entmythologisierung oder Entkerygmatisierung der Theologie' (*Kerygma und Mythos*, Band II, pp. 85ff.) and 'Theologie der Existenz' (*Kerygma und Mythos*, Band III, pp. 81ff.).

[2] *Ein Versuch*, p. 55.   [3] *Theologie der Existenz*, p. 106.

has become bogged down in confusions and difficulties, all because of Bultmann's stubborn adherence to the idea of a *kerygma*. Thus the disciple of Bultmann turns into a critic, in the sense that he finds Bultmann's work inadequate, and wishes to carry it a stage further. Demythologizing cannot be arbitrarily halted when a theologian thinks that he has had enough of it. It must be carried through in a radical way. As Buri sees it, the theology of Bultmann cannot be left as it stands, for there are two grave objections to it.

The first objection is that Bultmann has got himself tangled up in logical inconsistency. Buri notices, as we have done also, that Bultmann speaks with two voices. One voice announces the end of myth, and proceeds to translate mythological into existential statements. But the other voice proclaims the *kerygma* and announces God's decisive dealings with man in the event of Jesus Christ. According to Buri, however, this *kerygma* is just a residue of myth which should be dealt with in the same way as other myths. Bultmann has demythologized miracles, resurrection, eschatology, and the like, but he stops short at the *kerygma*. It is not to be taken away by demythologizing, but set free. Perhaps Bultmann is suffering from a kind of hangover, resulting from his close association in the early days with the kerygmatic theologians. Perhaps by making a concession to the *kerygma*, Bultmann may have saved himself from an accusation of heresy. Perhaps he has not wished to overturn too many altars at once. But whatever his underlying motives may have been, he has, according to Buri, paid too high a price in retaining the idea of a *kerygma*. The price is a radical inconsistency and obscurity in his thinking. Indeed, Buri goes so far as to say that Bultmann has made lack of clarity into a principle of his theology! And he declares roundly that there is *no way out* from Bultmann's difficulties.[1]

Even from this summary of his argument, we may well be driven to wonder whether Buri has not overstated his case. He may be too hasty in concluding that there is 'no way out'. He gives no consideration to the possibility which we ourselves have in view, namely, that the ambiguities in Bultmann may be of the nature of paradoxes rather than of irreconcilable contradictions. Not for Buri is the patient working out of

[1] On these points, see *K.u.M.*, II, pp. 85, 93, 96.

paradox. He does not seem to appreciate that paradox may be inevitable in theology, though elsewhere he does recognize plainly enough that living religion is one thing and the theology, which seeks to give conceptual expression to it, is another thing. Buri is making the demand that all shall be clear and consistent, and perhaps no theology can fully meet this demand without sacrificing some aspect of the truth. Of course, Buri might reply that the traditional conception of the task of theology is no longer tenable, and that the very fact that theology seems to keep landing itself in antinomies is a proof that it is following a mistaken course.

But however that may be, there is justice in that part of Buri's criticism which points to the obscurity in Bultmann's thought on these matters. It is certainly not obvious, in reading Bultmann, that we have to do with paradox rather than with flat contradiction. If Buri has overstated his case, at least he has drawn attention to a very real problem. If we accept demythologizing, have we any right to go on talking about a *kerygma*? Is the appeal to paradox just an excuse to cover up loose thinking? Is the retention of the *kerygma* just an attempt to cushion the blow which demythologizing gives to traditional Christian beliefs? These questions, raised by Buri's criticisms, make all the more urgent the task of seeking to vindicate the paradoxes in Bultmann.

Buri's second objection to Bultmann's theology is even graver than the one which we have just examined. He perceives a certain arrogance in the introduction of the *kerygma* into the discussion. It is the arrogance of the man who claims that there are open to him possibilities of insight and of action which are shut off from other men. Bultmann is prepared to enter into a conversation with certain philosophers. He finds common ground between their teaching and that of the New Testament. In particular, he finds such common ground in what they have to say about the fallenness of man, and in their quest for an authentic existence. But just as this conversation is proceeding smoothly in a shared language, that is to say, in terms of existential analysis and self-understanding, Bultmann, says Buri, suddenly appeals to the *kerygma* and maintains that it is only God's gracious act in Christ which enables any man to attain to an authentic existence. Bultmann 'recoils before the dissolution of theology'. He wants to cling to something exclusive, and represents the Christian way as quite different from the way of the philosophers. Indeed, he even seems to suggest that the philosopher's quest for authentic existence is at bottom a subtle form of sin, in so far as it is something which man seeks to do in his own power (*eigenmächtig*). But Buri denies that there is any such difference between the Christian theologian and the secular philosopher. If we follow Bultmann in interpreting the cross existentially—in 'making Christ's cross our own'—how does this differ from that 'turning from the world' (*Entweltlichung*)[1] of which philosophers can speak without reference to the cross of Christ? Or if we follow Bultmann in interpreting the resurrection existentially, as something which takes place in the self-understanding of the disciples who experience the cross as a victory, how does this differ from that 'liberation' (*Erlösung*) which philosophers— again apart from Christ—recognize as following upon the 'turning from the world'? Buri thinks that Bultmann wants to make a difference where there is in fact none. Nor will he even allow Bultmann to make the distinction that whereas the Christian life is a work of grace, the authentic existence of which the existentialist philosopher speaks is something to be achieved by human effort. Perhaps some philosophers speak in that way, but if they are guilty of arrogance, as Bultmann suggests, the same sin can be imputed to Bultmann himself in so far as he makes an exclusive claim for Christianity. But it is not necessary that philosophers should think of authentic existence as something to be attained by man's own powers. The idea of grace is not exclusively a Christian idea. Buri asks whether Bultmann does not know that Jaspers speaks of authentic existence as a gift, and interprets its gift-like character in terms of the concept of grace. This grace, however, is not tied to any particular event, such as God's act in Christ. It is a grace which belongs to existence itself. Thus it is argued that Bultmann's appeal to a *kerygma* in Christianity, understood as something which differentiates it from all philosophies and makes it somehow superior to them, is both mistaken and arrogant. Bultmann with

[1] It is hard to find a good equivalent for this term in English. 'Turning from the world' is to be understood not as an ascetic 'world-renunciation', but rather as being 'in' the world, but not 'of' the world.

his existentialist terminology may look like a philosopher to kerygmatic theologians, but to philosophers themselves he appears as just another myth-maker, because of his appeal to the *kerygma*. Such an appeal, in Buri's view, rules out the possibility of a genuine conversation between theologians and philosophers.[1]

On looking at this second criticism which Buri offers, we may again think, as in the case of the first one, that he has overstated his case. It is surely absurd to maintain, as he does, that when a theologian accepts a *kerygma*, he is *ipso facto* debarred from the possibility of a dialogue with the philosophers. That would be equivalent to saying that a dialogue is possible only if the theologian is prepared to become purely and simply a philosopher; that the pre-condition of such a dialogue is the complete capitulation of the theologian, who is to acknowledge that there is really nothing distinctive in his own discipline! If the theologian ever came to acknowledge this, it would come after the dialogue had ended, not before it had begun. To be really fruitful, a dialogue needs contributions from both sides, and it must begin on the assumption that both sides have something to offer. The possibility of such a dialogue is destroyed if the theologian begins on the assumption that he has a monopoly of the truth; it is equally destroyed if the philosopher begins with the assumption that the theologian has nothing worthwhile to contribute. There is a possibility of a genuine conversation when theologians and philosophers find a zone of common interest upon which light may be thrown from both sides to the benefit of both disciplines. But surely this is how Bultmann understands his relation to certain philosophers. He recognizes that they have matters of common concern, he is willing enough to learn from the philosophers, and yet he believes that as a Christian theologian he has his own distinctive contribution to make.

Yet, even if Buri has overstated his case, we must concede that once again he is coming to grips with a real problem. An appeal to a *kerygma* may easily enough lead to arrogance. It may easily enough appear as just a convenient shortcut to preconceived conclusions. We have to ask whether Bultmann's appeal to the *kerygma* is something well founded or something quite arbitrary. Does the Christian theologian really offer

[1] On these points, see *K.u.M.*, II, pp. 90-2, 94.

some distinctive contribution which cannot come from the side
of philosophy?

The remedy which Buri proposes, in order to remove the
difficulties which he finds in Bultmann, is simple and drastic.
This remedy he designates by a term which introduces a new
cacophony into the long-suffering theological vocabulary—
'dekerygmatizing'. A *kerygma*, he holds, is neither necessary nor
possible. Demythologizing is to be carried through to the end,
and in the process the *kerygma* will go the way of myth, since
this *kerygma* is itself only 'the last remnant of mythology'.[1] But
when we stop looking at things through apologetic spectacles,
wondering how much of the traditional Christian faith can be
rescued, then, according to Buri, we shall see that to give up
the *kerygma* will bring gain rather than loss. On the one hand,
there will be gain in clarity, and we shall no longer be faced
with what he regards as the insoluble difficulties besetting
Bultmann's position. We shall no longer have on our hands the
problem of relating existential interpretation to the idea of a
kerygma, for the *kerygma* will have disappeared, and all will
be existential interpretation. On the other hand, we shall
avoid the sin of arrogance. The New Testament teaching will
be set free from its mythical and kerygmatic setting so that we
can recognize it as simply the expression of a concept of authentic existence which is not restricted to either the New Testament
or the Church, but is to be found elsewhere as well. Salvation
has nothing to do with a once-for-all event, and the value of the
New Testament does not lie in the fact that it speaks of such an
event, but in the fact that it gives expression in mythical terms
to authentic existence. If the New Testament itself sometimes
says otherwise, this is an element in the myth which must be
discarded.[2] But all this, in Buri's view, is a positive gain. By
giving up the arrogant claim that there is something in the New
Testament which is inaccessible to human philosophizing, and
by frankly admitting that it deals in nothing other than possibilities of human existence, the theologian will be able to
enter into a discussion with the philosopher in the only way in
which Buri conceives that such a discussion can genuinely take
place. And he is so carried away with enthusiasm for dekerygmatizing that in spite of all his warnings against exclusiveness

[1] Loc. cit., p. 96.   [2] Loc. cit., p. 97.

and arrogance he tells us that such dekerygmatizing is '*the*
way in which a Christian theology is still possible today'.[1]

In turning now to a more detailed discussion of the points
at issue between Buri and Bultmann, we shall try first of all to
get a clearer picture of the kind of theology which Buri develops
on the basis of dekerygmatizing (Section 21); then we shall
examine his conception of grace, for here we shall find the focal
point of his disagreement with Bultmann (Section 22); and
finally, in the light of this, we must try to decide whether
Bultmann is right in retaining the idea of a *kerygma* (Section 23).

21 *The Theology of Existence*

As we have seen, Buri believes that the only kind of theology
which is possible today is the theology which frankly accepts
dekerygmatizing. But dekerygmatizing is a negative principle,
and Buri describes the theology which he develops from it in a
more positive way as the 'theology of existence'. Such a theology
treats dogmatics as the explication of the self-understanding
belonging to an authentic existence as experienced in Christian
faith.

In the systematic application of his principle to the various
fields of Christian doctrine, Buri is able to find a place for most
of the traditional ideas of Christian theology, though often
they are drastically re-interpreted. He shows real insight, and
has many enlightening things to say. As an example of his
approach, we may take his treatment of the unpromising
doctrine of predestination.[2] One might have supposed that there
could be no room for such a doctrine in a theology of existence.
Buri indeed rejects it if it means a fatalism, for such a view would
exclude that responsibility which is intrinsic to existence. But
the interpretation of predestination which equates it with
fatalism rests on a misunderstanding. It has perverted an
existential statement of faith into a general metaphysical
assertion. The truth in the doctrine of predestination lies in the
fact that it gives expression to the believer's experience that
he has not just chosen a certain kind of existence, but that in
some way that existence has laid hold on him, that he is chosen.
'Election', says Buri, 'even in the thoroughgoing mythological
sense of double predestination as we already find it in the

[1] Loc. cit., p. 98.   [2] *Theologie der Existenz*, pp. 66ff.

apostle Paul[1] and after him in Calvin and Calvinism, represents for existence the most adequate expression of its experience of getting itself as a gift, in the grace which comes to the sinner.' But this experience takes place against a 'dark background'— the possibility of being lost, that it might have been otherwise. This 'dark background' is the truth in the idea of reprobation, which has meaning only from the standpoint of an experience of election. God does not have two activities, electing and rejecting. He elects only, but in experiencing election we perceive what the other possibility might have been.

Of course, someone may ask whether this is not just Bultmann's demythologizing over again. It is indeed—or at least it is something very like it—and Buri handles other doctrines— creation, christology, and so on—in a similar fashion. But where he differs from Bultmann is in carrying his existential interpretation beyond the point at which Bultmann leaves off.

The full implications of a thoroughgoing theology of existence will become clear if we ask two questions. First of all, what has become of the record of the New Testament in the theology of existence? The answer is that the record has now purely and simply the status of a myth. Buri says explicitly: 'The theology of existence is founded not on the objectivity of a salvation-history, but on its own self-understanding in existence.'[2] He can speak quite readily of the Christ-myth.[3] Presumably, unlike some earlier writers who used this term, Buri does in fact believe that there is some historical substratum to the myth, and that there actually was a Jesus of Nazareth round whom the myth grew up. But that is not of the slightest importance from his point of view. Any objective historical reference in the narrative of the Gospels is completely irrelevant. The entire significance of the New Testament lies in the understanding of existence to which it gives expression. Buri finds an advantage in this position, since of course it renders theology completely invulnerable to any possible findings of the historians. Here Buri's position is certainly more radical than that of Bultmann, who, in spite of his depreciation of objective history, clearly wants to maintain some link with it and to distinguish between the Gospel narrative and the purely mythical stories of the Hellenistic cults. We have ourselves seen good reasons for

[1] Rom. 9.11.   [2] *Theologie der Existenz*, p. 63.   [3] *K.u.M.*, II, p. 97.

believing that theology, if it is not to get lost in speculation, must have some anchor in empirical fact.[1] But Buri's concern is purely with human possibilities and not at all with matters of fact. Yet although the New Testament record is to be regarded as a myth with an existential significance, Buri attaches some value to the mythical form itself—perhaps more than Bultmann does. A dramatic and concrete story, even though a myth, can have a remarkable power as a symbol of authentic existence.[2] To the Christian myth he is willing to assign an almost unique power. He says: 'In the sea of mythological ideas and images, there are only a few really great redeemer-myths of the kind which we have in the story of the eschatological Christ. As archetypes, they emerge from the unconscious, in great moments of humanity they are formulated by prophets, then they grow from generation to generation— until even they grow old and die.'[3] This particular myth, he thinks, with its imagery of the irruption of a complete new creation through the appearing of the Messiah, expresses symbolically 'an intense awareness of existence as grace', and he declares that it must have great depth 'to have survived so many variations and still be "revelation" '.[4] Men can be moved by this symbol of authentic existence to participation in, and acceptance of, such existence, far more powerfully than they could be by any description of authentic existence in the abstract language of philosophical analysis. Thus although the New Testament record is reduced to the status of a myth through and through, Buri thinks that it has a very important psychological function.

If such is the fate of the New Testament record for one who accepts dekerygmatizing, we must now ask a second question: what has actually become of Christian theology itself when it is transformed into a 'theology of existence'? In one sense, such a theology of existence has been merged into philosophy. Buri plainly states that 'between our theology of existence and a philosophy which founds itself on the same concept of existence, there is in principle no difference'.[5] Buri tells us that we are not to be alarmed about this. On the contrary, we are invited to see in this happy union the attainment by theology of what is

---

[1] See above, pp. 90ff.   [2] *K.u.M.*, II, p. 99.
[3] *Theologie der Existenz*, p. 86.   [4] Op. cit., pp. 90-1.   [5] Op. cit., p. 28.

usually called 'intellectual respectability'. No longer will
theology be a discipline of doubtful status. We may think,
however, that the price paid for this advantage is rather high,
since it is virtually the end of theology. It must abandon its
claim to be different; it must deal in no mysteries beyond the
reach of the natural understanding; it must meet on equal
terms with secular philosophies and become part of that
philosophical enterprise which is concerned with the exploration of human possibilities and the quest for authentic existence.
These are happy results, in Buri's eyes. Here again his position
differs completely from that of Bultmann, who explicitly denies
that Christian theology can be merged into the philosophy of
existence.[1] In another sense, however, Buri seems willing to
leave to Christian theology a certain distinctiveness even
within the wider field of existential analysis into which it has
been merged. The distinctiveness of theology lies in the fact that
it speaks out of the rich tradition of symbolic material which
belongs to the Christian religion. Christian theology has to do
with only a part of the tradition of mankind, albeit a very
significant part, especially for our Western culture. On the other
hand, 'philosophy cannot tie itself down to a sector; its tradition is the tradition of mankind as a whole'.[2] This difference
does not seem to amount to very much. The business of theology
is to explore the powerful symbols of the Christian faith so as to
bring out their existential significance, that is to say, to show
how they depict an existence founded on love. But although it
works within its peculiar tradition, theology must frankly
recognize that secular philosophers may arrive at pretty much
the same results without reference to the Christian tradition—
though whether any modern Western philosophy can be
regarded as independent of the Christian tradition is surely
very doubtful. However that may be, it would seem that, on
Buri's view, the more successful any theologian is in translating
his symbols into clear existential statements, the less need there
will be for theology. In so far as he is willing to leave to theology
any vestige of independent status at all, Buri seems to visualize
the former queen of the sciences leading a somewhat precarious
life on the fringes of philosophy, and the more she pursues her
task, the nearer does she come to being swallowed up altogether.

[1] See above, p. 23.   [2] *Dogmatik als Selbstverständnis*, I, p. 39.

It may not be inappropriate at this point to make a short digression in order to draw attention to the remarkable resemblance which there seems to be between Buri's dekerygmatized theology of existence and the view of religion which has been put forward by the English empiricist philosopher, Professor R. B. Braithwaite.[1] We have pointed out already that contemporary philosophical theology is primarily interested in trying to elucidate the *meaning* of religious statements, and recognizes that this question is prior to the question of their *truth*. We have suggested that demythologizing may be regarded as one of the ways in which the question of meaning is being approached, but that there are other approaches, such as that of logical empiricism which, in Britain and America, has been far more influential than existentialism. These different approaches seem, however, to have gone on in watertight compartments, and neither has had any influence on the other. Braithwaite and Buri are out of different philosophical worlds. Their interests are different, they represent divergent traditions, their terminologies have hardly anything in common, yet they seem to have arrived at very similar results so far as their interpretation of the Christian religion is concerned. Just as Buri thinks that Christianity expresses an authentic existence, so Braithwaite regards it primarily as a way of life, and both would put Christian love at the foundation. Again, just as Buri finds the same authentic existence outside of Christianity, so Braithwaite thinks that the same way of life is common to the major religions of the world. Buri sees the *differentia* of Christianity in its treasury of myth and symbol; so Braithwaite believes that what is distinctive in the major religions is the set of stories belonging to each of them. Some of these stories may refer to events which actually happened, but Braithwaite would agree with Buri that this is of no importance, and that even if one were an adherent of the Christ-myth school, the value of the stories would remain unaffected. For both men, that value is psychological. Buri thinks of the myths as powerful symbols, derived from unconscious archetypes, and able to move men and to bring them into authentic existence. Braithwaite's way of expressing this is

[1] See his Eddington Memorial Lecture, *An Empiricist's View of the Nature of Religious Belief* (Cambridge University Press, London, 1955). For a comparison of Braithwaite and Bultmann, see the present writer's article, 'A New Kind of Demythologizing?' in *Theology*, LIX, pp. 451ff.

to say that when the stories are entertained in the mind, they prove to be a powerful aid towards following the way of love. One could pursue the comparison further, and, of course, one could find differences between the two as well, but enough has been said to show that here we have an interesting case of two thinkers working quite independently in different traditions and yet arriving at points of view which are not very far apart. One might almost speak, in Bernard Bosanquet's phrase, of a 'meeting of extremes in contemporary philosophy', and the meeting-ground is the interpretation of religion. Radical empiricism and radical existentialism have converged at this point, and they unite in offering us a view of religion which interprets it in terms of human existence or activity.

But here we must leave our digression and return to the main theme. We now have before us an outline of Buri's 'theology of existence' and we can see plainly enough that it differs from Bultmann's in being considerably more radical. In particular, it abolishes the *kerygma* and to all intents and purposes rubs out the dividing line between theology and philosophy. Bultmann will not agree to do either of these things. Is he right or is Buri right? On the face of it, Buri's theology looks simpler and free from some of the embarrassments which trouble Bultmann. But the question of which is right can be settled only by investigating which of them gives the more adequate account of the living religious experience which they are trying to explicate.

22 *Nature and Grace*

The basic difference between Bultmann and Buri can perhaps be brought into view most clearly by comparing what each of them has to say about the function of grace in the Christian life. We may begin by recalling how Bultmann sought to draw the line which, as he believes, separates Christian theology from the philosophy of existence, and throws into relief that kerygmatic character of theology which prevents its dissolution into existential analysis. Bultmann willingly acknowledges that the existentialist philosopher may perceive that the being of man is not in order, and that in so far as the philosopher does perceive this, he must also somehow conceive of an authentic existence for man. Bultmann acknowledges further that the philosopher may conceive of such an authentic existence in a way which may come very close to the New Testament teaching on the Christian life. But at this point Bultmann feels himself obliged to part company with the philosopher and to take a different path. He maintains that the fallen nature of man alienates him so radically from his authentic existence that though he may conceive it, he cannot of himself attain it. Only an act of grace from beyond man himself can put the possibility of his true life within his grasp; and Bultmann, of course, claims that Christian faith does know of such a gracious act. This act lies beyond the horizons of existential analysis. It is God's decisive act in Christ, as proclaimed in the *kerygma*.

Now Buri, as we have seen, rejects the notion of a *kerygma*, and along with that he must reject Bultmann's view of grace, which is bound up with the *kerygma*. But Buri, while rejecting Bultmann's understanding of grace, by no means denies that grace has its function in the Christian life. If he did, then the matter would be relatively simple. We could say that whatever might be the merits of Buri's views considered as a humanistic philosophy, they could not be reckoned as belonging to Christian theology, which speaks of a religious experience to which grace is quite essential. However, Buri does assign a place to grace, and affirms that it is an important place—though the very fact that he deems it necessary to tell us that the term is being used legitimately by him may make us wonder whether he himself does not have some doubts in his mind. Is he really using the word in a clear and proper sense, or not? Indeed, although Buri has claimed that his principle of dekerygmatizing is going to lead to clarity, his conception of grace turns out to be more obscure and mystifying than anything to be found in Bultmann.

Of course, the distinction between 'nature' and 'grace' has never been a very happy one. The word 'nature' is a highly ambiguous term, not only in ordinary usage but in theology as well. We have noted this ambiguity already, in connection with Bultmann's rejection of 'natural theology'.[1] What he rejects is the belief that we can argue successfully to God from nature, where 'nature' means something like 'the ordered

[1] See above, pp. 25, 48-9.

universe and its processes'. He does not reject the belief—
on the contrary, he affirms it—that the quest for God, and
therefore some understanding of God, arises from our own
nature, where 'nature' means something quite different, and
may be defined as 'the constitution proper to anything, in
virtue of which it behaves as it does'. Bultmann holds that
grace is continuous with nature, in the second of the two
senses which we have distinguished, and for this reason Barth
is able to say that for Bultmann the Christian life is man's
'truly natural' existence.[1] 'Grace', on the other hand, must
mean something which is 'gifted' to man 'in addition to' his
natural endowment—*donum superadditum*. But we cannot draw a
hard and fast line between nature and grace. We cannot point
to a fixed stock of characteristics and say, 'That is human
nature, and anything not on the list must be grace'. Least of all
can we do that if, like Buri and Bultmann, we think that man
has no fixed essence, but that his essence is his existence, his
potentiality for being. What one man may experience as natural
may be experienced by another as a work of grace. The
Christian in particular, believing that man is created by God
and that therefore his whole being is a gift from the Creator,
may extend the idea of grace to such a length that nature is
swallowed up, or else is identified only with man's fallen or
sinful nature; though this is surely most confusing, since sin is
not man's nature but a perversion of his nature. Thus Calvin
attributed the virtues of the ancients not to natural endowment
but to grace which God made available to them.[2]

We have indicated that no sharp distinction can be drawn
between 'nature' and 'grace' in the sense that one cannot draw
up two lists of characteristics and then label the one 'nature'
and the other 'grace'. These are relative terms with a very
variable application. What one man does 'naturally' may be
very difficult for another. But what does seem clear is that men
sometimes have the experience of being enabled to do what was
not, as they say, 'in their nature' to do, and this they call an
experience of grace. Grace is therefore conceived as something
which comes to the recipient from beyond himself—it is something which he experiences not as his own but given to him.
Yet it does not come to him as something utterly foreign. The

---

[1] *Ein Versuch*, p. 15.   [2] *Institutes*, II, iii, 3.

recipient can and must make it his own. There may be what theologians call 'irresistible grace', but grace can never be imposed. It is appropriated. It must therefore lie somewhere within the recipient's horizons of being or, in other words, be continuous with his nature. These points seem to be satisfied very well on Bultmann's view of grace. It comes from beyond man, from the God who acts in Christ—indeed, Bultmann identifies grace with this act—yet the act addresses itself to the self-understanding of man and presents him with a genuine possibility for which he can make his own decision. Grace is at once transcendent of nature and a fulfilment of nature.

It is more difficult to disentangle the ideas which Buri, almost apologetically, wishes to designate by the term 'grace'. He tries to steer a middle course between Heidegger who, as he thinks,[1] conceives authentic existence to be attainable without grace by man's unaided effort, and Bultmann who thinks that authentic existence is attained through God's act of grace in Christ. Buri finds a clue in Jaspers, who seems to have had a strong influence on his thought about these matters. Jaspers can speak of authentic existence as having the character of a gift. There is a grace in existence itself—existence includes grace. In contrast to this conception Bultmann, it is said, envisages existence as graceless. But here, surely, we find confusion entering in—and perhaps it is inevitable when we use such slippery terms as 'nature' and 'grace'. If grace brings a gift, something not my own—and we have indicated that it must do so, if it is grace properly so called—then all existence, prior to the working of grace, must be graceless, as Bultmann conceives it. For if grace is already immanent, so to speak, in existence, then it is already my own. It is not a gift and indeed it is not grace in the proper sense but rather nature. What Buri calls 'grace', however, is already there in existence. It is not something from beyond me, but something which already belongs to me. Certainly it has nothing to do with a saving act, such as the *kerygma* proclaims. It is already given with my existence itself.[2]

And yet, although grace is given with existence and so belongs

---

[1] But Buri misrepresents Heidegger. In his later writings, Heidegger speaks of Being as 'calling' or 'claiming' man who experiences the 'graciousness' of Being —much as Buri himself speaks of the experience of being 'elected' to and 'gifted' with an authentic existence.

[2] On these points, see *K.u.M.*, II, pp. 94, 97.

K

to me, Buri maintains that the working of such grace is experienced as a gift. It conduces to authentic existence, which I
recognize as something which is not at my disposal but is
presented to me. In this experience I understand myself as
created and elected, and as related to a transcendence which
meets me as a personal God.[1] So now the transcendent element
is brought into the picture. God is seen to be the author of
grace, but he confers it not in a saving act such as the *kerygma*
proclaims, but in man's original endowment of existence.

Buri supports his view by citing a number of scriptural
passages which illustrate the grace of existence. One of his
illustrations is from the story of the fall.[2] The more familiar
part of the story tells of man's eating of the tree of knowledge
and his fall into sin. The immediacy of his relation to God is
broken, and he becomes a responsible being, knowing good and
evil. Yet, says Buri, Christian theologians have always seen in
the myth a *protevangelium* or anticipation of the gospel in the
promise that the seed of woman shall bruise the serpent's head.[3]
Buri interprets this to mean that, in the biblical view, human
existence has been from the beginning onwards both guilty and
reconciled. Existence is the creation of grace, and in knowing
sin it also knows grace.

Elsewhere he illustrates the same point from the story of
Isaiah's vision in the temple. The prophet's awareness of his
sinfulness is at the same time the call to a new life, and this
is all that is necessary for the grace of a new creation. 'That I,
as a sinner, need not perish before   holy God, that this fire
does not consume me, that I . . . experience the purifying
power of the divine presence and the call to God's service—
that is the grace of a new creation.'[4]

In another book, Buri makes his point more clearly still.
This time he illustrates it from the parable of the prodigal son.
'The lost son did not first need to accept a doctrine of atonement, and then, on the basis of his confession of faith, dare to
believe in the grace of God. There is no mention here of all
those things which bar the way to grace for so many men,
because they can reconcile them neither with their thought nor
their experience. Forgiveness does not depend on a past event

---

[1] *K.u.M.*, III, p. 86.   [2] *K.u.M.*, III, pp. 88-9.   [3] Gen. 3.15.
[4] *Theologie der Existenz*, p. 65. Cf. Isa. 6.1-8.

which we must accept as true in order to be accepted again by the Father. No! Forgiveness takes place here and now in the life of the man who knows himself guilty. . . . In so far as he recognizes and acknowledges that he is a sinner, he is no longer merely a sinner. Recognition and acknowledgement of his sin before God is no longer sin. With this he has turned in a new direction towards salvation.'[1]

Buri shows both good sound common-sense and genuine religious insight in the passages which we have just quoted. He blows away some of the theological cobwebs and gets to grips with important matters. His point that recognition of sin is no longer sin is true and important. But is it adequate as an account of grace? Buri claims that 'by acknowledging its perversion, existence wins back its lost responsibility and freedom'.[2] But does it really? Is it not sometimes the case that when a man recognizes his own guilt he becomes morally paralysed and cannot advance one step towards soundness or salvation without some more positive help? Is Buri's account of the grace of existence anything more than Bultmann's recognition that there arises from man's natural self-understanding the awareness that his being is not in order, and with this the quest for authentic existence and for God, and therefore some understanding of these? But Bultmann holds that something more is required, before we can properly speak of grace. Again, Buri is right in saying that the Church has always regarded the promise to Eve as a *protevangelium*. But the *protevangelium* is not yet the gospel, but only a pointer to it.

It is interesting to notice that throughout his remarks on grace, Buri makes repeated use of a German verb, *innewerden*, for which there is no precise equivalent in English. In its etymological sense, the word would mean, 'to get in'. As ordinarily used, it means 'to perceive' something, but in a more active sense than the English verb suggests, and which we might express as 'to awaken' to something. It implies both becoming aware of something and becoming alive to it. This is not without importance for understanding Buri's view. He seems to believe that because of the indwelling grace of existence man can both perceive his true life and become alive to it and

---

[1] *Die Reformation geht weiter*, pp. 54-5. Cf. Luke 15.11-32.
[2] *Theologie der Existenz*, p. 64.

enter into it. There is no human effort in this. Authentic existence, he says, cannot be compelled. It comes as a gift. But the grace of existence confers the gift—to perceive is the same as to awake.

However, if the use of this verb helps to throw light on Buri's meaning, it also points to a fundamental weakness in his view, for what he describes would seem to be in flat contradiction with the experience reported by a good many Christians. When he criticizes Bultmann for representing human existence as without grace, Buri asks if he has never read of Jaspers' conception of the gift-like character of existence. We might well ask Buri in turn if he has never read some classic Christian accounts of the experience of grace, Saint Paul's among them. For Saint Paul was well enough able to *perceive* where his true life lay, but to *become alive* to it and to enter into it proved to be a different matter altogether. He speaks of conscience, of the law of the mind, of the inner man. These all directed him to life. But against that inmost self which delighted in the law of God there was working another side of his being, and that other side frustrated him and held him in 'this body of death'.[1] And it was not the grace of existence which delivered him from the misery of his situation, but God's concrete act of grace in Christ.

The truth would seem to be that although he is looking for a middle way between Heidegger and Bultmann, Buri has not really advanced beyond the position which he (mistakenly) attributes to Heidegger. He has indeed introduced a personal God into the picture, and the somewhat vague conception of an indwelling grace which is given with existence. But he still believes that man has only to perceive his true life in order to turn towards it, and that man has power to do this because of the grace which belongs to him from the beginning. Bultmann is surely more realistic in recognizing that fallen man can conceive his true life but may not be able to lay hold on it apart from an act of grace which comes from outside of himself. The cause of Buri's error is twofold.

In the first place, he fails to make the distinction, to which Bultmann attaches considerable importance, between an existential possibility and an *existentiell* one. This is probably due once more to the influence of Jaspers, who explicitly

[1] Rom. 7.24.

rejects such a distinction.[1] The distinction is common to both Heidegger and Bultmann, and is directly relevant to our present discussion. An existential possibility is one which is revealed by existential analysis and which belongs to all human existence in virtue of the way this existence is constituted. An *existentiell* possibility is one which is open to me in a particular situation so that I can decide for it. All *existentiell* possibilities must lie within the horizon of existential possibility; but there may be existential possibilities which are not *existentiell* possibilities for a given individual at a given time. It may be the case, for instance, that because of past decisions I have cut myself off from some existential possibility. Love is an example of an existential possibility in the sense that it is a possible way of being for human existence as such, the way in which one person can authentically 'be with' another. But there may well be some unfortunate person who, because of past experiences, has lost the possibility of loving. For him, there is no *existentiell* possibility to love, even if to love is an existential possibility. A good illustration would be Victor Hugo's hero, Jean Valjean.[2] When we meet him, he is an embittered man, after serving twenty years as a convict because he stole a loaf to feed some starving children. It seems that all good has died in his breast. He is an enemy of all mankind. When he receives an act of kindness from the bishop of a provincial city, he repays it with a theft. But when his theft is still met with kindness from the bishop, Jean Valjean undergoes the crisis of a conversion experience, and eventually becomes a man capable of love and self-sacrifice in the highest degree. It is in some such way that Bultmann understands God's act of grace. 'Only those who are loved', he says, 'are capable of loving.'[3] This is also the New Testament teaching: 'We love, because he first loved us.'[4] All these cases visualize something more than the grace of existence, as Buri understands it. Fallen man, just because he is still man, has an existential possibility of authenticity, but this may not be an *existentiell* possibility for any given individual in a particular situation. It may require a gracious act from beyond himself to make the possibility one which he can choose in his

---

[1] Cf. *K.u.M.*, III, p. 15, where Jaspers says that he does not know whether it was Heidegger or Bultmann who first thought of this distinction.
[2] See the opening chapters of *Les Misérables*.
[3] *Kerygma and Myth*, p. 32.   [4] I John 4.19.

situation. Yet this act will not be something utterly foreign, the grace is not imposed but received, because the existential possibility is already there. For Buri, all possibilities are alike. His failure to distinguish among them leads him to believe, on the one hand, that just to have an existential possibility is to be in a position to lay hold on it, and, on the other hand, that a saving act of God must be something utterly foreign to man and unrelated to his existence.[1]

In the second place, Buri may well have underestimated the effects of sin in man, as alienating him not only from God but from his own authentic self. In this also, the influence of Jaspers may be discerned. Jaspers attacks Bultmann for representing fallen man as hopelessly sinful, and says that the idea of justification by faith is the strangest of all thoughts from the philosophical point of view.[2] And let us acknowledge at once that there can be an extravagant talk of 'total depravity' and 'justification by faith alone' which Jaspers is fully justified in criticizing. But what he and Buri are agreed upon is that no specific saving act of God is necessary. In language which is strongly reminiscent of T. H. Green and the nineteenth-century idealists, they can speak of a 'Christ in me', and understand this expression as a mythological symbol for man's *nobilitas ingenita*, as Jaspers calls the grace of existence.[3] There is of course an important element of truth in the thought of the event 'in me'. This is fully recognized by Bultmann in his conception of the eschatological event—an event which is not simply past, but is present as it happens over and over again whenever the *kerygma* is proclaimed and accepted. But by insisting that it is still the event of Jesus Christ, Bultmann clearly maintains that it is not only an event 'in me' but also an event 'for me'. 'All this is from God.'[4] The act of grace transcends my existence and comes to me from beyond myself. And it is

[1] When we speak of grace as 'supernatural', presumably we mean that it is 'additional to nature', in the second of the two senses of 'nature' distinguished on p. 144; not that it is 'above' or 'beyond' 'nature' in the first of the two senses. Grace is in fact always experienced in an action or event which from one point of view could be regarded as perfectly 'natural', e.g., the bishop's act of kindness.

[2] *K.u.M.*, III, pp. 22, 42.

[3] When an expression like *nobilitas ingenita* is used, it would seem that we ought to speak of 'nature' rather than of 'grace'. But when this 'nature' is believed to be itself 'gifted', it really becomes a matter of words whether we choose to speak of 'nature' or of a 'common grace' available to all men.

[4] II Cor. 5.18.

precisely this point which is left vague and indeterminate in Buri and Jaspers, with their talk of an indwelling grace. For them, there is certainly an event 'in me' but in spite of their talk of the gift-like character of authentic existence, they do not make it clear that there is any event 'for me'.

But what kind of event is adequate to man's fallen situation? Need it be only 'in him' or must it be 'for him' also? Bultmann's view is that the consequences of sin are so disabling that we need some gracious act for us, such as the one which the *kerygma* proclaims. His opponents, with their thought of an indwelling grace, are content with an event in us. Which view is to be judged correct will depend on how serious a view we take of sin. Another possibility, at which we have already hinted, is that, because of individual differences, what is 'natural' to one man needs a 'work of grace' in another. But there can be no doubt that it is Bultmann who stands closer to the New Testament and to Christian experience. And if theology, as distinct from the philosophy of religion, speaks out of a concrete living faith, if it is, as Bultmann describes it, faith interpreting itself, then Bultmann is theologically correct, as against Buri. One can hardly fail to get the impression that Buri has first of all developed a philosophy of religion, based upon Jaspers, and has then proceeded to clothe it in the language of the New Testament, at the expense of the latter.

23 *The Vindication of the Kerygma*

With this discussion of grace, we are now in a position to judge of Buri's theological enterprise, and so to answer our question about what happens when the limit which the *kerygma* sets to demythologizing is removed. The answer is that we find ourselves in what we must paradoxically call a kind of theistic humanism. If we were to use the language of William James, we might say that the religion upon which Buri bases his theology is a religion for the healthy-minded. He deals in the analysis of human possibilities, and sets before us the possibility of an authentic existence which we are to realize with the aid of such endowment of grace as may have been bestowed on us with our existence.

That God's grace is not restricted to certain channels (and certainly not to ecclesiastical channels), and that there are fortunate souls who have only to perceive the true life in order to come alive to it, no one, perhaps, would deny. That there is grace outside of the Christian religion, that either by 'nature' or by 'common grace' (call it what you will) some men attain to wholeness or salvation, that men 'turn from the world' and are 'liberated' apart from the *kerygma*, neither Bultmann nor any reasonable person would wish to gainsay.[1] But the point is surely this, that if there is one sick soul in the world, then the kind of theology which Buri expounds is inadequate to the needs of mankind. And we may remember William James' own question, 'whether the sentiment of human helplessness may not open a profounder view . . . of the situation'.[2] It is certainly the case that the great leaders of the Christian Church—Saint Paul, Saint Augustine, Martin Luther, to mention only three—began their spiritual pilgrimages as sick souls who could find no way out from their difficulties, and were transformed not by any indwelling grace of existence but by the encounter with God in his gracious act in Christ.

One positive result emerges from our discussion. It is that, in adhering to the idea of a *kerygma*, Bultmann is holding fast to something which is quite essential to Christianity. It involves him in paradox, admittedly, but it is true to the faith which he seeks to interpret. There may be an existentialist theology, but there can scarcely be a theology of existence. There can be only an anthropology of existence, dealing in human possibilities; and if we care to question such remnants of the transcendent as are still to be found in Buri, we find that it is only a step further on to the position of Sartre, where God, if we speak of him, means simply my ideal of myself. On the kind of interpretation which we are offered when the limit to demythologizing is removed, Christianity ceases to be a religion of saving power and becomes just another view of human existence. It may still have a message for the healthy-minded, for the man who is *naturaliter Christianus*, but it has no longer any gospel and it no longer holds out any hope to the multitudes of the weary, the guilty, and the heavy-laden. It was not mere facetiousness

---

[1] See, for instance, a passage in his *Essays*, pp. 301ff., where he says that 'the way to God' means just this 'turning from the world', and visualizes a community in which 'confessed nihilists and atheists' as well as 'the pious' are authentically 'with' one another.

[2] *The Varieties of Religious Experience* (Longmans, London, 1952), p. 133.

which prompted the comparison at the beginning of this chapter between our exploration of the dekerygmatized theology of existence and Dante's visit to the underworld. For as far as the sick soul is concerned, the realm which we have surveyed might well be labelled with the same ominous words which Dante read above the dark portal: 'Abandon all hope, ye that enter.'[1]

[1] *Inferno*, Canto III, 9.

VI

DEMYTHOLOGIZING AND PHILOSOPHY

24 *Liberalism and Orthodoxy*

To those conservative people who take fright at the mere mention of demythologizing and who tend to look on Bultmann as a dangerous radical, intent on undermining the foundations of Christianity, it must come as a very considerable surprise that the same Bultmann who has so shocked them is accused from another quarter on the grounds that he is the champion of a most illiberal orthodoxy. Yet this is precisely the charge brought against him by Professor Karl Jaspers, who has entered the demythologizing controversy as the defender of liberalism.[1]

We have asked whether demythologizing may hold out some prospect of a *rapprochement* between theology and philosophy,[2] and it might have been expected that Bultmann's work would get a sympathetic response from Jaspers. For this philosopher, himself usually reckoned an existentialist, puts forward a point of view which, in some respects, seems not far removed from Bultmann's. Both of them distinguish three areas of being. There is the world of objects, including not only physical objects but also human ideas and activities so far as these are objectifiable. Then there is the realm of existence, our own being which we cannot objectify or derive from anything other than itself and of which we are aware in the experiences of

---

[1] Strictly speaking, Jaspers upholds the cause of *Liberalität*, not of *Liberalismus*. We might have followed the example of Dr A. R. Vidler and used the English word 'liberality', but this word has so many unwanted connotations, especially in Scottish ecclesiastical usage, that we have thought it better to speak of 'liberalism'. The word will be used in this chapter to denote not the views of any particular school of theological or political thought, but an attitude of openness towards religious problems. See further on p. 157 below.

[2] See above, p. 32.

deciding and acting and the like. Finally, there is being-itself, transcendence, or God, which speaks through the world but lies beyond it.

Moreover, Jaspers is well-known as the exponent of a 'philosophical faith'[1] which, on the surface at least, might be supposed to have a good deal in common with a demythologized version of Christianity. Like Bultmann, Jaspers looks for a third way when he is confronted with what he calls the 'facile alternatives' of a fixed dogmatic type of religion on the one hand and a shallow secularism on the other. He finds this third way in what he calls 'philosophical faith'. Such a faith is not, of course, a new system of dogmas intended to replace the old one. For Jaspers, as Ronald Grimsley has well expressed it, 'to philosophize is to be engaged in an active striving—to be "on the way" and to ask questions from the midst of a personal situation'.[2] The faith which arises in such philosophizing is not an assent to general propositions, nor are its truths held to be demonstrable. It does not deal in objective truths, such as dogmas are often supposed to be. Yet on the other hand, such faith is not purely subjective; it is not just a believing state of mind. To express the wholeness of the subjective and objective sides of faith, Jaspers speaks of 'the comprehensive' (*das Umgreifende*). 'We call the being that is neither only subject nor only object, that is rather on both sides of the subject-object split, the "comprehensive".'[3] Here we seem to be very close to Bultmann's existential conception of faith.

When we inquire about the content of Jaspers' philosophical faith, we learn that it involves recognition of a transcendent God, of an absolute imperative, and of the dependent status of the empirical world.[4] When we learn further that 'the absolute imperative confronts me as the command of my authentic self to my empirical existence, as the command, as it were, of what I am eternally in the face of the transcendent to the temporality of my present life', we might think that we are very near indeed to Bultmann's existentialist interpretation of Christianity.

[1] See especially his book, *Der philosophische Glaube*, which, in the English translation by Ralph Manheim, has been renamed *The Perennial Scope of Philosophy* (Routledge & Kegan Paul, London, 1950).

[2] *Existentialist Thought* (University of Wales Press, Cardiff, 1955), p. 150.

[3] *The Perennial Scope*, p. 14. [4] Op. cit., p. 34ff.

It is true that so far there has been no mention of the Bible in this philosophical faith. But it is soon brought into the picture. Although such a faith must be lived out in the existence of the individual, so that it has its being in the present and cannot shelter under the past, it is nevertheless in a tradition. We in the Western world have 'our specific roots in biblical religion'.[1] Thus Erich Dinkler can say that 'Jaspers must be characterized as an extreme liberal Protestant who, concerned with Jesus as a type for failing mankind, uses him to support his "philosophical faith" '.[2] Jaspers himself thinks that we have an urgent duty to transform and revive our traditional religion so that its power may again be felt. Our religious beliefs call for a 'change as far-reaching as all the other changes that have taken place in our era—or else the eternal truth of biblical religion will recede beyond the horizon of man'. This would be a disaster, and so we have a duty 'to do everything in our power to restore the eternal truth; we must plumb its very depths and, unconcerned over what is transient and historical, utter this truth in a new language'.[3]

Since this is exactly what Bultmann is trying to do in his demythologizing, and since, furthermore, the 'new language' which he uses is, as we have seen, pretty close to Jaspers' own, then we might indeed have expected that Jaspers would recognize in Bultmann a fellow-seeker. But this is not the case. In those of his writings which deal specifically with demytho-logizing,[4] Jaspers will not allow that Bultmann's theological enterprise has anything in common with a philosophical faith or even that it makes any worthwhile contribution to that task of refurbishing biblical religion of which Jaspers has spoken. Whatever its superficial resemblances to a philosophical faith may be, Bultmann's theology is alleged to lack the one quality which is fundamental to any philosophical faith—a genuinely liberal spirit.

---

[1] Op. cit., pp. 24-7 and p. 41.   [2] *Christianity and the Existentialists*, p. 115.
[3] Op. cit., p. 107.

[4] Jaspers' principal essay on demythologizing, 'Wahrheit und Unheil der Bultmannschen Entmythologisierung', which first appeared in the *Schweizerische Theologische Umschau*, is reprinted, along with a reply by Bultmann, in *Kerygma und Mythos*, Band III. For the complete discussion, which includes a second essay by Jaspers and a further brief rejoinder by Bultmann, see *Die Frage der Entmytho-logisierung* (Piper, Munich, 1954). Cf. Ian Henderson, 'Karl Jaspers and De-mythologizing', *The Expository Times*, LXV, pp. 291ff.

For Jaspers, a truly liberal attitude towards religious questions is our only safeguard against a deadening orthodoxy on the one hand and a disruptive unbelief on the other. He tells us what he understands such a liberalism to mean. It must speak out of the living experience of the individual, without any appeal to an external authority. Yet it is not arbitrary, for it arises within a tradition, and brings to life that which has been handed down and which would otherwise have stagnated. Liberalism is never exclusive for it is open to every way in which the transcendent speaks to man. Faith must always remain 'a venture of radical openness'. Liberalism is never final, for it recognizes a hiddenness in transcendence beyond what man can grasp—'the *deus absconditus* recedes into the distance when I seek to fathom him'. Such liberalism is opposed to orthodoxy whose characteristics are the antitheses of those which we have just noted. Orthodoxy is authoritative, and claims to have precise information about what God says and wants; it is exclusive, denying truth to any heterodox point of view or at the most grudgingly conceding a partial glimpse of the truth; it is final, claiming that the truth which it possesses is imperfectible. But liberalism is equally opposed to that secularism which confines man's view to the phenomenal world and deprives him of his relation to transcendence, thereby depriving him at the same time of the fulness of his existence. This liberalism of religious thinking Jaspers finds in Kant, Lessing, and Goethe. He has also praise for Buri's courage in seeking to liberalize theology along the lines of a radical dekerygmatizing. But he says that he can find nothing of the liberal spirit in Bultmann.[1]

Jaspers very readily acknowledges the greatness of Bultmann as a scientific historian and New Testament critic, and confesses how much he himself has learned from Bultmann's researches into Christian origins. These researches were carried out in a spirit of free inquiry, unhindered by prejudice or irrelevant considerations. But when Bultmann turns from history to theology, then, according to Jaspers, he misleads us altogether. His theology is 'the strangest mixture of false enlightenment and vehement orthodoxy'. From the philosophical

---

[1] On these points, see *Die Frage der Entmythologisierung*, pp. 37ff., or *K.u.M.*, III, pp. 33ff. Cf. *The Perennial Scope*, pp. 16, 39.

point of view, it is untenable, and from the religious point of view, it is unproductive. It may displease the orthodox because it takes away so much from them, but although it seems to make concessions to the liberal attitude, it does not really do so, for it falls back on the idea of a special and unique revelation, the notion of a saving act of God in Christ. In the last resort, Bultmann's vaunted demythologizing is itself nothing but orthodoxy and illiberalism all over again in a new form.[1] Thus there arises the situation to which Buri drew our attention: to the orthodox theologian, Bultmann looks like the exponent of a liberal and philosophically oriented theology; but to the philosopher, he looks like just another orthodox theologian, whose orthodoxy may admittedly be veiled but is none the less rigid and illiberal. In spite of his claim to be free from myth and dogma, and in spite of his enthusiasm for the philosophy of existence, Bultmann in the philosopher's eyes falls into the same condemnation as Barth and all the others.

Even though Jaspers' attitude to demythologizing, as briefly introduced above, may seem to be quite unsympathetic and even unexpectedly hostile, the very fact that a philosopher of such renown has chosen to enter a theological controversy is to be warmly welcomed. By a *rapprochement* between theology and philosophy, we do not mean that the two should speak with one voice. Apart from the fact that such a state of affairs would be very dull, each of the two disciplines has its own task to perform, and by their very nature there must always be a certain tension between them, each criticizing the other. By a *rapprochement* we mean a resumption of the exchanges which characterized the relations of theology and philosophy at various times in the past. In our own century, there was for a long time little intercourse between theologians and philosophers. There have been theological positivists who tend to despise philosophy as the wisdom of this world, and who suppose that they have nothing to learn from it. On the other side, there have been not a few philosophical positivists who regard the utterances of theology as nonsense, in the strict meaning of the term, and as therefore unworthy, or rather, incapable of discussion. Such an isolation of the disciplines is

---

[1] On these points, see *Die Frage der Entmythologisierung*, pp. 37ff., or *K.u.M.*, III, pp. 33ff. Cf. *The Perennial Scope*, pp. 16, 39.

surely not desirable. But now we may hope that the period of estrangement is ending.[1] To borrow the language used by the diplomatic correspondents of our newspapers, we may say that talks have been resumed at a high level. Indeed, when we consider the eminence of the interlocutors, the discussion between Jaspers and Bultmann might be thought to rank almost as a summit conference.

The comparison with diplomacy is not altogether inappropriate. Anyone who reads the exchanges between Jaspers and Bultmann must derive some amusement from the cautious way in which they approach each other. It is reminiscent of hard bargaining at the United Nations when neither side is willing to allow that it can give anything away. Jaspers will scarcely concede that there is any merit in Bultmann's theology at all. Bultmann is reluctant to admit that Jaspers has anywhere properly understood his meaning. Jaspers alleges that Bultmann has put himself outside the sphere of philosophical discussion. Bultmann denies that Jaspers appreciates the theological problem. There is a good deal of fencing, but at the same time shrewd blows are being dealt on either side. Meanwhile, lesser protagonists have entered the debate. All this could happen only because, in spite of some of the disclaimers, there is common ground between the two sides and genuine problems for discussion.

There is some cause for regret at the way in which the debate has ended, so far as the two principals are concerned. Jaspers' critique of demythologizing provoked a detailed reply from Bultmann. To this reply, Jaspers made a further equally detailed rejoinder. But this time Bultmann applied the closure, for the time being at least, with a polite note of three sentences. Long before his discussion with Bultmann, Jaspers had written: 'It is among the sorrows of my life, spent in the search for truth, that discussion with theologians always dries up at crucial points; they fall silent, state an incomprehensible proposition, speak of something else, make some categorical statement, engage in amiable talk, without really taking cognizance of what one has said—and in the last analysis, they are not really

---

[1] Of course, it is not only the Jaspers-Bultmann debate that gives rise to this hope. The past few years have witnessed a remarkable revival of interest in religious questions among logical empiricists.

interested. . . . No one who is in definitive possession of the truth can speak properly with someone else—he breaks off authentic communication in favour of the belief he holds'.[1] Has Jaspers had the same experience again with Bultmann? And if so, have we been too hasty in thinking that a genuine conversation has taken place? Or have we to look behind the diplomatic language for the real issues?

Jaspers' criticism of Bultmann is certainly one of the most far-reaching of any that have appeared up till now. It ranges from his epistemology to his exegesis, and even contains a section on Bultmann's personality as an important factor in his theology! As Jaspers sees it, Bultmann's theology is like a building supported by two pillars, and both of these pillars are faulty and unable to carry the weight of the superstructure. One pillar is Bultmann's conception of the modern man—and here Jaspers makes some of his best points, though a consideration of this topic must be deferred until the final chapter.[2] The other pillar is that of the philosophy of existence, or rather of one particular expression of that philosophy. That we have to do in Jaspers with a type of criticism similar to that which we have already encountered in Buri is made very clear by Jaspers himself in a passage from his second essay on demythologizing. 'The main point of my first essay', he says, 'was this. I have followed your demythologizing as something which is true in so far as it takes away from the ciphers[3] of a faith the kind of significance which belongs to a material reality. However, what I meant was that your way must be pursued to its end. For even a word of God, made material (or incarnate) through the fact that it arises at a place and time in the world as the only decisive truth for men, could be merely a myth when represented as an action of God.'[4] He goes on to say, however, that the language of myth, as a cipher-language, seems to him indispensable, and that to get rid of it would be a mischief.

Into all the details of Jaspers' criticisms we need not go.

---

[1] *The Perennial Scope*, pp. 77-8.   [2] See below, pp. 233ff.

[3] 'Cipher-language' is Jaspers' term for the way in which transcendence speaks. Myth is one kind of cipher-language. Unlike Bultmann, however, Jaspers does not think that cipher-language can be translated into a language of concepts.

[4] 'Erwiderung auf Rudolf Bultmanns Antwort' in *Die Frage der Entmythologisierung*, p. 77.

With some of his points we have already made acquaintance in our discussion of Buri who, as we saw, is strongly influenced by Jaspers. Thus we have noted how Jaspers thinks that Bultmann takes too pessimistic a view of the helplessness of fallen and sinful man. This is not because Jaspers himself takes an optimistic view of man. Few writers have drawn attention more urgently than he has to the many dangers and possibilities of perversion which beset our human nature in the technological age.[1] He can speak of man's becoming enslaved to the collective mass and so losing his authentic existence, and the picture which he gives is very similar to Bultmann's interpretation of the New Testament teaching on man, as lost in a world which has become hostile to God and to man's true life. But perhaps for Jaspers the evil is not so radical for, as we have also seen, he can speak of an inborn nobility in man, which is gifted to him by his Creator and which makes any act of grace from outside of himself unnecessary for his salvation. All the difficulties and obscurities which arise in connection with Buri's conception of grace reappear in Jaspers, and indeed that is only to be expected, since it is from him that Buri derives his ideas.

We have noted also how Jaspers rejects the distinction between existential analysis and *existentiell* thinking.[2] He regards Bultmann's existential interpretation as an academic undertaking, the result of which can be only to make the Bible and its teaching more distant from us than ever. In attempting to translate a cipher-language into an exact conceptual language, Bultmann is simply gathering up dead leaves from the tree. For Jaspers, the true transformation of myth lies in living it out in concrete *existentiell* situations, and he sees this taking place above all in the work of the parish priest who is living out his calling. Jaspers has much to say here that is of the greatest interest. But while there is always the danger that theology may become scholastic, in the bad sense of a speculation detached from the living experience of religion, there is surely a place for an academic as well as a practical theology, provided that the two do not lose touch with each other. And

[1] See especially his book, *Man in the Modern Age*, trans. E. and C. Paul (Routledge & Kegan Paul, London, 1951).
[2] See above, p. 148. Cf. *Die Frage der Entmythologisierung*, p. 13, or *K.u.M.*, III, p. 15.

L

surely also, Jaspers is scarcely doing justice to Bultmann's real concern to let the message of the Bible speak to man in the very core of his existence. There would seem to be more substance in the complaint of the dogmatic theologians that Bultmann exhibits Christianity purely as a way of life than in Jaspers' complaint that he makes theology too academic. But neither complaint takes the whole truth of the matter into account, and again we are confronted with the paradoxical nature of Bultmann's thought.

But into these points in Jaspers' critique we shall not go further, and there are other points which we must leave aside altogether, since they are not directly relevant to our own inquiry into the limit to demythologizing. We shall therefore concentrate on three objections which he brings against Bultmann. All three are designed to show up the anti-philosophical and illiberal bias of Bultmann's thought, and they all concern us closely.

The first of Jaspers' objections is that Bultmann is selective in his philosophy; he has taken one single item from the vast field of philosophy and made it basic to his theology (Section 25). The second objection is that he is selective in his exegesis of the Bible and in the interpretation of the Christian religion which results from his exegesis; he has taken one part of the New Testament, ignoring the rest, and built his views upon it (Section 26). The third objection is that he is selective in his understanding of revelation as a whole; he has taken the event of Christ as definitive, and speaks as if there can be no true knowledge of God apart from that event (Section 27). These three prejudices, as Jaspers regards them, are held to be fatal to Bultmann's theological enterprise, to exclude any possibility of a *rapprochement* with philosophy, and to demonstrate the contention that Bultmann's demythologizing is at bottom illiberalism and orthodoxy all over again. The consideration of these objections will bring us to face yet another aspect of the problem presented by the limit to demythologizing (Section 28).

25 *A Prejudiced View of Philosophy?*

We consider first of all the objection that Bultmann is selective in his understanding of philosophy, and that his selectiveness amounts to an anti-philosophical prejudice. In

Jaspers' view, the essence of philosophizing lies in its openness and freedom from prejudice. He who would truly philosophize must expose himself to divergent currents of thought. He must give genuine consideration to alternatives. Now Bultmann, it is argued, has not done so. He has confined himself to a single philosopher, Martin Heidegger. More than that, he has restricted himself to a single book by this philosopher, *Sein und Zeit*. Worse still, it is suggested that he has not even properly understood this book! The result, if these allegations are true, is that Bultmann has really excluded himself from philosophy altogether. 'Not a breath of the thought of Kant or Plato, for instance, seems to have touched him', says Jaspers. Thus the seeming interest of Bultmann in philosophy is quite deceptive. The attitude revealed in his theology is utterly at variance with the true philosophizing spirit. He has set up as a dogma his own doubtful interpretation of a single book by a single philosopher, he has taken that for philosophy and built his theology upon it.[1]

Certainly, if this charge of Jaspers could be substantiated, it would prove Bultmann to be a remarkably prejudiced and illiberal thinker and his apparent interest in philosophy a sham. The charge, moreover, does have some plausibility. It may be that Bultmann himself has taken it to heart and sought to free himself from an exclusive preoccupation with Heidegger. We have already noted how he relies in his Gifford Lectures primarily upon Collingwood; though we have also noted that Collingwood comes in for criticism precisely at the point where his thought seems to diverge from that of Heidegger, so that it might seem that the only thing which Bultmann cannot abide is any hint of deviationism from the Heidegger line![2] However that may be, Jaspers' accusation calls for serious examination.

We must first look more closely at the way in which Jaspers conceives philosophy to be related to religion and theology. 'Religion', he says, 'is no enemy of philosophy, but something that essentially concerns and troubles it.' The two differ in many ways—religion has its cult, its myths, its community, while philosophy has none of those things. Yet, in spite of their

[1] On these points, see *Die Frage der Entmythologisierung*, pp. 11ff., or *K.u.M.*, III, pp. 14ff.

[2] See above, p. 89.

differences, both outward and inward, religion and philosophy converge at certain points. They are both interested in the question of God. Their respective ideas of God may seem to have little in common, but it is the same God who concerns them and, in Jaspers' view, the religious idea of God is the more powerful but the philosophical idea is the clearer intellectually. There are other points at which Jaspers sees the two activities converging. An interesting example which he mentions is prayer. In some of its forms prayer, he thinks, stands at the frontier of religion and philosophy. When prayer is free from any seeking for practical results, it comes near to the philosophical activity of contemplation.[1] We may indeed recall how in some of the great Christian theologians—Saint Augustine and Saint Anselm are examples that come to mind—prayer and speculation stand side by side and merge into each other. Sometimes these writers address the reader directly, but sometimes their words are addressed to God, and the reader, as it were, overhears what is said. Jaspers does not believe that religion can be transformed into philosophy or superseded by it. He does not think that even a philosophical faith of the kind which he expounds can take the place of religion, with the majority of mankind at least; for he concedes that in spite of the intellectual clarity claimed for it, a philosophical faith lacks the power to move men as they can be moved by a historical religion working through ritual, scriptures, an organized community, and so on.[2]

But if philosophy can never annex to itself the province of religion, the case may be very different, thinks Jaspers, with theology. For theology is not religion. It is rather the kind of reflection which takes for its subject-matter the truths underlying religion. Jaspers names Plato, the Stoics, Origen, Saint Augustine and Nicholas of Cusa as thinkers in whom theology and philosophy were closely conjoined. Philosophy too is interested in the truths underlying religion, and the unification of theology and philosophy appears to Jaspers to be the 'natural development' for liberalism.[3] Here Jaspers' view of theology and of its relation to philosophy comes very close to Buri's, except that whereas Buri seems to lay stress on the notion that

[1] *The Perennial Scope*, pp. 82-3.
[2] *Die Frage der Entmythologisierung*, p. 51, or *K.u.M.*, III, p. 43.   [3] Ibid.

any particular theology, such as Christian theology, confines it-self to some definite sector of tradition,[1] Jaspers seems to think of theology as concerning itself with the truths of religion in general.

This glance at Jaspers' view of the relation of philosophy to religion and theology would appear to indicate that, like Buri, he misconceives the nature of a discussion between theology and philosophy. For, like his disciple, he seems to suppose that such a discussion is possible only where the theologian is prepared to turn purely and simply into a philosopher. But we have already argued that a discussion between the two dis-ciplines is not made possible by merging them. Any genuine discussion needs contributions from two sides, and the results of such a merger as Jaspers and Buri envisage would be to make a discussion impossible, for there would be only one voice left. Moreover, the reservations are not all on the side of the theologian, as Jaspers would have us believe. It is not only the theologian who sometimes 'falls silent' or 'talks of something else'. Jaspers tells us that when confronted with the concrete ciphers of a religion, 'philosophy stops and looks at something different'.[2] And rightly so, for the business of philosophy is with the conceptual. But perhaps theology can only speak out of a concrete religion. Philosophy and theology have different functions, and they go about their tasks in different ways. Nevertheless, this does not rule out the possibility of a conversa-tion between them. For although the two disciplines are not identical, there may be zones of common interest between them. These zones will occur at certain points, and there contribu-tions can be made from both sides and a genuine discussion can take place. In an article on the relations of theology and philosophy, Professor Robert M. Brown has well said: 'The problem is not that of relating Christian faith to philosophy *qua* philosophy, but of seeing what its affinities and dissimilarities are with a given philosophy.'[3] But this is precisely what Bult-mann has tried to do. In expounding Christian theology in terms of human existence, he has found a zone of common interest with Martin Heidegger in that part of Heidegger's

---

[1] See above, p. 140.   [2] Ibid.

[3] 'Christian Faith and Contemporary Thought', in *The Student World*, XLIX, p. 419.

philosophy which is expressly concerned to analyse the structures of our human existence. In this zone of common interest the philosopher contributes a conceptual analysis of existence in general; the theologian contributes that understanding of existence which arises in the Christian life of faith. And it may be contended that Bultmann very properly confines himself to this particular zone, and does not wander over the whole field of philosophy as Jaspers seems to demand that he should.

If Jaspers misconceives the relation of philosophy to theology, he is even further from appreciating the task of the Christian apologist. Bultmann is an apologist rather than a philosopher of religion. Apologetics is distinct from the philosophy of religion, in that it is not a disinterested study of religion but a function of the Church. The apologist's task has been recognized as a service within the Church almost from the beginning of Christianity. His task is to commend the Christian faith as a living issue for his own day, and in order to do that he employs contemporary language and ideas. Jaspers complains that we find no trace of Platonic or Kantian philosophy in Bultmann. To this it might well be replied that if Bultmann had been an apologist of the early Church, he would have used Plato, and that if his birth had taken place a hundred years earlier than it actually did, he might have used Kant. He is well enough acquainted with the writings of both philosophers. One has only to read his works on Christian origins to appreciate his grasp of Greek thought; and when we remember that he was a student under Wilhelm Herrmann, while the Ritschlian theology was still in the ascendant, we shall understand that he is not ignorant of Kant. Failure to discuss the views of these great thinkers does not imply ignorance of them, and still less does it imply disrespect for them, since everyone knows that the achievements of contemporary philosophy are possible only on the basis of work done in the past. But as an apologist, Bultmann is writing for the mid-twentieth century, and accordingly his thought is directed towards men of his own time, and to the way in which they understand themselves. Therefore, as far as his apologetic work is concerned, he uses Heidegger rather than the philosophers of past generations, because Heidegger's language and ideas afford him a point of entry into contemporary thought and debate. Of course, Bultmann might have paid more attention to other contemporary philosophical movements, such as logical empiricism, or to other contemporary existentialists, such as Jaspers himself; and probably he should have done so. Yet obviously there must be some selection if we are not to get lost in an inconclusive eclecticism. Thus when we have regard to the proper task of apologetics and its orientation to contemporary thought, we see that Bultmann's preoccupation with Heidegger is not so arbitrary as Jaspers would have us believe. Within limits, it is a defensible procedure.

Still another consideration must be taken into account, and perhaps this is the most important point which we must bear in mind in trying to assess Jaspers' objection. When Jaspers claims that Heidegger's philosophy of existence is like a pillar on which Bultmann proceeds to rear the superstructure of his theology, he is giving us an entirely misleading picture of the situation. It is a distortion of the facts to suggest that Bultmann takes Heidegger's philosophy as his foundation, and then tries to build the Christian faith on to it. Rather is it the case that Heidegger's existential analytic becomes for Bultmann a hermeneutic tool.[1] As we have seen, Bultmann believes that when we turn to the Bible, the important questions which we ask are not factual questions or speculative questions but questions about our own existence in the world—the existence which is always one's own and for which each one is responsible. But in order that such questions may be asked with clearness and with understanding of what they involve, we must grasp as clearly as we can what this existence of ours is. Heidegger's existential analytic helps to provide concepts for understanding the structures of human existence, and so enables us to formulate our questions clearly. But it in no way prejudices the content of the answers. These come from the Christian faith itself. Bultmann can say that the philosophy of existence is the 'right' philosophy for the work of the theologian,[2] but this does not mean that he takes it as his foundation; what he does is to use it for the conceptual clarification of his subject-matter. Gogarten has remarked, concerning the application of Heidegger's analysis in demythologizing: 'This truth does not have to be learned from Heidegger. If one thinks one can learn it

---

[1] See above, pp. 55ff. [2] K.u.M., II, p. 192.

better from another source, all well and good. But, in one way or another, learned it must be'.[1] When this is understood, we again see that Bultmann's interest in Heidegger is not just the arbitrary choice of a congenial philosophy. The existential analytic is not the source of Bultmann's theology. The New Testament is the source. But the existential analytic provides the conceptual tools for eliciting the meaning of the New Testament.

When we consider these various replies which may be made to Jaspers' criticism that Bultmann is prejudiced in his philosophy, we see that this criticism turns out to be something of a damp squib. Admittedly Bultmann puts himself in a vulnerable position by his seemingly exclusive preoccupation with a certain area of Heidegger's thought, and in his more recent writings we see Bultmann trying to widen the scope of his philosophical contacts. But the fact that he is interested in one particular kind of philosophy and steadfastly refuses to let himself be 'carried about by every wind of doctrine'[2] does not prove that he is in any sense illiberal or prejudiced. It shows rather that he has a sounder conception of the relation between theology and philosophy than Jaspers has. As regards Jaspers' subsidiary charge, that Bultmann misunderstands Heidegger, little need be said. Heidegger is, of course, not easy to understand, but the only person who could pronounce whether Bultmann has properly understood him or not would be Heidegger himself. So far as the present writer is aware, Heidegger has made no pronouncement on the subject. But when we remember that Bultmann and Heidegger were colleagues together at Marburg and that they have been in correspondence over many years, it would not seem at all likely that Bultmann has been guilty of any serious distortion of Heidegger's thought. And it cannot be said that this thought is being applied by Bultmann in an illegitimate way, since Heidegger himself explicitly declares more than once that theological problems stand in need of precisely that kind of existential-ontological clarification which Bultmann seeks to provide for them.[3]

---

[1] *Demythologizing and History*, p. 52 n. 1.
[2] Eph. 4.14.
[3] Cf. *Sein und Zeit*, pp. 10, 180.

26 *A Prejudiced View of the Bible?*

We must now turn to Jaspers' second major criticism, which represents Bultmann as selective and prejudiced in his biblical exegesis. This is held to be further evidence of an illiberal and anti-philosophical attitude of mind. Jaspers concedes that as a biblical critic Bultmann has shown himself interested in all parts of the Bible, but contends that as a theologian Bultmann is selective. It is said that he is almost indifferent to the Old Testament, that he is sceptical about the Synoptic Gospels, and that he attaches most value to the Pauline and Johannine writings, stressing in particular the idea of justification by faith. For him, revelation does not lie in what we can know of the historic Jesus, but rather in the disciples' conception of a saving event. Jaspers, on the other hand, asks us to keep our minds open to the biblical writings as a whole, without any such arbitrary selection. From his point of view, the 'spiritualized Christ' of the Fourth Gospel, attractive though he is in his own way, is a lesser figure than the 'real Jesus' of the Synoptic Gospels. More than this, Jaspers claims that if we are open to the teaching of the Bible as a whole, we shall not be forced to share Bultmann's pessimistic view of man as so radically sinful that he can be saved only by an act of grace from outside himself. Jaspers thinks that we shall be able to find another point of view in the Bible which supports his own belief that man possesses a nobility which is at once inborn and yet given by God.[1] Here we may recall how Buri sought to support a similar point of view by citing biblical passages—the promise to Eve, Isaiah's vision, the experience of the prodigal son—taken from outside of the area on which Bultmann is said to concentrate.[2] Thus Jaspers maintains that in his exegesis of the Bible, Bultmann has shown himself to be prejudiced in favour of an illiberal orthodoxy.

It may be thought that Jaspers is somewhat rash in leaping into the field of biblical exegesis where, as he acknowledges, he is not an expert, while his opponent is universally admitted to be one of the outstanding biblical scholars of our time. Nevertheless, Jaspers' criticism has some plausibility, and exactly

---

[1] On these points, see *Die Frage der Entmythologisierung*, pp. 23-4, 50; or *K.u.M.*, III, pp. 22-3, 42.

[2] See above, pp. 146ff.

the same point has been made by other critics of Bultmann, some of whom are well versed in biblical studies. Thus Barth thinks that Bultmann tends to make the Pauline writings a 'canon within the canon', as followers of Luther have often done.[1] Most people would agree that divergent points of view can be found in the Bible, and it is well-known that almost any theological position, however extravagant, can be buttressed by an arbitrary selection of texts. One has only to glance at Saint Augustine's controversies with the Pelagians to see how the latter were able to find biblical support for their view of man —a view which was not very different from Jaspers' own. The exegete must, as Jaspers says, be open to the Bible as a whole. Yet at the same time, he must select, for not all parts of the Bible say the same things, and not all parts are of equal value. The question to be asked about Bultmann or any other exegete would seem to be not whether he is selective, but whether his selection is an arbitrary one, made in the interests of a pre-conceived theory, or whether he concentrates on that material which is most likely to yield a theological interpretation of the authentic message of the Bible.

First of all, we should beware of exaggeration. It is true that Bultmann has a special interest in the Pauline and Johannine writings, but it is not true that he ignores the rest of the Bible. Recently he published a collection of his university sermons, delivered at Marburg over a period of twenty years.[2] It is interesting to notice how he has selected his themes. Of the twenty-three sermons in the book, only two are based on texts from the Old Testament, which would seem to support Jaspers' contention that Bultmann regards it with indifference. But when we proceed to examine the sources of the remaining twenty-one sermons, which are models of expository preaching, we get a rather surprising result. Ten expound texts from the Synoptic Gospels; six are based on the Fourth Gospel; three on the Pauline epistles; and the remaining two are from other parts of the New Testament. A book of sermons of this sort might be held to give us a fair cross-section of Bultmann's thinking about the Christian faith. And we should have to conclude that, as far as the New Testament is concerned, he gives us a fairly well balanced presentation.

[1] *Ein Versuch*, p. 46.   [2] *Marburger Predigten* (J. C. B. Mohr, Tübingen, 1956).

When we look at his more specifically theological work, then we do find the preoccupations of which Jaspers complains. In his general exposition of New Testament theology, Bultmann gives pride of place to the Pauline and Johannine writings, and in addition he has written an extensive commentary on the Fourth Gospel. Yet is this to be wondered at? We are now talking about Bultmann as a theologian, so we ought not to be surprised if his interest is concentrated on the more theological parts of the Bible. As a Christian theologian, he is naturally more concerned with the New Testament than with the Old Testament, and within the New Testament he is concerned primarily with those writings which are most distinctly theological in their tone—the Pauline and Johannine literature. It is difficult to understand why such a procedure should be regarded as arbitrary and prejudiced.

In his major work on the theology of the New Testament, Bultmann points out at the very beginning that the teaching of Jesus is a presupposition of this theology rather than a part of it,[1] but he gives a full exposition of the teaching of Jesus and also of the teaching of the primitive Christian community, before he goes on to expound the more developed theology of Saint Paul and the Fourth Gospel. If, as we have argued, Christian theology is not a general philosophical study of religion but the interpretation of Christian faith—faith bringing itself to articulate expression—then clearly it must be primarily concerned with those parts of the New Testament in which the task of such interpretation has been explicitly recognized, and the writers have gone furthest in the direction of carrying out the task.

These considerations lead us into another. Everyone knows that the picture of Jesus given in the Fourth Gospel differs markedly from the one which we find in the Synoptic Gospels. It is generally agreed that the picture in the Fourth Gospel has been idealized, and that the interests of historical accuracy have been subordinated to the theological interest. But it is also generally agreed nowadays that the same kind of theological interpretation which is so marked in the Pauline and Johannine literature is present in some degree throughout the New Testament. Jaspers contrasts the 'spiritualized Christ' of the

[1] *Theologie des Neuen Testaments,* pp. 1ff.

Fourth Gospel with the 'reality of Jesus' in the Synoptic Gospels. But the earliest of the Synoptic Gospels opens with the words: 'The beginning of the gospel of Jesus Christ, the Son of God.'[1] And although some ancient authorities omit the phrase, 'the Son of God', it is clear enough from the use of the terms 'gospel' and 'Christ' that we have to do here not with a presentation of what Jaspers calls the 'reality of Jesus' (if by that he means a straightforward biographical account), but with a presentation of Jesus as the Messiah. The picture is already interpreted for faith; it is theologically coloured. Again, Jaspers refers to the legendary character of the Fourth Gospel. But it is in the Synoptics that we find such stories as those of the virgin birth and the ascension, not in the Pauline or Johannine writings. It is hard to avoid the conclusion that Jaspers is rather out of date in his New Testament studies. It seems that he still holds to the belief of the old 'liberal school' that we can distinguish a simple Jesus of history, presented in the Synoptics, and a supernaturalized Christ, presented in Saint Paul and the Fourth Gospel. As Bartsch remarks with some justice, philosophical circles have not yet acquainted themselves with the work done on the New Testament during the first half of the present century.[2] So far then as Jaspers' criticism rests on an outmoded view of a supposed opposition between the Synoptic Gospels on the one hand, and the Johannine and Pauline literature on the other, it fails to strike home.[3]

Before we leave the subject of Bultmann's attitude to the Bible, one further point may be briefly made. It is that in the Pauline and Johannine writings, Bultmann claims to find precisely that existential interpretation of the mythical which is so central to his thought. Saint Paul, for instance, can speak of the world as subject to the demonic powers of darkness, but he can speak also of man's idolizing of the creation—an idolizing which makes it a hostile power, yet leaves the responsibility with man himself. The Fourth Gospel can speak of Christ's coming again, but its typical thought is that of an eternal life

---

[1] Mark 1.1.   [2] *K.u.M,,* III, p. 71.

[3] Jaspers has another objection to the Fourth Gospel. Its attitude to the Jews seems to him to contain the seeds of that anti-semitism which, as we should all agree, has been a recurring disgrace in our Western civilization. There may be some truth in his complaint. But this point may be deferred for the present, since we shall discuss the question of exclusiveness and intolerance in the next section.

upon which men enter here and now, rather than the apocalyptic notion of a future age to be ushered in with catastrophic
happenings.[1] Thus in the most mature reflection of the New
Testament, Bultmann claims to find confirmation for his
existential interpretation of the Christian faith.

When all these points are taken into account, Bultmann's
preoccupation with the Pauline and Johannine literature as the
main source for his theology appears to be justified, and Jaspers'
accusation of prejudice and illicit selection turns out to be far
less damaging than it appears at first sight. We have still not
found that illiberal and anti-philosophical element in Bultmann
of which Jaspers complains.

27 A Prejudiced View of Revelation?

We come now to the third and most far-reaching of Jaspers'
major criticisms. Bultmann gives a special place to the revelation of God in Jesus Christ, and to this Jaspers takes strong
exception. In his view, God does not confine revelation to one
particular event—indeed, we place an arrogant restriction
upon God if we say that he does. There are ways to God without
Christ. Asians have found them in their great religions, and
any man, thinks Jaspers, can learn of God if he is open to God
instead of laying down in advance how God must reveal himself.
Revelation is everywhere and always. For me, it must be
present, and cannot lie in an event which took place long ago in
another place. Furthermore, to maintain that God's self-
revelation is confined to one particular event leads to intolerance, and even to the belief that all who think differently
are damned. Jaspers thinks that it is in their respective view of
revelation that orthodoxy and liberalism are most sharply
differentiated. And he has no hesitation in classing Bultmann
with the orthodox, for Bultmann does claim that it is in the
crucified and risen Christ that God reveals himself to men.
Thus, behind Bultmann's apparent concessions to philosophy,
Jaspers sees once again an illiberal and even intolerant orthodoxy.[2]

What is this revelation which is possible everywhere and

---

[1] Cf. *Primitive Christianity in its Contemporary Setting*, pp. 190-1, 197-200.
[2] On these points, see *Die Frage der Entmythologisierung*, pp. 41-6; or *K.u.M.*,
III, pp. 36-9.

always? It is to be understood in connection with Jaspers' well-known doctrine of the 'limit-situation'. In our existence we cannot help coming into such a situation where, so to speak, we come up against a wall. 'We become aware of the pheno-menality of empirical existence' and, in becoming aware of this, we gain awareness of transcendence. Guilt, suffering and death are examples of such limit-situations. The Bible, in Jaspers' view, 'is the deposit of a thousand years of human experience on the limit'. But revelation cannot consist in past events—it occurs now, when, for instance, a man 'takes the cross upon himself' and enters the area of the limit. This sounds very much like Bultmann, except that Jaspers would insist that revelation is not tied to any particular event, such as the cross of Christ.[1]

In a criticism of this view of Jaspers, Karl Barth denies that men learn about God from limit-situations. He points out that 'millions and millions of our contemporaries have, for many years, seen themselves falling out of one limit-situation (in the strongest sense of the term) into another. And what has this meant for them in practice? Has anyone encountered the wholly other, and in this encounter with the wholly other become just a little bit "other" himself, through the fact that he has fought in Russia or Africa or Normandy, or endured the Hitler terror, or undergone air-raids, or suffered hunger and imprisonment, or lost dear ones, or been dozens of times in extreme danger of his life, and in all this become somehow guilty himself?'[2]

Despite its rhetoric, this criticism of the view that there is revelation at the limits is remarkably lacking in bite. In the first place, we have to notice that Jaspers is perfectly well aware that men can often be in tight corners without learning any-thing. In a passage which pretty effectively draws the teeth from Barth's comments, Jaspers says almost exactly the same things in more sober language: 'It is a terrifying fact that today despite all the upheaval and devastation, we are still in danger of living and thinking as though nothing really important had happened. It is as though a great misfortune had merely dis-turbed the life of us poor victims, but as though life might now be continued in the old way. . . . For the great danger is that

---

[1] Cf. *The Perennial Scope*, pp. 33-4, 101, 103.
[2] *Kirchliche Dogmatik*, III/2, p. 135.

what has happened may pass, considered as nothing but a great misfortune, without anything happening to us men as men, without our hearing the voice of transcendence, without our attaining to any insight and acting with insight.'[1] In other words, we can find ourselves in difficult situations without perceiving them as limit-situations or finding any revelation of transcendence in them.

Thus, in the second place, Barth seems to misunderstand the nature of a limit-situation. He seems to think that any overwhelming event which overtakes us becomes automatically a limit-situation. But this is not so. The limit-situation belongs to the realm of what Jaspers calls the 'comprehensive',[2] which is said to be on both sides of the subject-object split. Revelation is not just objective happening, but includes our response to the happening. In the course of his remarks on Jaspers, Barth says that 'the Lord was not in the storm, or in the earthquake, or in the fire'.[3] This is true enough; but Jaspers is not saying that God is revealed in these events themselves. What he is saying is that sometimes experience of such events brings men to awareness of the limits of existence in such a way that they also become aware of transcendence. But Jaspers knows as well as anyone the tendency of human nature to level down such events, to rob them of their significance for existence, and to treat them just as inconvenient happenings.

In the third place, it must be noted that Barth's remarks can easily be turned against his own position. For if the limit-situations experienced in the past few generations seem to have had little result in making men aware of the wholly other or in making them a little bit 'other' themselves, it might be said that the same is true of the preaching of the Christian gospel over a very much longer period. After nineteen centuries of it, we stand on the verge of nuclear warfare. This simply goes to show that God is not revealed in any objective happening to which one can point and say 'Lo, here'; and that the same toughness which brings men unchanged through what might

---

[1] *The Perennial Scope*, p. 162. Presumably Barth had no time to read these words, since they appeared almost simultaneously with his own comments in 1948. His criticisms are based on a much earlier work of Jaspers, *Philosophie* (Springer Verlag, Heidelberg, 1932), Band II, p. 201ff. Yet even there Jaspers makes it clear enough that to undergo a misfortune is one thing, to experience it as a limit-situation is another.

[2] See above, p. 155.   [3] Ibid.; cf. I Kings 19.11-2.

have been limit-situations makes them equally resistant to the Christian proclamation.

While we shall argue that in a sense the Christian revelation has a certain definitive character, we may accept Jaspers' contention that there is no restriction of revelation to one single event or series of events, and that there are ways to God apart from the Christian revelation. Some superstitions are relatively harmless, but the superstition that there is only one way to God lies at the root of all the fanaticism and intolerance which is the very antithesis of the religious spirit. The most objectionable feature of Barthian theology is just its arrogant insistence that apart from the Christian revelation there can be no genuine knowledge of God but only idolatry. We must ask how far Bultmann has freed himself from this point of view. His position is admittedly ambiguous. As Jaspers sees it, Bultmann is on the side of intolerance. In spite of his superficial interest in philosophy, he is held to be at bottom quite illiberal. The three adjectives which Jaspers applies to the conception of the revelation in Christ, as said to be held by Bultmann and the orthodox, are 'exclusive', 'once-for-all', and 'absolute'.[1]

None of these three adjectives, however, is really particularly appropriate to Bultmann's point of view. 'Exclusive' is an ugly word, and it stands for an even uglier idea. Whoever thinks that he is in exclusive possession of the truth in religion has made the symbols of his own thinking ultimate, and has identified them with the reality which they are supposed to illumine. But this identification of the symbols with that which they symbolize is a kind of idolatry, and like all idolatry it issues in demonic results. Such exclusiveness, it must be confessed, has appeared from time to time in the Christian Church, not only with regard to other religions, but as between different branches of the Church. Christians have unchurched and persecuted other Christians because of the delusion that they were in exclusive possession of the truth. This is a perversion of Christianity. Now it must be noticed also that Bultmann occasionally uses the word 'exclusive' and speaks as if there could be no genuine knowledge of God or of man's authentic existence apart from the Christian revelation.[2] If

---

[1] *Die Frage der Entmythologisierung*, p. 42; or *K.u.M.*, III, p. 36.
[2] Cf. *Essays*, pp. 109ff.

this is what he really means, then we can only disagree with him, take sides with Jaspers, and acknowledge that the charge of an illiberal attitude has been made out. But Bultmann is highly ambiguous on these matters. We find him also saying that it is 'turning from the world' which is the way to God, and that Christians and non-Christians who have taken this step are unified in a 'community of the transcendent' which has nothing exclusive about it![1] The question must be pursued further.

Jaspers' second adjective, 'once-for-all', is liable to lead to misunderstanding, and as we are already aware, Jaspers blames Bultmann for maintaining the once-for-all character of the Christian revelation whereas some orthodox theologians blame him for abandoning it. This time, however, the ambiguity is more easily pinned down, for Bultmann has fortunately given an explanation of what he understands by 'once-for-all'. Jaspers takes the word to designate an objective event which occurred at a definite point of time; and perhaps this is the natural way to interpret the word. Bultmann, however, explains that for him the word does not refer to a datable event which occurred once, but has rather the meaning of 'once-for-all-times'. That is to say, it refers to what Bultmann calls an 'eschatological' event—an event which indeed happened in the past but is made present or re-presented now, as in the proclaiming of the *kerygma*. The possibility of existence embodied in the past event can be understood as a possibility of existence now. It is clear that this is very close to Jaspers' own teaching that 'history becomes to me the present that I myself am'.[2] For Bultmann as for Jaspers, revelation is in a sense only in the 'now' for each individual. But while Jaspers appears to misunderstand Bultmann's peculiar use of the term 'once-for-all', there is certainly a difference between the two thinkers. For Bultmann, the present revelatory event is the proclaiming of the *kerygma*—that is to say, it is always related to the event of Jesus Christ. For Jaspers, on the other hand, with his belief that revelation is everywhere and always, it would seem that any present event has the possibility of becoming a revelatory event. But just how far this difference extends is still not clear,

[1] Cf. *Essays*, pp. 301ff.
[2] *The Origin and Goal of History*, trans. Michael Bullock (Routledge & Kegan Paul, London, 1953), p. 270.

M

for Bultmann on his side can say: 'In every moment slumbers the possibility of being the eschatological moment. You must awaken to it'.[1]

Jaspers' third adjective, 'absolute', turns out to be as slippery as the two others. One might suppose that to claim 'absolute' truth for anything amounted to saying that it is true for everyone under all circumstances. But we find that both Jaspers and Bultmann have a curious habit of talking of religious truth as 'absolute' *for those who accept it*.[2] If, however, anything is absolute *for me* but possibly not *for you*, it is in some sense not absolute at all but relative. To say that something is absolute for a particular person means presumably that it makes an unconditional claim on that person. If this use of the word 'absolute' is not actually a misuse of language, it is at least highly misleading, since it is only too easy to slip over to the more normal meaning of the word, according to which that which is 'absolute' possesses its character apart from its relation to anything else.

To avoid the confusions which arise from Jaspers' three adjectives, let us substitute for them the term 'definitive'. It is clear that Bultmann wants to claim for the Christian revelation a definitive status; and it is clear also that this claim is particularly annoying to Jaspers. What we have to inquire is whether it is possible to find a sense in which the definitive claim of the Christian revelation can be defended without falling into that exclusiveness and intolerance which Jaspers rightly condemns.

It must frankly be admitted at the outset that we cannot defend the claim to a definitive character if we are thinking in terms of objective historical events which took place in Palestine some two thousand years ago. This point emerged plainly enough in our discussion of the historical nature of Christianity.[3] Perhaps people of New Testament times could look upon the event of Jesus Christ as in itself having a definitive status. For them, the universe was a relatively compact place, with the earth in the centre and man the chief end of creation. The world-process—equated, as we have seen, with human history—was supposed to have begun only a few thousand years

---

[1] *History and Eschatology*, p. 155.

[2] For Jaspers, see *The Perennial Scope*, p. 89; for Bultmann, see *Die Frage der Entmythologisierung*, p. 69; or *K.u.M.*, III, p. 56.

[3] See above, p. 60.

before, and to be shortly coming to an end. For people who held such beliefs, it may have been possible also to believe that God had made all ages a preparation for the coming of his Son, and that the event of Jesus Christ has a central and definitive place in the unfolding of universal history. But for us, the picture is very different. The old compact universe has vanished away, the earth and man have been deposed from the centre of things, the mind reels when it tries to comprehend the immensity of space with its multitudes of universes, the time-scale has been so extended that we cannot even begin to imagine its vastness. In saying this, we are not being so foolish as to be frightened by mere size. It has often enough been said, and truly said, that the value of anything is not affected by size. But at the moment we are not discussing the value of the Christ-event, but its alleged place at the centre of an objectively conceived cosmic process. Its value might indeed entitle it to be placed at the centre if there were a centre as people once believed, but what we learn from modern cosmology is that there is no centre.[1] Against the background of the cosmic process, as it is understood in the post-Copernican era, any event which takes place on this earth, even the event of Jesus Christ, can be only very local and very temporary, in so far as it is conceived as objective happening.

The point, however, which Bultmann has been chiefly concerned to stress is that we do not or should not look upon the event of Jesus Christ as purely objective happening. We do not seek to be spectators of all time and all worlds so that from this godlike point of view we can pronounce that such and such an event is absolute, unique, final, central or however we may care to express it.[2] We see events only from the limited standpoint of human existence. It is from this standpoint alone that we can see the event of Jesus Christ, and any definitive status which is assigned to this event must be understood in terms of its existential significance. But we shall now argue that

[1] On the philosophical significance of Copernicus, see R. G. Collingwood, *The Idea of Nature*, pp. 96ff.

[2] Jaspers thinks that within human history we can discover an axis or turning-point. 'This axis', he tells us, 'would be . . . the point most overwhelmingly fruitful in fashioning humanity.' He identifies it with the 'spiritual process that occurred between 800 and 200 B.C.' Cf. *The Origin and Goal of History*, pp. 1ff. Bultmann denies that we can have the overall view which Jaspers' theory seems to demand. For his comments on Jaspers' view of history, see *History and Eschatology*, pp. 129-30.

when the event of Jesus Christ is regarded from the point of view of our existence, we find that we must assign a certain definitive character to it, and that this comes about in two ways.

The first point is that our existence never begins from scratch. As Heidegger expresses it, we are always 'thrown' into a situation which determines the possibilities of decision actually open to us. At any moment the possibilities before us are limited by our own past choices, by the choices of past generations, and by a great many other factors which have never been chosen by anyone but are simply given. Among other things, we are thrown into a historical tradition—in our case, the Western tradition, which is also a Christian tradition. Thus Western man learns about God in terms of a tradition which has been shaped by the Christian revelation. In an essay with the title, 'Why We Cannot Help Calling Ourselves Christians',[1] Benedetto Croce remarks that his object is 'simply to demonstrate by an appeal to history that we cannot avoid acknowledging and confessing that we are Christians, and that the name merely registers a fact'. Christianity, he argues, is an integral part of our Western heritage, and sometimes the essential Christian values are kept alive and developed better by men outside our churches than by men within them. 'The truth is that, though we are children of the whole of history and its blood flows in our veins, yet ancient ethics and religion were taken up and dissolved in the Christian idea of conscience and moral inspiration, and in the new idea of God in whom we live and move and have our being'. For us, as the children of Christianity, God cannot be Zeus or Yahweh or Wotan. Croce indeed concedes that 'no man can tell whether another religious revelation, equal or superior to what Hegel calls "absolute religion", will come to pass for the human race in some future of which today we can see no dawn'. But that is matter for speculation. 'This we know, that in our times, our thought inevitably works on the lines laid down by Christianity.'

It is the case that the revelation which meets us within our own historical tradition speaks to us as no other revelation can. Even the atheism of the West is a kind of Christian atheism, determined at every point by its relation to Christian-

[1] In *My Philosophy*, trans. E. F. Carritt (Allen & Unwin, London, 1949). See especially pp. 37, 45-6.

ity, as Jaspers' own study of Nietzsche very well shows.[1] We cannot, in our historical situation, get away from Christianity. This does not mean that truth is to be denied to other revelations—far from it. But hardly anyone in the West ever grasps a revelation outside his own tradition *as* a revelation. Whoever has tried to study more than superficially a religion other than his own knows how difficult it is to penetrate into its ethos. Islam, for instance, is not for the ordinary Western man a live option—if we may borrow a useful expression which was introduced into the demythologizing controversy by Professor Ian Henderson.[2] But presumably Islam is a live option and a genuine revelation to the West African who may find himself faced with a decision between Islam and fetishism. For the Western man, however, the real possibility of decision into which he is thrown by his historical situation is between Christianity, orthodox or unorthodox, and secularism in its various forms. Thus for the Western man, in virtue of the factical conditions of his existence, Christianity has an inescapably definitive character. At the beginning of the present century, when it seemed as if Western culture was on its way to becoming the first world-culture, it might have seemed also that Christianity was on its way to attaining a definitive status for all men. But the awakening of African and Asian nationalism, the reaction against colonialism, the association of Christianity with Western imperialism, and the revival of Islam and Buddhism, make it appear likely that for a long time yet different religions will need to live together on the earth.

It is interesting to note that the kind of definitive status here claimed for Christianity was very clearly stated a long time ago by one of Bultmann's own teachers, Wilhelm Herrmann. After saying that he would 'by no means wish to assert, even for a moment, that the savages of New Holland have no knowledge of God', Herrmann goes on to say: 'We stand in such historical relationships that Jesus Christ alone can be grasped by us as the fact in which God . . . reveals himself to us. The knowledge of God and the religion which have been and which are possible to men placed in other historical conditions are impossible to us.'[3]

[1] *Nietzsche und das Christentum* (Seifert, Hameln, 1938).
[2] In *Myth in the New Testament* (SCM Press, London, 1952).
[3] *The Communion of the Christian with God*. Third Edition, trans. J. S. Stanyon and R. W. Stewart (Williams & Norgate, London, 1909), pp. 62-3.

There is a second way in which, from the standpoint of existence, it may be claimed that the revelation in Christ has a definitive character. As well as the fact that man is thrown into a historical tradition within which his understanding is shaped, there is to be considered the nature of revelation itself. To recognize a revelation is to recognize that God speaks; and when God speaks, he makes an absolute claim upon us. God makes himself known to us as our 'ultimate concern', in Tillich's expression. The point is very well put by Bultmann himself[1] when he says that wherever there is revelation, there is also the assertion and command: 'I am the Lord your God. You shall have no other gods besides me.'[2] By its very nature, a revelation of God must have a definitive character. Jaspers seems to confuse the recognition of a revelation as revelation for me with the recognition that there may be revelation for others which is not revelation for me. The two are not incompatible. To accept a revelation is to accept its definitive and ultimate character. But this is not to deny that some men may have knowledge of God in other ways. We should no more wish to lay down restrictions for revelation than we did for grace, in discussing Buri's position.

Saint Paul makes it clear that he recognizes that there is in the Old Testament revelation the same truth that he has learned in Christ, as when he says, 'They drank from the supernatural rock . . . and the rock was Christ'.[3] Saint Justin the Martyr extended the idea to Greek philosophy, when he described as Christians 'such as Socrates and Heraclitus among the Greeks, and those like them . . .'.[4] To recognize the Logos in the Church's kerygmatic word is to recognize an ultimate so that one does not look elsewhere; but this is not to deny that the Logos speaks elsewhere.

We have tried to show that to assign a definitive status to the Christian revelation is not necessarily to fall into the illiberalism and intolerance of which Jaspers rightly complains. To that extent, we may have succeeded in turning aside his objection. But it is by no means certain that Bultmann would go with us in our interpretation of the definitive character of Christianity. His own position is so equivocal that it is not at all clear that he

---

[1] *Die Frage der Entmythologisierung*, p. 69; or *K.u.M.*, III, p. 56.
[2] Ex. 20.2-3.   [3] I Cor. 10.4   [4] *First Apology*, xlvi, 4.

can wholly escape Jaspers' criticisms. We must now attempt to define still more precisely the difference between the two men, and ask whether that difference is quite irreconcilable.

28 *Revelation and Communication*

From the foregoing discussion, it is clear enough that Jaspers and Bultmann have a good many things in common, yet the fact remains that their conversation has broken down. Let us ask first what it is that Jaspers holds to be of vital importance. Stated briefly, it is 'complete openness of communication'.[1] In his view, no concession can be made to that man-made exclusiveness which separates men and embitters their relations to each other. And with this we must agree.

But what does this imply for religious faith? Is Jaspers advocating what is usually called a 'private religion'? We would not wish to deny that a private religion may be adequate to the needs of the person who holds it, and that it may produce the fruits of the spirit and make him a whole or saved person as much as an orthodox religion would. But we should criticize a private religion as inadequate on the grounds that religion has a social or communal function. Religion should be a leaven for the whole culture, and this a private religion cannot be. But Jaspers is not advocating a private religion. In his philosophical faith he finds—unlike some other existentialists—an important place for tradition. He thinks it a matter of urgent importance that biblical religion should be renewed. He acknowledges the power of a historical religion, and values such religion himself.

Is Jaspers then advocating a syncretistic faith, a merging of religions in which the best elements in each would be combined? Although such a merger has had an appeal for certain minds from classical times onwards—one calls to mind the Roman Emperor Alexander Severus who is said to have had in his oratory statues of Orpheus, Abraham, Jesus, and others—the effect is usually a loss of vitality and a vague confused sentimentalism. Jaspers is too wise to advocate anything of the sort. He knows that the different roads cannot 'be travelled all at once'. He asks us 'to become concerned with the historically different without becoming untrue to our own historicity'.

[1] See *The Perennial Scope*, pp. 172ff.

What Jaspers seems to be advocating is a liberal Christianity in which the believer can be loyal to his own faith without denying that others may have found God in different ways. His point of view seems not far removed from that of Arnold Toynbee, who advocates a kind of peaceful co-existence among the higher religions. Toynbee says: 'The missions of the higher religions are not competitive, they are complementary. We can believe in our own religion without having to feel that it is the sole repository of truth. We can love it without having to fear that it is the sole means of salvation.'[1]

This is surely a quite reasonable point of view. We have noted that for a long time to come it is likely that there will be a variety of religions existing together on our planet. They have much in common, especially in their ethical teaching and in their spiritual conception of life. Faced with the rising tide of secularism and of that grasping materialism which threatens to undo mankind, is it not possible for the various religions, each remaining loyal to its own traditions, to work together for common ends, just as the various Christian denominations have learned to co-operate without losing their individuality? And has not the Christian apologist a big enough job in commending the faith to the present generation, without being expected to prove in addition that every other approach to God is false and idolatrous?

Now let us ask what is vital to Bultmann's position in his discussion with Jaspers. Briefly, we may say that it is the concreteness of revelation. Jaspers' talk of a revelation which is possible everywhere and always and his tendency to equate awareness of the limits of existence with awareness of God makes revelation something very tenuous and indefinite. Bultmann is right in asserting that in revelation God addresses us, there is a movement from the divine side to man. Here he is rightly recognizing another limit to demythologizing, in so far as demythologizing confines itself to talking of human existence. In our historical situation, the vehicle for this concrete revelation is the Christian *kerygma*, and Bultmann is right in insisting that it be retained. But there is no reason why he should maintain that God never addresses men through any other vehicle; and if he maintains this (it is difficult to know whether he does

---

[1] *An Historian's Approach to Religion*, p. 298.

or not) it must be accounted a weakness in his theology.

We must conclude that the gap between Jaspers and Bultmann, at least, on these main issues which we have considered, is a narrow one. They are divided not by a question of principle but rather by a difference of emphasis. Jaspers, as the philosopher, lays the stress on openness of communication. Bultmann, as the theologian, attaches importance to the concreteness of revelation. These two are not irreconcilable, as we have tried to show. Although the conversation between Jaspers and Bultmann has ended in an apparent breakdown, we can acknowledge that something has been accomplished towards the desired *rapprochement* between philosophy and theology, if we are prepared to consider the two points of view dispassionately and sympathetically.

VII

DEMYTHOLOGIZING AND LANGUAGE

29 *Existentialism and Logical Empiricism*

WE have seen that demythologizing may be regarded primarily as a method of interpretation. Its aim is to elucidate the meaning of Christian language by bringing out the existential content of mythical and even historical statements.[1] Bultmann's enterprise may therefore be regarded as standing in relation to the current philosophical interest in exploring the meanings of different kinds of languages. Bultmann expounds an approach to the language of myth, and it would be natural to expect that among his critics we should find some of those logical empiricists who have directed their attention to religious language. It is necessary, however, to say at the beginning that the exchanges between demythologizing and logical empiricism have as yet been on a very restricted scale. Although there are at present a good many logical empiricists who interest themselves in the problems of religious language, very few of them have shown any interest in Bultmann; and their lack of interest in him has been matched by his indifference not only to them but to the whole philosophical movement within which they work.

This mutual indifference may well be symptomatic of the present state of philosophy. The breakdown in the present century of traditional ways of thinking has brought about, as one of its consequences, a fragmentation of philosophical activity. We find nowadays several well-defined schools of philosophy which seem to go their independent ways with very little communication among themselves. Of course, there always have been different schools of thought in philosophy, but they used to criticize and stimulate one another. We cannot read

[1] See above, p. 33.

very far in F. H. Bradley, for instance, without being made aware that there are other points of view than the idealist one. Even if he does not think very highly of them and writes most scathingly about them, Bradley at least takes note of them and says why he thinks they are wrong. But one can read quite extensively in the literature of existentialism without coming across any serious discussion of logical empiricism. Equally, one can read a lot of logical empiricism without realizing that there is such a thing as existentialism—except, perhaps, for a few impatient references which represent it as scarcely worthy of serious consideration.

When we remember that the two movements mentioned have certain common roots in the history of philosophy, it is the more surprising that they should show themselves so indifferent to each other. There is a danger that contemporary schools of philosophy are becoming unhealthily introverted. Perhaps any new school of thought needs some time to sort out its own ideas before it is ready for conversation with another point of view. But if there is no such conversation, then each school—be it existentialist, empiricist, neo-Thomist, or something else— tends to develop a dogmatic and exclusive attitude.

In the case which is of special concern to us, we have already noted[1] that in his approach to the problems of hermeneutics Bultmann relies exclusively upon existentialism—and, indeed, as Jaspers has indicated, upon one particular version of existentialism. He shows no interest in logical empiricism and does not even betray any awareness of it. For this reason, Bultmann's thought appears 'foreign' to British readers, of whom at least the younger generation have grown up in an empiricist atmosphere and look to Wittgenstein rather than to Heidegger. When confronted with demythologizing, such readers might be expected to ask how it stands up to the acids of the logical analysis with which they are familiar. But they are just as likely to dismiss Bultmann without further consideration because he is unfamiliar to their way of thinking and employs a jargon different from their own. The fault is not on one side only. A few years ago, Professor George E. Hughes felt himself constrained to protest against the tendency not uncommon in logical empiricists to suggest that their point of view 'is the

[1] See above, p. 56.

only one, or at least that it is the only one which any sensible man can now hold'.[1] If we look through those writings on religious themes which have come from the side of logical empiricism, we find that with few exceptions they take as little notice of Bultmann as he takes of them.

It is surely desirable that the existentialist and empiricist approaches to religion should be taken out of their sealed compartments and brought into confrontation with each other. Just where do the differences lie? Are the two approaches incompatible or are they, perhaps, directed upon different aspects of the problem so that each needs to be supplemented by the other? Here we can get some help from Professor John Macmurray. Noting that logical empiricism and existentialism are the two main forms of philosophizing which have emerged after the breakdown of the traditional systems, he has this to say about them: 'Both rest upon the decision that the traditional method of philosophy is incapable of solving its traditional problems. But whereas the logical empiricists discard the problems in order to retain the method, the existentialists relinquish the method in wrestling with the problems. So the latter achieve a minimum of form; the former a minimum of substance. The logical empiricists are content to elaborate the subtleties of formal analysis . . . the existentialists, determined to grapple with the real problems, find no formal analysis that is adequate to the task. They are constrained to quit the beaten track, to wallow in metaphor and suggestion.'[2] This characterization of the difference between the two types of philosophy may be exaggerated, and it fails to do justice to individual cases in both philosophical camps. Surely there are some logical empiricists who get to grips with substantial problems and equally there are some existentialists—Heidegger and Bultmann among them—whose interest is in the formal structure of existence. Demythologizing is itself an attempt to get away from pictorial language. Even in the case of those existentialists whose interest is an *existentiell* rather than an existential one and who express their ideas through the medium of plays and novels, it seems rather hard to say that they 'wallow' in metaphor and suggestion, since the word 'wallow' is itself suggestive of rude comparisons with the behaviour of farmyard animals! But

[1] *New Essays in Philosophical Theology*, p. 58.   [2] *The Self as Agent*, pp. 27-8.

allowing for an element of exaggeration, we may accept Macmurray's comments as a generalized description of the current situation, and as true within limits. There is a danger that form and matter are being torn apart. As far as the special problems of philosophical theology are concerned, Macmurray's estimate lends support to the contention that if we are to have a balanced view, the existentialist and empiricist approaches should not be kept separate. Each should take heed of what the other is doing.

The demythologizer, on his side, ought to pay more attention to what the logical empiricists are saying. Perhaps theologians are inclined to steer clear of logical empiricism because many of them have a suspicion that it is inherently hostile to religion. In particular, Bultmann would presumably have made his acquaintance with the movement through the writings of the Vienna circle which at one time advocated a positivist or 'physicalist' position and would have excluded theology from the realm of meaningful discourse. Even if the movement were hostile to religion, that would still, of course, be no reason for ignoring it. But a theologian looking for help with his problems would scarcely be attracted to a philosophy which told him in advance that his utterances were senseless.

Logical empiricism, however, like existentialism itself, is a way of philosophizing rather than a body of doctrine. Just as there are believers and unbelievers among existentialists, so there are among logical empiricists. Indeed, a glance through the literature of the latter group shows that within it we can find just about every possible attitude to religion imaginable. Some of these attitudes are hostile or indifferent to traditional religious belief. Ludwig Wittgenstein taught that 'the solution to the problem of life is seen in the vanishing of this problem', that is to say, that religion is *inexpressible*; A. J. Ayer regards religious utterances as pseudo-propositions which are senseless and simply evince *emotion*; J. N. Findlay, as we have seen, advocates a *religious atheism*. In other writers we find attempts to salvage religion from positivist attacks. R. B. Braithwaite puts forward a *conative* interpretation which comes near to assimilating religion to morality; Ian Crombie and John Wilson stick to a more conservative point of view, and think that religious statements tell us about *supersensible* realities. A further group of writers believe that religious language cannot be simply characterized but has a complex function involving more than one factor—a view which would accord with the results at which we arrived in our discussion of demythologizing and dogma. Thus R. M. Hare speaks of religious language as both *'descriptive and prescriptive'*, because it is 'too factual to be called specifically moral, and yet too closely bound up with our conduct to be called in the ordinary sense factual'; Ian T. Ramsey takes it to be an 'odd' kind of language which refers to situations involving both *'discernment and commitment'*; Willem Zuurdeeg prefers to call religious language *'convictional'* and holds that the 'conviction' which it expresses is a complex attitude combining several factors.[1] Of course, it is not being suggested that one can arbitrarily pick and choose among these different points of view or that logical empiricism provides a climate equally congenial to all of them. Obviously, they can hardly all be correct. But the diversity of viewpoints which is *in fact* found among thinkers with a background of logical empiricism is mentioned to show that the theologian can approach this type of philosophy with an open mind. He certainly cannot afford to ignore it. He has indeed much to learn from it if it can help to clarify his own ways of speaking, to introduce consistency into his theories, and to show up the weak points in his thinking.

If the existentialist theologian ought to take note of logical empiricism, it is equally the case that the logical empiricist who is interested in religion ought to pay attention to existentialism. Sometimes he is tempted to discuss language in the abstract, as if it were something that existed by itself in a kind of vacuum. It may be true that there are some kinds of language which can be properly discussed in this way, such as the language of mathematics. But the language of religion is so bound up with the person or persons by whom it is used that if

---

[1] For these various points of view, see: L. Wittgenstein, *Tractatus Logico-Philosophicus*, trans. C. K. Ogden (Kegan Paul, London, 1922); A. J. Ayer, *Language, Truth and Logic*, Second Edition (V. Gollancz, London, 1946); J. N. Findlay in *New Essays in Philosophical Theology* (SCM Press, London, 1955); R. M. Hare and Ian Crombie in *Faith and Logic* (Allen & Unwin, London, 1957); R. B. Braithwaite, *An Empiricist's View of the Nature of Religious Belief* (C.U.P., London, 1955); John Wilson, *Language and Christian Belief* (Macmillan, London, 1958); Ian T. Ramsey, *Religious Language* (SCM Press, London, 1957); Willem F. Zuurdeeg, *An Analytical Philosophy of Religion* (Abingdon Press, New York, 1958).

it becomes isolated we no longer have any possibility of getting a proper understanding of it. Such language has to be understood as a factor in the existence of the person who uses it—in a sense, indeed, it *is* his existence, since in such language he expresses *himself*. We must therefore have an understanding of the existence of this person—his situation, possibilities, limitations, and so on. Thus it may be argued that the logical empiricist who would give us an adequate analysis of religious language must also undertake an adequate analysis of the human existence out of which such language arises. This point is grasped very clearly by Zuurdeeg, who supplements his linguistic analysis with existential analysis. He writes: 'Language is not only a terminology, a grammar, though language always implies these elements. It is misleading to concentrate in linguistic philosophy upon sentences or words. We should never lose sight of the man who speaks.'[1]

In these preliminary remarks, we have tried to show the desirability of bringing together the existentialist and empiricist approaches to religion. The remainder of the chapter will be devoted to some topics within this field. First we shall explore in more detail the relations between language and human existence (Section 30). Then we shall turn to the criticisms of demythologizing which have been made by one of the few empiricist writers on the subject—Dr R. W. Hepburn. In a short but penetrating essay,[2] Hepburn shows us just how salutary and needful it is to apply the tests of logical analysis to an apparently well-founded theological position. We shall consider two of the most important points which he raises— whether Bultmann's basic terminology is confused (Section 31) and whether demythologizing helps towards establishing the validity of the Christian faith (Section 32).

30 *Language and Existence*

Let us take as our starting-point some remarks of Heidegger on the subject of language.[3] He makes a distinction between 'talk' or 'discourse' (*Rede*) and 'language' (*Sprache*). Discourse, we are told, is an *existentiale*, that is to say, one of the basic

---

[1] *An Analytical Philosophy of Religion*, p. 60.
[2] 'Demythologizing and the Problem of Validity' in *New Essays in Philosophical Theology*, pp. 227ff.
[3] *Sein und Zeit*, pp. 160ff.

possible ways in which man exists. It is the way in which man expresses *himself*. Discourse is one of the *existentialia* which have to do with the disclosedness of existence, for man's existence is such that it always carries with it some understanding of existence. It is an existence which is disclosed to itself. Furthermore, it is disclosed to itself as 'being-in-the-world'. We do not begin with a subject (self) and an object (world) which have somehow to be brought into relation with each other; rather, subject and object, self and world, get sorted out from the concrete actuality of being-in-the-world. Language (words and sentences) is said to be based upon discourse (the possibility of expressing oneself as being-in-the-world). Thus 'the phenomenon (of language) has its roots in the existential constitution of man's disclosedness'.

What this somewhat cryptic doctrine means can perhaps best be seen by looking at Heidegger's own use of language, which is sometimes notoriously difficult to follow. It was Paul Tillich who said of him that he had exploited 'the genius, or rather the demon, of the German language'; while linguistic philosophers like Rudolf Carnap have severely criticized his habit of talking on such topics as 'being' and 'nothing'.[1] Yet Heidegger's language is far from being as woolly and amorphous as it is sometimes represented. Formidable it may be in some respects, but it has a definite structure. Heidegger has certain principles in view, and he is remarkably consistent in the use of his vocabulary.[2] One can be pretty certain that anything which seems unintelligible when first encountered will soon click into place as one reads a little further.

The strangeness of Heidegger's language arises largely from his conscious rejection of much of the traditional philosophical terminology. For instance, he thinks that philosophy has traditionally regarded the self as a substance, and talked about it in language appropriate to a 'thing'; but in Heidegger's

---

[1] Especially in his essay, *Was ist Metaphysik?* (V. Klostermann, Frankfurt, Fifth Edition, 1949), where he formulates the metaphysical question as 'Why are there entities at all, and not rather nothing?' This question forms the starting-point for his further treatise, *Einführung in die Metaphysik* (Niemeyer, Tübingen, 1953).

[2] The present writer makes these remarks after having spent some years, in collaboration with Professor E. S. Robinson of the University of Kansas, in the task of translating *Sein und Zeit*, and they apply principally to that work. Heidegger's later works, especially some of his essays, raise new problems of language.

view, this way of talking about human existence is most inappropriate. Here we might venture to suggest a comparison with Gilbert Ryle's critique of 'mind-talk', even if the outcomes are very different. Heidegger's language is strange not because he is being arbitrary, but because he is trying to get away from a kind of talk which he regards as misleading.

How does Heidegger set about getting away from such misleading kinds of talk? Partly, he does it by devising new terms of his own. His works abound in terms which will not be found in the dictionary. One even comes across such a linguistic *tour de force* as the ending of the present participle suffixed to the stem of the past participle! Of course, philosophers have always had a habit of inventing new terms, or giving new meanings to existing words, and sometimes the new usage eventually becomes standard. Heidegger himself points out that Aristotle is much harder to read than Thucydides. Partly, however,—and this is of special interest from the point of view of our inquiry—Heidegger tries to get behind the traditional connotations of words by returning to what he supposes to have been the original meanings. Commentators have sometimes remarked on the archaic impression conveyed by his style. This is not just an affectation, but is a way of reflecting the author's intention of going back to the original sources of philosophizing, while as yet these sources had not become choked by dead traditions.[1] His interest in the origins of words is parallel to his interest in early Greek philosophy.

In particular, Heidegger makes much of etymologies. For instance, he fastens on the fact that, according to some philologists, the preposition 'in', which we normally use to designate a spatial relation between entities, is derived from an old verb, *innan*, 'to dwell'. It is maintained that the preposition has been derived from the verb, and not *vice versa*. Now it is obvious that 'to dwell in' means very much more than merely 'to be located in'. Certainly, 'to dwell' includes the spatial relation, but it involves a host of other relations besides—what we may call existential relations, such as practical concern, familiarity, affection, and so on.[2] A process of abstraction has taken place in

---

[1] Cf. *Sein und Zeit*, p. 21.

[2] Cf. the Latin verb *colere*, which means 'to dwell', 'to cultivate', 'to take care of', 'to reverence', etc.

the meaning of the word 'in', whereby the sense of spatial location has more or less displaced the other possible senses. But Heidegger does well to remind us of the existential matrix of meaning behind the word, especially as we may still hear someone saying that he is 'in' love or a theologian declaring that God was 'in' Christ, where we would completely misunderstand what was meant if we thought that 'in' had a spatial sense. Again, the word 'world' is a very old compound of which one of the component elements is *wer*, 'man'. Heidegger's philosophical concept of the world represents it as the field of human concerns, which give to it its 'significance'. This existential concept of the world is not opposed to the objectified concept of the world as a self-regulating cosmos of which man can be the spectator, but, in Heidegger's view, the existential concept is the more primordial one, and the other has been derived from it by a process of abstraction. Such a process of abstraction is both valuable and necessary for certain purposes, but Heidegger wishes to remind us that in so far as we are more than cognitive beings, our everyday understanding of the world is not merely and not even primarily in terms of pure observation. We stand in a broad existential relation to the world, and our everyday understanding of it is in terms of our manifold concerns with it.

Although the linguistic interest has become so pronounced only within the last generation or so, it is perhaps worth recalling that one of the first scholars to be appointed to the Gifford Lectureship in Natural Theology, back in 1888, approached the problems of religion largely from the viewpoint afforded by a study of language. We refer, of course, to Friedrich Max Müller. Many of his etymologies, if they are correct, fit in with Heidegger's instrumental concept of the world, and show us that the words by which we name things originated from the use which man made of these things in the practical concerns of his existence. We are told that when men said *dar-u*, 'tree', what they said was 'splitting-here', and 'they must have been men who had learned to use trees for certain purposes'; when they called a horse *as-va*, 'quick runner', 'they must have been men to whom the horse had become useful as a runner'.[1] Heidegger points out that the Greek word for a 'thing' is πράγμα, a thing which we do, not a thing which just stands over against us.[2]

---

[1] *Natural Religion* (Longmans, London, 1889), p. 281.   [2] *Sein und Zeit*, p. 68.

But what value is there supposed to be in this somewhat antiquarian approach to words? When Heidegger exploits the derivations of words in his arguments, or when he allows two well-defined meanings of the same term to ring together in the same context, his readers may well become impatient. They may ask what kind of verbal sleight of hand—or tongue—is being practised upon them in such passages. Heidegger acknowledges that we have to guard against what he calls a 'word-mysticism'. But he adds: 'Nevertheless, in the end it is the business of philosophy to preserve *the power of those most elemental words* in which man expresses himself, and to prevent them from being levelled down to unintelligibility through the ordinary understanding of them'.[1] Admittedly, in some of his writings Heidegger appears to forget his own warning against a 'word-mysticism'. For instance, he can speak of language as the 'domain of being' where one can listen to the 'dictation' of being.[2] His thesis could obviously be carried to extravagant lengths. Yet apart from possible extravagances, there is justice in his claim that language is intimately related to existence, and that one function of philosophy should be to preserve the existential force of language when it is in danger of being eroded away.

Heidegger's view of language raises a number of questions. Does he think of the development of language as having been really a deterioration and impoverishment? And if so, is he not entirely wrong, and would it not be more true to say that the development of language has been in the direction of greater precision, and that in the process anthropomorphic and animistic ways of speaking have been largely eliminated? Is it not, for instance, a very good thing that modern man can talk about a tree as an object for botanical study, without thinking of it as firewood to be split up, still less as the abode of a spirit to which he ought to take an expiatory offering? Why should there be this apparent glorification of the primordial sources of language—or, for that matter, of philosophy? Has every development from early times down to our own day been nothing but aberration so that we have to go back to the

---

[1] Op. cit., p. 220.
[2] See the essays 'Wozu Dichter?' and 'Der Spruch des Anaximander' in *Holzwege*, Third Edition (V. Klostermann, Frankfurt, 1957).

sources and begin all over again? And is this not an absurd suggestion—as well as an impossible one?

It is indeed, but all of these questions rest on a misunderstanding. Heidegger is not glorifying primeval language nor is he decrying the language of modern science and philosophy. He would readily admit that this language has its own field, but what he deplores is that it has become so predominant that it is fast on the way to becoming the only kind of language that 'makes sense' for a modern man, and that we are losing the power to understand any other kind of language. For language will indeed have undergone an impoverishment if we are left with nothing but the languages of science and factual description, of logic and mathematics. Bradley's famous phrase, 'an unearthly ballet of bloodless categories', comes to mind. It should, however, be added that we would never be content with such a language, just because we are human beings with a wide range of existential possibilities. It would soon happen that convictions which are not in the least scientific would express themselves in scientific language. We can see this happening today. Scientific language has a tremendous prestige, and if non-scientific convictions can be expressed in the jargon of a science they acquire for the uncritical mind something of the prestige of that science. Thus we may be offered a 'scientific ethic' purporting to be based on the facts of evolution though it does not require much reflection to see that 'we cannot infer what men *ought to do* from what nature *does*'.[1]

In these days when propaganda has been raised to the status of a fine art, we hardly need to be reminded of the extraordinary power of language. If anyone can get the discussion of a subject going in language of his own choosing, he is already well on the way to securing acceptance of the point of view which he wishes to establish. A government, for instance, will speak of its colonial problems in terms of 'terrorism' and of 'preserving law and order', thereby justifying in advance its own oppressive policies. What is less obvious is that there is a continual rivalry between different kinds of languages[2] and that each tends to expand its sphere of influence. In the past, religious language

[1] Cf. H. J. Paton, *The Modern Predicament* (Allen & Unwin, London, 1955), pp. 303ff.
[2] Zuurdeeg appropriately calls this phenomenon the 'imperialism' of languages. See *An Analytical Philosophy of Religion*, pp. 69ff.

was one of the worst offenders and sought to establish its claims in such areas as cosmology and biology. But now scientific language is the aggressor, and seeks to invade fields where it may be quite inappropriate.

It is in the light of this situation that we must understand Heidegger's belief that philosophy should 'preserve the power of those elemental words in which man expresses *himself*'. The language of science is one kind of language which has developed out of the primordial matrix of language, but it is not the only kind or even, in Heidegger's view, the fundamental kind. Of course, most logical empiricists would nowadays recognize that there are different kinds of languages. Nevertheless, scientific language and its canons are taken as the norm, and there is a tendency to regard any other language as something of a curiosity—if not actually suspect. Certainly there is little tendency to accept Heidegger's view that language is to be understood primarily in terms of man as the being who has the existential possibility of discourse, ζῷον λόγον ἔχον. Scientific language would seem to be a depersonalized kind of language in which we can largely ignore the question of who speaks it. Yet there are other kinds of language in which man expresses *himself*—and religious language is surely among them —where the relation between what is said and the person who says it is so close that any linguistic analysis would need to be correlated with an existential analysis.

The language of the great religions has its roots in a period before scientific language had properly developed or attained its present prestige. Such religious language is now therefore at a disadvantage. Who nowadays, apart from theologians and others who have studied the problem, understand what Saint Paul means by such words as 'the flesh', 'the world', 'the spirit'? And here perhaps even the most uncompromising critic of Bultmann would admit that he has done something to restore the power and significance of these words. How can the modern theologian speak of 'dogma', 'faith', 'sin'—words which have been either distorted or trivialized—without grave danger of being misunderstood? An amusing example of the threatened deterioration of a religious word appears in a recent newspaper report. Describing the ceremony whereby Britain's new automatic system for trunk telephone calls was inaugurated

at Bristol, the report states that this was done 'by operating a
switch making GRACE (Group Routing And Charging Equip-
ment) available at once to eighteen thousand Bristol sub-
scribers . . .'.[1] How widespread will become the habit of
using the word 'grace' to designate this latest convenience, it
is hard to predict. But it seems safe to say that most of us
nowadays find it easier to understand the kind of 'grace' which
can be made available by operating a switch, than the kind
which is said to be experienced in the Christian and other
religions.

If we are to be fair to religious language, therefore, we must
not only avoid treating it as if it were scientific language but
we must also avoid starting with the assumption that it is somehow 'inferior' to scientific language. We have to try to re-
capture the force of words that have long since been trivialized,
and to guard against the domination of one kind of language.
Does religious language have a legitimate function in expressing *ourselves* in certain aspects of our being? And does
theological language have a legitimate function in helping to
elucidate the insights of religious language in a more systematic
and reflective way?

Bultmann's demythologizing professes to offer us a refurbishing of religious language by interpreting it in relation to the
human existence which it expresses. But the word 'demythologizing' points to the fact that Bultmann considers the primary
language of religion to be myth, and we must now ask how
exactly he understands this term.

31 *A Discussion of Terminology*

When we ask about the meaning of myth, we should remember that there are two quite distinct questions here, and we must
be clear about which of them we have in mind at any particular
time. We may be asking about the meaning of mythical discourse, the principles on which we should seek to interpret it,
and so on. Or we may be asking a formal question about the
meaning of the term 'myth', how we define it and to what areas
of discourse we propose to apply it. As regards the first of the

[1] *The Scotsman*, Saturday, December 6, 1958. No doubt the telephone engineers
adopted the word not directly from theology but from its derived use as a girl's
name.

two questions, we may say that if myth is a kind of language in which man expresses *himself*, then, in the light of our foregoing remarks on language and existence, the elucidation of the meaning of myth is to be accomplished by existential rather than logical analysis. And indeed all through this book we have spent a good deal of time in exploring the possibilities and the limitations of existential interpretation. However, we cannot avoid the second question. Demythologizing offers us not just interpretations of actual myths, but a theory about myth. It is here that logical analysis must come into its own. Such analysis may be of little avail when it is a question of interpreting a language whose 'grammar' seems to be quite different from the logic of everyday thinking.[1] But when we start theorizing about myth, we must at once submit ourselves to the ordinary canons of logic. And perhaps the first thing we should do is to ensure that when we talk about myth, we use the term in a consistent manner.

Bultmann, as is well-known, does in fact put forward a formal definition of 'myth', or rather of 'mythology'. He says: 'Mythology is the use of imagery to express the otherworldly in terms of this world and the divine in terms of human life, the other side in terms of this side'.[2] Thus he at least sets out to use the term in a clearly defined sense—though the definition offered is itself by no means a model of clarity. But does he abide by his definition and use the term consistently? And if he wobbles in the use of this key-term, does not this go far to invalidating his whole theory of demythologizing? These are questions for logical analysis, and we find one analytical philosopher who has shown pretty conclusively that Bultmann's concept of 'myth' is quite confused. Dr Hepburn writes: 'Any instability in the concept of myth itself would be found to imperil the discussion at point after point. Yet Bultmann neither offers a satisfactory definition, nor abides by the definition he does offer.' And Hepburn goes on to point out that by Bultmann's own test, even his definition itself 'is partly couched in mythological language, which is cause enough for bewilderment'.[3]

Not only Dr Hepburn but other writers as well have expressed

[1] Cf. Ernst Cassirer, *Language and Myth*, trans. Suzanne Langer (Constable, London, Dover Books Edition, 1957).
[2] *Kerygma and Myth*, p. 10 n. 2. [3] *New Essays in Philosophical Theology*, p. 229.

grave dissatisfaction with Bultmann's handling of his key-term. Four main objections may be noted. (1) Dr Hepburn's own major criticism is that Bultmann's definition of myth is too *wide*. It is, he thinks, 'sufficiently wide in its scope to include all pictorial, analogical and symbolical speech whatsoever'.[1] 'Myth' becomes a generic word with 'analogy', 'symbol', and so on, as species. But nearly all theologians—Bultmann among them—would agree that we can speak of God only in oblique language, and if 'myth' is the general term for such language, then the possibility of demythologizing is ruled out from the beginning. (2) Looking at the matter from a different point of view, Professor Henderson concludes that Bultmann's definition of myth is too *narrow*. He has in mind modern ideologies like that of the Nazis, and these, he thinks, 'one can best describe as mythological'. But 'if room has to be found within mythology for the Nazi myths of blood and soil—and they are certainly neither history nor science—then can mythology still be described as the conceiving of the divine as if it were human and the other-worldly as if it were the this-worldly?'[2] Clearly, some modern world-views look very much like myths, yet since they lack any transcendent element they do not fall within the scope of Bultmann's definition. (3) H. P. Owen, as well as reinforcing Hepburn's criticisms, makes the point that Bultmann's use of the term 'myth' makes it little more than a label for designating a very *heterogeneous* collection of items. 'Myth' is the word used by Bultmann to cover all the 'meaningless elements' in the New Testament, and his list of such meaningless elements 'includes such heterogeneous items as miracles, demonic powers, the fall of Adam, the sacrificial idea of atonement, the Pauline conception of the Spirit'. Owen rightly points out that it is not easy to see what there is in common between, say, a miraculous *event* and a spatial *notion* of divine transcendence.[3] We are left wondering whether the word 'myth', as Bultmann uses it, is not an entirely vacuous term which is being employed for rhetorical effect to designate an arbitrary collection of odds and ends. (4) In an earlier discussion of Bultmann, the present writer criticized him for including *primitive science* under the heading of myth. It would be excluded

---

[1] *New Essays in Philosophical Theology*, p. 229.
[2] *Myth in the New Testament*, pp. 52, 54.   [3] See *Revelation and Existence*, pp. 1-6.

by his definition, but before he gives the definition, he has already described the ancient cosmology of the Bible as mythical. I wrote: 'But this is not myth within the sense of his own formal definition. It is primitive science or primitive world-view, not a description of the divine in terms of this world, but a description of this world itself as these early thinkers imagined it to be.'[1]

When we consider these criticisms, it certainly appears that Hepburn is right in pointing to confusion in Bultmann's central concept. Just how damaging this might prove to his whole enterprise is not yet clear. But it seems quite clear already that his formal definition of myth must be scrapped. As Owen very charitably puts it, 'Bultmann is not saying what he wants to say'—and Owen distinguishes his own approach to Bultmann from that of G. V. Jones who makes Bultmann mean what he says (a reasonable enough thing to do!) and draws the inevitable conclusions.[2] Bultmann's mistake was to introduce too rigid a definition of myth at too early a stage in the discussion. As we have seen, he does not adhere to it himself. If we look at his writings as a whole, we find that in various passages he comes to grips with the questions raised in the four objections cited above. The question which we must ask is whether there emerges to take the place of his discredited definition a conception of myth which is sufficiently clear and stable not to throw into confusion the whole theory of demythologizing.

Needless to say, there is no intention in what follows of attempting anything so presumptuous as the delineation of a concept of myth in general. There is great need for a comprehensive and up-to-date treatment of the whole subject, and it would be a boon to theologians and others if someone of sufficient competence were to correlate the vast amount of material on myth brought to light in recent years by philosophers, psychologists, anthropologists, historians of religion, and other investigators. All that will be attempted here is to make a few suggestions for the clarification and reconstruction of Bultmann's conception of myth. Whether this conception has any value as a conception of myth in general is a question

---

[1] *An Existentialist Theology*, p. 167.

[2] Op. cit., pp. 6, 18-9. Cf. G. V. Jones, *Christology and Myth in the New Testament* (Allen & Unwin, London, 1956).

not raised. We are concerned only to ask whether, after the false start of his formal definition, a reasonably consistent view of myth can be derived from Bultmann's writings, for as Hepburn indicates this is vital to Bultmann's whole position. The clarification and reconstruction will be done by making four distinctions, corresponding roughly to the four objections mentioned above, and involving some refinements of terminology.

The first distinction which has to be made is that between *mythology* and *analogy*. Both Hepburn and Owen rightly pointed out that Bultmann's formal definition of myth would also include analogy. But Bultmann has obviously had second thoughts on the matter, for in a later essay he makes it clear that he wishes to distinguish analogical language from mythological language. He says that when we speak of an 'act of God', this is not pictorial but analogical language in which 'we represent God's act as analogous to a human act'.[1] The very fact that he uses the word 'represent' (*vorstellen*) would seem to indicate that we have not entirely got away from images and pictures, and although Bultmann wants to make the distinction between mythology and analogy, it is not at all clear on what he bases it. Is the suggestion that when the symbol is taken from human existence—such as 'act of God', 'love of God'—the language is analogical, whereas when the symbol is taken from nature—such as 'height' or 'light' when applied to God—it is mythological? But this will not do, for Bultmann recognizes that one can speak mythologically of an act of God, and in such a case it is regarded as a 'wonder' breaking into the course of nature. It may be worth pointing out that in the Bible the expression, 'the acts of the Lord', belongs to the Old Testament rather than the New, and usually refers to 'his acts which he did in Egypt'.[2] These acts would be mythical enough by Bultmann's standards, as, for instance, when 'the Lord rained hail on the land of Egypt'.[3] We cannot classify the symbolic words which we use about God and say that some are analogical and others mythological. The same symbol may be analogical in one context and mythological in another. In spite of his formal definition of myth, Bultmann obviously wants to distinguish analogy from mythology, but he never makes the distinction clear.

[1] *Kerygma and Myth*, p. 196.   [2] Deut. 11.3, etc.   [3] Ex. 9.23.

Nevertheless, the distinction is a genuine one, and it may be suggested that it lies in the relation of the speaker to the symbol which he employs. In myth, this relation is a direct one. The symbol and the thing symbolized have not been sorted out. This is not to say that the myth was taken just 'literally', but that it contained a whole matrix of meanings which were not differentiated. Its language was 'symbolical' as well as 'literal', but the symbolism was unconscious and there was no distinction between 'symbolical' and 'literal'. In analogy, on the other hand, the relation of the speaker to the symbol which he employs has become more detached. The immediacy of the myth has given way to a conscious symbolism. The New Testament contains the sentence, 'God is light'.[1] Presumably the usage here is analogical. The writer is not identifying God with light, but consciously using the symbol of 'light' to point to characteristics of the divine nature. Yet there would be people living at that time who did identify God with light, and for whom the sentence would be a mythological utterance. We must remember, however, that for such people light was not just a natural phenomenon, as it is for us, but was a mysterious effluence having all those characteristics which we still think it appropriate to apply to God when we speak analogically of God as light.

The distinction may be expressed in another way. Psycho-analysts like Freud and Jung have shown us the close connection between myth and dreams. Both have the same non-logical, pictorial and, if we may say so, existential character. The transition from mythology to analogy may be likened to waking out of a dream. The immediate relation to the imagery has ended, and the imagery is recognized as imagery. If we may borrow a vivid expression of Paul Tillich, we may call the process whereby we become conscious of the symbolic character of the myth the 'breaking of the myth'.[2]

We must not think of this process as sudden. Rather, it takes place gradually. In the New Testament itself there are mytho-logical and analogical elements alongside one another. In the Church today, a large part of the myth remains intact for many believers. Presumably, however, the process will continue until the symbolic character of the entire myth is consciously

[1] I John 1.5.   [2] *Dynamics of Faith* (Harper, New York, 1957), p. 51.

recognized—as indeed it has been by many Christians for a good many generations now. And if anyone asks if we shall be left with 'only a symbol', we may refer again to Tillich: 'He who asks this question shows that he has not understood the power of symbolic language, which surpasses in quality and strength the power of any nonsymbolic language. One should never say "only a symbol", but one should say "not less than a symbol".'[1]

Consider the following expressions: 'God is in heaven'; 'God is the most high'; 'God is the supreme being'; 'God is transcendent'. In each of them we have a word which is associated with the idea of 'height'. In the first and second expressions, this idea is very plainly present, and suggests actual spatial elevation. In the third and fourth expressions, the idea is present only in the etymologies of the words 'supreme' and 'transcendent', and the suggestion of spatial elevation has disappeared as completely as when we talk of the High Court. What has happened here? It would be wrong to think that men began with the idea of spatial elevation, and then transformed it into power or something of the sort. We must remember what was said on the topic of language and existence[2] and on the histories of words like the preposition 'in'. In an admirable analysis of the 'height' symbol as applied to God, Edwyn Bevan shows us that when men first thought of God as high up, they were thinking not just of spatial elevation but of all that height means for human existence—power, vision, value and so on.[3] What seems to have taken place in the transition from the mythical picture of God in the sky to the theological idea of divine transcendence is an increasing concentration on the existential significance of height—a significance already present at the mythological stage—and an increasing relinquishment of the 'objective' significance of height as spatial elevation. However, even if we move from mythology to analogy, we never get away from a symbolic element, since we are still 'representing' the divine in terms drawn from our finite experience in the world. Dr Hepburn quotes what he calls a 'crucial statement' from Bultmann, to the effect that 'there are certain concepts which are fundamentally mythological,

---

[1] Op. cit., p. 45.   [2] See above, pp. 191ff.
[3] *Symbolism and Belief* (Allen & Unwin, 1938), pp. 82ff.

and with which we shall never be able to dispense, for instance, the idea of transcendence. In such cases, however, the original mythological meaning has been lost, and they have become mere metaphors or ciphers'.[1] Hepburn comments: ' "*Mere* metaphors", note; the phrase suggests that these concepts are "as near literal as makes no difference". But in fact it makes a great deal of difference. The gulf between literal (or direct) and oblique language cannot be bridged so lightheartedly.'[2]

Reluctant though he may be to admit it, Bultmann seems to

[1] *Kerygma and Myth*, p. 102. Bultmann's remarks quoted here were written before the essay in which he wishes to distinguish analogical from mythological language. In the first sentence of the passage which Hepburn quotes, Bultmann would now perhaps write 'analogical' or 'symbolical' instead of 'mythological', since he obviously has a conscious symbolism in mind. A full analysis might well demand further distinctions among 'symbol', 'analogue', 'cipher', 'metaphor'. In current philosophical usage, a 'symbol', as distinct from a mere 'sign', is supposed somehow to participate in the being of the reality to which it points. 'Analogy' in our talk of God is an idea that has been specially studied by the neo-scholastics, and in Cardinal Mercier's text-book, *A Manual of Modern Scholastic Philosophy*, trans. T. L. and S. A. Parker (Routledge, London, 1952), II, p. 506, we find analogical knowledge defined as 'knowledge of something through a proper knowledge of something else which is by its nature different from it but because of certain resemblances is capable of representing it'. It is obvious that Bultmann now recognizes the need for making distinctions, but he has not done so systematically. He has contented himself with *ad hoc* distinctions designed to meet particular objections to his view of myth, and the total result is rather confusing.

Thus we may compare with the passage quoted by Dr Hepburn the following remarks of Professor Bultmann, from a correspondence with the present writer. He says: 'I believe that myth and symbol must be sharply distinguished. Perhaps symbolic language is not dispensable if we wish to talk about God and his acts. But I believe that desymbolizing (*Entsymbolisierung*) must be carried as far as possible.' In this passage, talk of God's acts is called 'symbolic', not 'analogical'; the contrast is now between 'myth' and 'symbol'; and we are being invited to embark on desymbolizing as well as demythologizing!

That these problems are still worrying Professor Bultmann may be seen from the fact that he has devoted a whole chapter of his recent book, *Jesus Christ and Mythology*, to 'The Meaning of God as Acting'. The reader, however, will be disappointed if he expects that Bultmann is now going to clear up the obscurities. He makes no real advance on his previous statements and, indeed, introduces some new and quite gratuitious difficulties. He begins by repeating his distinction between mythological and analogical language. An 'act of God' (and also the 'love of God', the 'wrath of God', the 'fatherhood of God') are said to be analogues. So far, we may say, so good. But now Bultmann makes the astonishing assertion that such analogical talk does not 'necessarily' involve us in 'symbols or images' (these terms are not defined), but 'must be able to convey its full *direct* meaning'—p. 68. If these remarks are to be taken seriously, we must ask two questions. If this talk of God is direct, then why is it called analogical, which implies that it is indirect? If this talk of God in human terms bears its 'full *direct* meaning', are we not committed to a fantastically naïve anthropomorphic understanding of God, since such talk could be fully direct only if God were *precisely* like one of ourselves?

The truth is that however perceptive Dr Bultmann may have shown himself in the interpretation of myth, he has failed to carry out any adequate logical mapping of the forms of religious language, and is still wide open to such criticisms as those of Ronald Hepburn. In this respect, Bultmann lags far behind Tillich.

[2] Loc. cit., p. 237.

admit in his most typical utterances that an oblique element remains in our talk about God, and that the desymbolizing which he advocates in addition to demythologizing can proceed only up to a point. We may contrast Bultmann's negative attitude to symbolism with the much more positive attitude of Tillich, who agrees with Bultmann on the need for demythologizing but is much more forthcoming about the indispensability of symbols. Tillich thinks that the myths must be broken and recognized as myths, but 'they should be maintained in their symbolic form and not replaced by scientific substitutes'.[1]

We may now sum up this part of the discussion. Bultmann's concept of myth needs to be more sharply defined by delimiting myth from analogical and consciously symbolic language.[2] The difference, we have maintained, lies in the fact that the myth gets broken, its symbolic character is recognized, and the symbolic imagery is refined and tends to be conceptualized. But, as Hepburn shows, we are still left with the problem of oblique language on our hands, and later we must return to this problem.[3]

The second distinction which must be made is between *myth* and what we shall call '*quasi-myth*'. Here we recall the objection that Bultmann's definition of myth is too narrow, since it would exclude such modern doctrines as those of the Nazis or the Marxists. Certainly some of these contemporary points of view seem to have many of the marks of myth. This would be true not only of extreme instances like Nazism, but of much popular pseudo-scientific talk, or again, talk of democracy and the Western way of life.[4] If anyone wishes to use the word 'myth' in these connections, he would seem to have considerable justification for doing so. The assumption underlying such a usage would seem to be that myth-making is a characteristic activity of modern man, as it has been of man in the past. The modern myths would differ from the ancient ones only in leaving out the gods.

[1] *Dynamics of Faith*, p. 51.

[2] It has not seemed necessary in this context to inquire into further possible distinctions between analogy and symbolism. For a recent discussion of this topic, see C. A. Campbell, *On Selfhood and Godhood* (Allen & Unwin, London, 1957), pp. 427ff.

[3] See below p. 216.

[4] See, e.g., S. Toulmin's 'Contemporary Scientific Mythology' in *Metaphysical Beliefs*, ed. A. MacIntyre (SCM Press, 1957).

Bultmann, however, is unwilling to apply the term 'myth' to these modern points of view. He prefers to call them 'ideologies'. And if we are to use the term 'myth' in a technical rather than a popular sense, he may be right to make this distinction. The reason for denying the term 'myth' to the modern ideologies, however, would seem to be not so much that these ideologies are secularized as that they lack the immediate unbroken character which, as we have seen, belongs to myth. Despite all the far-fetched views to which men have subscribed in the twentieth century, there is a sense in which we live in a post-mythical age. Fritz Buri remarks that the concept of myth does not exist for a mythical age but emerges only when the myth has been called in question.[1] The very fact that Alfred Rosenberg called his book *The Myth of the Twentieth Century* indicates a certain distance from myth, a recognition of myth as myth. In the same way we may presume that those who, like Erich Ludendorff, returned to the old Germanic cults, did so with a certain sophistication. The old gods were not to them what they had been to the ancient worshippers. In this connection, we have to remember also that the word 'myth' occurs occasionally in the New Testament itself. Its writers certainly did not move in an entirely mythical climate of thought. To some extent, they were already in a post-mythical world. Myth could be recognized as such, and the criticism of myth was already established. Of course, the 'godless and silly myths'[2] which are condemned were pagan or heretical myths, and the term, which carries a pejorative sense, is not applied to the Christian message. Yet according to Bultmann the demythologizing of the Christian message has already begun in the New Testament, for instance, in the Johannine conception of 'eternal life' as a kind of existence which men may enter here and now.

It would seem that Bultmann wishes to confine the term 'myth' to the productions of certain periods in the history of cultures when different kinds of language had not been sorted out or had been only partly sorted out. Of course, the myth might survive unbroken into later and more sophisticated periods, but these periods would not be capable of producing new myths, and would increasingly cease to understand the

[1] *Dogmatik*, I, p. 198.   [2] I Tim. 4.7.

traditional myths. The point is made more explicitly by another demythologizer, Fritz Buri, who claims that 'the time when the great myths arose preceded the emergence of critical scientific thinking'. He goes on to say: 'In the sea of mythological ideas and images, there are only a few really great redeemer-myths of the kind which we have in the story of the eschatological Christ. As archetypes, they emerge from the unconscious, in great moments of humanity they are formulated by prophets, then they grow from generation to generation—until even they grow old and die.'[1] Bultmann would agree that myths arise in certain epochs, but he would be less happy about the suggestion that they have a natural life-span, ending in senescence and death.

What Buri says in this connection is indeed strongly reminiscent of Oswald Spengler. This historian of culture also thought that there are myth-producing periods in the histories of culture, and he has some vivid language about the 'dream-heavy' consciousness which characterizes the 'spring-time' of a culture. After remarking on the 'mythic world' which developed around the 'young soul' of our Western culture in the early medieval period, and observing that men in those days 'could not even detach themselves sufficiently to "know" it' because 'they lived in it', he claims that 'to us who are separated from these ancestors by thirty generations, this world seems so alien and overpowering that we always seek to grasp it in detail, and so misunderstand its wholeness and undividedness'.[2] But Bultmann, while accepting that in certain periods the myths arise and in certain other periods they lose their meaningfulness, would not agree that they must simply die when they have run their course. His belief is that they may contain important insights which can be lost to view by more sophisticated generations, and demythologizing presupposes the possibility of recovering such insights, though in a different form. What Bultmann rejects is the deterministic element in Spengler, and he does so quite explicitly. In Spengler, he says, 'the understanding of history became radically naturalistic'.[3] The culture and its characteristic mythology is regarded as an organism

[1] *Theologie der Existenz*, pp. 85-6.
[2] *The Decline of the West*, trans. C. F. Atkinson (Allen & Unwin, 1932), II, p. 188.
[3] *History and Eschatology*, p. 84.

running its natural course from birth to death, and such a view is not reconcilable with Bultmann's own existentialist understanding of history.

Whether Bultmann or Spengler is right, or whether the thesis, common to both, that the creation of myth belongs to a particular period or periods in the history of a culture, is correct, are questions which need not detain us, for we are concerned here not with the general question of myth but simply with delimiting Bultmann's conception of 'myth' more precisely. We have now seen that his exclusion of the modern ideologies is not due to confusion but to a deliberate view of myth, whether that view is sound or otherwise. When we consider that the modern ideologies have so much in common with myth—illogicality, symbolism, persuasive power, the delineation of a way of life, the inculcation of ideals, and so on —we may wonder whether they should not be included within myth. But the relative sophistication of our age, its distance from traditional myths which now seem alien, and its employment of different kinds of languages, make Bultmann's exclusion of the ideologies from the realm of myth a point of view with some plausibility. We may suggest that by designating the ideologies 'quasi-myths', we can at once preserve the distinction which Bultmann wants to make, and yet recognize the kinship of these ideologies with the traditional myths.

Our third distinction is between *myth* and *legend*. We took note of the question of how Bultmann manages to include such diverse items as, let us say, the story of a miraculous happening and the notion of divine transcendence in spatial terms under the general heading of myth, without thereby making the term 'myth' quite hazy in its signification. A partial answer at least may be found in distinguishing here between myth and legend. This distinction turns up almost accidentally in Bultmann, but it should be made explicit if his conception of myth is to be clarified and made consistent. Thus on a single page[1] we find Bultmann speaking of the 'myth' of the resurrection and of the 'legends' of the empty tomb.

The nature of the distinction is, in principle, clear enough. The word 'myth' is used to refer to the central Christian story of incarnation, atonement, resurrection, and exaltation,

[1] *Kerygma and Myth*, p. 38.

o

represented as a cosmic drama of redemption. The word 'legend' is used of peripheral stories and anecdotes which serve to illustrate aspects of the central myth. Thus, according to Bultmann, Saint Paul believed in the resurrection but does not appear to have known about stories of the empty tomb.[1] Again, he believed in the incarnation but does not appear to have known about stories of a virgin birth; or in the exaltation without knowing the story of a bodily ascension into heaven.

The various heterogeneous items—miracle-stories and the like—are not themselves myths, but they may be loosely included under the heading of 'myth' because their function is to illustrate and apply the central myth. They may not be consistent among themselves, yet they may nevertheless perform an illustrative function—for instance, Bultmann thinks that 'the virgin birth is inconsistent with the assertion of pre-existence'.[2] In practice, it may not always be easy to make a sharp distinction between the central myth and its illustrative legends, and Bultmann himself says that there can be no selection, as we have noted.[3] The various items, including even reports of historical facts, have been incorporated into the mythical framework, that is to say, they have been referred to the central cosmic drama of redemption.[4] A legend which in itself might have no particular religious significance acquires such significance when it is read in the light of the central myth. Thus, to go back to an example which engaged our attention earlier,[5] the story of the stilling of the storm would, as we have said, have no more religious significance than a story from the Arabian Nights, if it is taken in isolation. It becomes an 'edifying story' only when it is read as a story of the Christ and understood against the background of the whole gospel.

The word 'legend' is not being used here in any pejorative sense—we have simply taken it over from Bultmann. We might equally well have used Braithwaite's more neutral term 'story'. The point is, however, that such legends or stories are told not for the sake of the incidents which they narrate but as illustrations or embellishments of the central myth, and it is from this

---

[1] Ibid. See above, p. 86.   [2] Loc. cit., p. 11.   [3] See above, p. 22.

[4] We may notice the frequency with which Bultmann uses the adjective 'cosmic' in connection with the mythical understanding of the cross and resurrection—*Theologie des Neuen Testaments*, pp. 287ff.

[5] See above, p. 17ff.

central myth that they get their meaning. They tend to become parables. We can sometimes see this kind of transformation taking place in the Synoptic Gospels.[1] Thus Saint Mark tells how our Lord cursed a barren fig-tree, which after an interval his disciples found to be withered. Saint Matthew makes the story more definitely miraculous—the fig-tree withered 'immediately'. Saint Luke, on the other hand, tells the parable of a man who planted a fig-tree, and the story gets a new meaning.[2]

It is at this point that Bultmann's work as a demythologizer needs to be more definitely related to his work as a form-critic. It will be remembered that, according to the form-criticism school, the Gospels can be analysed into elements which may then be classified according to their literary forms—legends, apophthegms, and so on. These constituent elements are supposed to have served the various apologetic and devotional needs of the early Church. But this means in effect that they served as embellishments, illustrations or applications of the central Christian myth, and of the way of life which the myth embodies. Owen is right in saying that Bultmann has lumped together a great many heterogeneous items under the heading of 'myth', but it does not follow that his conception of myth is therefore hopelessly confused. In principle, it is possible to analyse these items and show the relation of each to the mythical framework into which they have been incorporated. Nor can we entirely blame Bultmann for not having done this in detail. He has simply set forth a programme for demythologizing, and has said himself that the working out of this programme would occupy New Testament scholars for a generation.

Incidentally, the distinction between myth and legend also serves to throw into relief the radical nature of Bultmann's enterprise. For a long time many theologians have criticized the legends, the peripheral stories of Christianity, but have left the central myth largely untouched. Bultmann's demythologizing challenges us to come to grips with this central myth itself, to recognize its symbolic character and to understand it as 'broken' myth in Tillich's sense.

Our fourth distinction is between *myth* and *cosmology*. To

[1] Cf. Mark 11. 12-4 and 20-5; Matt. 21.18-22; Luke 13.6-9.
[2] Cf. the interesting comments of H. D. A. Major in *The Mission and Message of Jesus* (Nicholson & Watson, London, 1937), p. 143.

the present writer's objection that, contrary to his own definition, he has included primitive science in the conception of
'myth', Professor Bultmann has replied: 'You make the objection that I talk of "myth" in a double sense. But if I call the
Babylonian cosmology a "mythological" one, I do so because
originally the idea of heaven and of the underworld was not the
idea of a primitive science. Originally, heaven and the underworld were "numinous" regions, the spheres of the divine and
the demonic. The myth represents these spheres in worldly
form and so it appears as if the myth dealt with the world-
picture of a primitive science. Admittedly, such ideas can lose
their original mythological character, and turn into the ideas of
scientific thinking. But this is not the case in the New Testament.
Is the meaning of γέεννα or of οὐρανός, for instance to be
found in world-pictures?[1] Or is it not rather the case that we
have to do with a mythological expression of the thought of
transcendence?'[2]

I would willingly concede the main point which Professor
Bultmann has made in his reply to my objection—and indeed
such a concession would be entirely in line with the remarks
made earlier in this chapter on the relation of language and
existence. It is hard for us, with our 'modern' outlook to get
away from the idea that myths are intended to 'explain', and
from attempts to rationalize them. This attitude towards myth
was probably almost universal a generation ago. One of the
standard reference-works of that period in its article on
'mythology' tells us that myths 'grew up or were invented
to explain certain phenomena, beliefs, customs, and names'.[3]
On this old-fashioned view of myth, a story like that of the
tower of Babel is interpreted as an etiological myth offering
a primitive—and fantastic—explanation of the origin of different languages; or belief in demon-possession is represented as a
primitive attempt to explain certain diseases. Nowadays, however, such rationalistic interpretations of myth have lost
favour. The myth is regarded rather as an attempt to bring to
expression the way in which those who told it understood their
own existence in the world. Thus in the case of the story of the

---

[1] Professor Bultmann cites passages in Matt. 10.28 and Acts 1.11.
[2] These remarks are quoted from correspondence with the present writer.
[3] *The Encyclopaedia of Religion and Ethics*, ed. James Hastings (T. & T. Clark, Edinburgh, 1913), IX, p. 120.

tower of Babel, attention would now be focused on the ambition of the builders to become as the gods, and on the frustration to which such an ambition conduces; while the belief in demon-possession would be understood as representing a primitive awareness that the world in which men live can be alien to their existence.

Nevertheless we must guard against exaggeration here. If the rationalistic view of myth as primitive science were wrong, it would surely be equally wrong to deny that there was any primitive science or any attempt to explain in the myth at all, or that it was only later that the myth began to be turned into science. If what has been said above on the subject of language and existence has any truth in it, then we must look on the myth as an undifferentiated matrix of meaning. Only later were the various meanings sorted out, but they were all latent in the myth from the beginning. If we may borrow a favourite word of Heidegger, we may say that they are 'equiprimordial'. This indeed follows from the fact that man's existence is being-in-the-world, so that to have an understanding of his existence is also to have some understanding of his world.

We should not therefore say that Babylonian cosmology was not primitive science, but that it included primitive science fused with other elements in the as yet undifferentiated matrix of myth. No doubt the process of differentiation would be a very slow one. Even when we come to Greece, and to Thales' famous doctrine that all things arise from water, we have not made a sudden transition from myth to primitive science. For presumably Thales thought of water very differently from the way in which we do—to us, it is 'just' H_2O—and it seems clear that he thought of the world as a kind of super-organism, ensouled and alive.

But while we must guard against the twin exaggerations of either reading too much science into the primitive cosmologies or of denying to them any element of an attempt at explanation, Bultmann is right in saying that as far as the New Testament is concerned, the interest is not in the world-picture *qua* world-picture but in the representations in mythical form of ideas like that of divine transcendence. To the extent that this is true, he again escapes the charge of confusion in his conception of myth. The ancient 'cosmologies'—or perhaps we should say 'cosmographies'—turn out to include a good deal more than 'cosmology' in the sense of a science of the universe.

The foregoing discussion, while it makes clear that Bultmann's formal definition of myth must be abandoned, also shows that he has developed implicitly a tolerably coherent conception of myth which is stable enough for his purposes. But before we go on to say anything further of this conception of myth, we must take note of another source of confusion. This one does not arise from Bultmann himself, but from some English writers on demythologizing who have adopted the habit of talking rather slickly of 'demything'. Apart from the fact that this word is a more than usually inelegant barbarism, it also betrays a fundamental misunderstanding of Bultmann's intention. If 'demything' meant anything, it would mean 'the elimination of myth'. Bultmann tells us often enough that, unlike the older liberal theologians, he does not want to eliminate myth but to re-interpret it. 'Demythologizing' means 'the elimination of mythology', and this is not the same as the elimination of myth.

What is the difference? The word 'mythology', of course, is used in various senses. Sometimes it is just a collective noun— when we speak of 'Iranian mythology' we may mean no more than the sum total of myths which were current in ancient Persia. Occasionally—though the usage is less common now than it was at the beginning of the century—'mythology' means the scientific 'study of myth', 'discourse *about* myth'. But 'mythology' also means—and perhaps most properly— 'mythical talk', 'discourse *in* myths'. It is in this third sense that the term is to be understood when we talk of 'demythologizing' as 'the elimination of mythology'. Just as Plato complained about philosophers who 'treat us as children by telling us some story or other (μῦθόν τινα διηγεῖσθαι)',[1] so Bultmann is saying that in this post-mythical age it is high time for theologians to give up discoursing in myths. But this does not imply 'demything' if this word means 'getting rid of myth', for the content of the myth is to be restated in existential terms. Demythologizing implies getting rid of mythology (as an outmoded and undifferentiated form of discourse), but it also

[1] *Sophistes*, 242c.

implies the recognition of myth as the vehicle for meanings which we must now try to express in other ways.

But if we now call to mind some of the distinctions which have been made above, we see that another limit to demythologizing emerges. Bultmann's intention was to translate all mythical statements into existential statements, but we have seen that he has had to find a place for analogical statements also. We must notice that there is all the difference in the world between a statement *about* human existence and a statement *in terms of* human existence which is supposed to refer analogously to God (as in talk of an 'act of God'). Either we must say that here there is a limit to demythologizing, or else we must redefine the aim of demythologizing, and say that it intends to translate myth into existential statements plus analogical statements or consciously symbolic statements, in which the immediacy of the myth has been 'broken'. But in either case, we come up against Hepburn's objection that we are no nearer to having solved the problem of oblique language about God. This problem would have been solved only if demythologizing, as purely existential interpretation, had been pursued without limit. This would have meant the abandonment of any attempt to talk about a transcendent God and the representation of Christianity as nothing but a possible way of existence for man. Obviously Bultmann does not want this.

We may now sum up the results of this section. We began by acknowledging that Hepburn has shown that there are inconsistencies in Bultmann's conception of myth, at least as far as his formal statements are concerned. We proposed to remedy this by abandoning Bultmann's premature definition of myth and by attempting a reconstruction of the conception of myth through making explicit certain distinctions which seem to be implied in Bultmann's thought. But even if we have had any success in showing that a tolerably stable conception of myth can be derived from Bultmann's writings, we have also discovered in the process that demythologizing does not do the job that it was supposed to do—namely, to translate mythical statements into existential statements. For analogical or consciously symbolic statements about God are still with us, having been introduced almost by the back-door. It is no doubt a gain to get away from the naïve unconscious symbolism of myth, to awaken from the dream, as it were, and become aware of the kind of language which we are using, but we have still to face Hepburn's more searching question about the validity of the theology which emerges from demythologizing. When Christian theology has been demythologized, has any advance been made towards showing that it is true?

32 *The Problem of Validity*

Dr Hepburn fears that the '*appearance* of directness' in a demythologized account of Christianity may be a menace towards clearly evaluating its claims and that its very plausibility may cause us to overlook the fundamental problems. The veiled obliqueness involved in a demythologized talk of God may be more dangerous than the obvious symbolism of mythology. 'The question which should be of greatest concern to the theologian is not whether this or that myth may be re-expressed in language less flagrantly pictorial, more abstract in appearance, but whether or not the circle of myth, metaphor and symbol is a closed one: and if closed, then in what way propositions about God manage to *refer*.' Or again: 'Overwhelmingly concerned with the phenomenology of faith and the life of faith, existentialist thought is in continual peril of failing to emerge from the subjectivist circle at all. A subjectivist account can provide an informative description of what it is like to think and act *as if* there was a God, of the "inward" metamorphosis which accompanies belief. But it is unable to go further . . . and say whether the belief is justified or unjustified, whether or not there exists a being before whom the believer has taken up the attitude of faith.'[1]

Two preliminary observations ought to be made here. The first is that we ought to remember that there is a difference between theology and the philosophy of religion. Theology is a function of the Church itself, and speaks from within faith. Its function is to make explicit what this faith is, and it may well be described as a phenomenology of faith. We cannot therefore blame the theologian (in this case, Bultmann) if he stays within the limits of theology proper and takes as his starting-point the faith which he is to elucidate. However, theology needs to be supplemented by the philosophy of religion,

[1] Loc. cit., pp. 237, 240.

which does raise the question of the validity of religious faith. Though this question is outside the sphere of theology proper, the theologian can hardly remain indifferent to it, and there is some justice in Hepburn's point that Bultmann deliberately evades this question.[1]

The second preliminary observation is that when it comes to testing the validity of religious statements, anything like a correspondence theory of truth is ruled out. The symbols of religious statements do not refer to an object in the same way in which a statement of fact refers to some state of affairs in the world. For one thing, we have seen that God is most properly described as 'being',[2] and since being is not another entity, a religious statement does not refer to any object comparable to the state of affairs to which a factual statement refers. For another thing, the possibility of establishing a correspondence between religious statements and God would seem to depend on our having a non-religious knowledge of God, which could be used to verify the religious statements. And even if there were such a knowledge, it would employ a non-religious symbolism, and could not establish the validity of the religious symbols. For instance, it is well-known that even if the traditional arguments for God's existence were valid, they would prove something much less than the God of religion— a first cause, a necessary being, a supreme intelligence, or something of the sort, but not the God of the Christian or any other religion. We seem therefore driven to the conclusion that if anything can be said for the validity of religious statements, it must come from the discrimination and analysis of religious experience itself.

At this point we may turn again to Martin Heidegger, whose philosophy sheds light on Bultmann's thought at so many points. In a discussion of truth, Heidegger rejects the view that the essence of truth consists in the agreement or correspondence of a statement with that to which it refers. Rather, it consists in making 'unconcealed' that which we are discoursing about.

---

[1] See also Bultmann's debate with Jaspers, who asks by what criterion a revelation can be recognized. Bultmann turns aside this question with the remark: 'As if God had to justify himself before man!' To which Jaspers replies: 'No, I do not say that God has to justify himself, but that everything that appears in the world and claims to be God's word, God's act, God's revelation, has to justify itself.'—*Zur Frage der Entmythologisierung*, pp. 42, 69, 85.

[2] See above, p. 126.

This view of truth, he argues, is a return to the most ancient tradition in philosophy—indeed, it represents man's pre-philosophical grasp of truth. As usual, he supports this contention with an etymological consideration. The Greek word for 'true' is ἀληθής. 'Is it', he asks, 'an accident that the Greeks expressed themselves in a *privative* manner about the essence of truth? Truth is ἀ-λήθεια, "unconcealedness". Do we not find proclaiming itself man's own primordial understanding of being in this way in which he expresses himself?'[1] The fundamental truth is the truth of existence itself—that is to say, as existing, we have some understanding of our existence, our existence is always more or less unconcealed to ourselves, we always exist more or less 'in the truth'. It is this basic truth which makes any other truth possible for us. In another passage which also exploits etymologies, Heidegger speaks of man as a 'clearing' (*Lichtung*). He is like a clearing in a forest because he is the *locus* where being becomes transparent to itself. Heidegger links up this thought of man as a clearing with the idea of light (*Licht*) and the traditional doctrine of a *lumen naturale*.[2] The peculiarity of human existence is that man not only has being but has some understanding of being. In human existence being is 'lit up', it is to some extent 'unconcealed', and there is a way into the 'truth' of being.

Heidegger's early work goes on the assumption that by phenomenological analysis man's understanding of existence, which is given with his existence, can be uncovered and clarified—in a way which is in some respects suggestive of Plato's doctrine of an anamnesis. Moreover, Heidegger believed that the understanding of man's own being (existence) provides the starting-point for an investigation into being in general, because man's being is the clearing in being itself. Yet he always recognized that there is a circle involved in such a procedure.[3] For if we are to understand the being of man properly, must we not already have some understanding of being in general? In his more difficult later writings, Heidegger reverses the procedure. Now thinking is a response to the claim of being. Being calls man, and shows itself gracious to him. 'Is it not', asks Richard Kroner, 'furnished with attributes which we can

---

[1] *Sein und Zeit*, p. 222.   [2] Op. cit., p. 133.   [3] Op. cit., pp. 7ff.

and should ascribe to the living God alone?'[1] Thus in his quest
for being Heidegger supplements his phenomenological analysis
of man's being with a religious or mystical experience of being
itself.[2]

Returning now to the problem of the validity of a demythologized theology, we must ask whether these considerations
from Heidegger can help us. We remember that the primary
aim of demythologizing is to express religious statements as
statements about human existence. Revelation, according to
Bultmann, is primarily self-understanding.[3] But to understand
the 'truth' of one's existence, to have this existence 'unconcealed', is also to penetrate into the understanding of
being, into the mystery of God. For this existence of ours is
understood as creaturely and incomplete, as pointing beyond
itself. Thus Saint Augustine tells us that it was when he
entered into his 'inward self' that he saw above it the 'unchangeable light'.[4] To understand one's own being is to be
pointed towards being itself.

But we remember that demythologizing also results in analogical statements. Religious experience is not only the understanding of one's own existence as pointing for its completion
to being beyond itself, it is also the experience of this being
coming to one's existence. Analogical language is in terms of
human existence but its reference is beyond such existence. It
does not speak of God as he is in himself, but tries to express our
experience of God as *something like* our experiences of various
items in our everyday existence. Bultmann is fond of saying that
God 'addresses' us. More common, perhaps, is the language of
God 'speaking' to men. A favourite word with modern theologians is 'encounter'.[5] Whatever the symbol used, it is meant

---

[1] See his instructive essay, 'Heidegger's Private Religion', in *Union Seminary
Quarterly Review*, XI, no. 4, pp. 39ff.

[2] Being takes the place of God in Heidegger's thought. He thinks that the
biblical God is an entity rather than being itself. We have pointed out that
Christian theology has wobbled between thinking of God as a kind of super-
entity and thinking of him as being itself—see above, p. 126. Following Tillich
and others, we have identified God with being. This, of course, is not pantheism,
which would be the identification of God with the totality of entities.

[3] See above, p. 25.   [4] *Confessions*, VII, 10.

[5] The word 'encounter' is perhaps usually understood as an encounter between
persons. In this sense, it has been criticized by Owen who points out that such
personal encounter does not have the paramount place in Christian experience
which Bultmann seems to assign to it, and that there are many Christians who have
never had such an encounter. Owen is right to assert the 'variety of religious

to point to a reality standing over against one's own existence. Human existence is correlated with the being which transcends existence. As E. L. Allen has well expressed it, 'The truth which wins me personally is at the same time the truth that is sovereignly independent of me.'[1] The true understanding of oneself leads to God, but God comes to man in such experiences as grace, so that there is, so to speak, a two-way traffic. We recognize this being as independent of our own existence, as a transcendent God. Yet we can speak of him only as we experience him, and even then we can express this experience only in terms of some everyday experience which is something like it.

Do these remarks help at all with the problem of validity? In one respect they do, for they help to clarify the functions performed by the statements—both existential and analogical—of a demythologized theology. These statements are meant to make 'unconcealed' our own being, so that we understand it in correlation with being itself which is gracious towards us. If we see clearly how the statements are supposed to refer, we have made some advance. As Hepburn himself remarks, 'to allow the logical structure of a theology to shine through its presentation is not only to prepare the way for assessing its validity; it is to have commenced assessment already. To see clearly what a theology demands is to begin seeing how plausible or implausible are those demands.'[2] In another respect, however, the problem of validity is still as far as ever from solution. Have we any guarantee that existence and being have really been unconcealed, or may we be the victims of an illusion?

Obviously no merely linguistic considerations can help here. And obviously the only kind of proof could be had by stepping right outside of human existence and viewing the whole of reality from some divine eminence. And this, of course, is

experience'. See *Revelation and Existence*, pp. 24ff., etc. Hepburn also criticizes the idea of personal encounter between God and man, and points out that such an encounter cannot be self-authenticating. See *Christianity and Paradox*, pp. 24ff. We should remember however that the word 'encounter' can be used in a wider sense—Heidegger frequently uses it of things as well as persons. The essential idea here is not that of a personal relationship but that of coming up against something which is not oneself.

[1] *Existentialism from Within* (Routledge & Kegan Paul, London, 1953), p. 14.
[2] Loc. cit., p. 227.

exactly what demythologizing and existentialism say is impossible. We can view things only from the standpoint of this finite existence of ours in the world. Our existence is such that we must walk by faith and not by sight. Considering that existentialism lays so much stress on the risk of faith and, moreover, tells us that this faith is not a permanent possession but something which must constantly be won afresh, it is surely rather unfair to suggest, as Hepburn does, that it glosses over the problem of the validity of religious belief. On the contrary, it tells us that so long as we exist in the world, we do not have certitude but only belief. Sometimes this belief may rise to heights of confidence, sometimes it may be assailed with doubts. Continually it will be tested, confirmed, or corrected by existence itself, from which its statements and symbols are drawn, and in the living of which they get their meaning.

Yet this faith is not baseless, not just a leap in the dark, as some say. It is based on an honest discrimination of our existence. It may well claim to be a reasonable interpretation of our experience. If its validity is challenged, we cannot prove it by stepping outside of existence and exchanging our worm's-eye view for a godlike one, if we may so speak. But we can ask the challenger to look in the same direction as we have done, to take account of the various aspects of our experience, to consider sympathetically the way in which the religious man seeks to express and interpret his experience, and then to make his assessment. And it may be claimed that demythologizing is a help rather than a hindrance to such an assessment.

VIII

TOWARDS VINDICATING
THE PARADOX

33 *A Survey of Results*

WE have now reached the point at which we must seek to bring together and assess the results obtained in the preceding chapters. We took as our starting-point that remarkable phase in Bultmann's theology when he leaves the way of existential analysis to talk of a *kerygma* which, although addressed to human existence, comes from beyond it. The question which has occupied our attention concerns the limit which the *kerygma* sets to demythologizing. We have asked whether, once we have set out on the path of existential analysis, there can be a limit which will be not just an arbitrary one. Can we hold together the method of demythologizing on the one hand and belief in a *kerygma* on the other—a method which aims at the description of human possibilities and a proclamation which asserts that God acts decisively in the human situation? Is the combination of the two to be considered a radical inconsistency from which there is no way out, or is it one of those paradoxes which appear to be inseparable from all theological thinking? In attempting to find answers to such questions as these, we have made a fairly comprehensive survey of the whole controversy which Bultmann's demythologizing has stirred up, and have examined those crucial points at which his thought has come into collision with the thought of his critics, both on the right and on the left.[1] At

[1] It should, of course, be said that while the rough classification of Bultmann's critics into right-wing and left-wing groups has proved very useful for the purposes of the foregoing inquiry, this classification must not be interpreted too rigidly. We have seen, indeed, that some of the most searching criticism of Bultmann has come from writers who have no particular theological or ideological axe to grind, and who could not properly be regarded as champions either of orthodoxy or of liberalism in religious belief.

each of these points, demythologizing was seen to come up against a limit, where the demands of theology cannot be met by an existential interpretation alone.

Broadly speaking, the critics on the right direct their onslaught against the method of demythologizing in order to rescue the *kerygma*, which they feel to be endangered by Bultmann's approach. We had little difficulty in showing that many of these criticisms fail to strike home, and in establishing that demythologizing and existential interpretation have a legitimate and valuable part to play in elucidating the problems of Christian theology. Yet, at the same time, we acknowledged that all of these criticisms have a certain value, in so far as they point to limits beyond which demythologizing cannot take us. They make it clear that existential interpretation does not supply the answer to every question which perplexes the theologian, and that it needs to be supplemented in various ways. Of course, it should be added that it is doubtful if anyone ever claimed that existential interpretation solves all the problems of theology. Bultmann himself, as we have seen, recognizes either explicitly or implicitly the various limits which are set to the scope of a purely existential interpretation, and the fears of some of his orthodox critics that he is dissolving away the substance of the Christian faith are grossly exaggerated.

Thus, when we considered the field of exegesis, our study of the nature of interpretation showed us that a strong case can be made out for an existential approach to the Bible. Bultmann's own careful analysis of the hermeneutical problem, his insistence that we formulate our questions in an appropriate fashion, his theory of the pre-understanding and its function, his demand for a properly clarified conceptual framework—all these factors combined to demonstrate, as against the critics, the scope of demythologizing in rendering the message of the Bible intelligible to the people of our time. Yet we had to admit that the message of the Bible cannot be exhausted in terms of an anthropology. When we turned to the difficult question of the historical element in Christianity, we tried various approaches, and again we were led to see the value of Bultmann's existential or existentialist approach, which directs our attention upon the existential possibilities disclosed in the sacred history. It was this approach, for instance, which enabled us to understand how the cross of Christ can have the character of an atonement for men who live nineteen centuries after the event. Yet there we saw the danger that we might get lost in a region of spurious and purely fictitious possibilities, unless some link is preserved between the possibilities set before us and empirical fact. In other words, an adequate theology would seem to demand not just an existential interpretation of the New Testament history but a certain minimum of factuality—at least, that there has been under the actual conditions of existence a life of the kind which is proclaimed in the New Testament, however the details of this life may fluctuate with the changing results of historical criticism. Our examination of the nature of dogma yielded parallel results. Here again we saw the strength of an existential interpretation. The obligatory character which is commonly attributed to dogma is intelligible only on the supposition that dogma commends to the believer a way of life for which he can decide—whether we think of it in pragmatic terms as laying upon him a duty to *do* something, or in existentialist terms as presenting him with a demand to *be* something. Yet we had to concede that the sense of dogma is not *only* practical or existential. At least when we take it as a whole, the body of Christian doctrine has ontological significance as well. We must, however, remind ourselves that in one way or another Bultmann himself makes provision in his theology for all these various limits to an existential or existentialist presentation of Christianity.

The left-wing critics reverse the procedure, and attack the *kerygma* in the interests of a more thorough-going demythologizing. Broadly speaking, they wish to remove the limit which Bultmann himself has set, and to merge theology into a philosophy of existence. But what happens when the limit to demythologizing is removed? To find an answer to this question, we examined Buri's conception of a dekerygmatized theology in which the method of demythologizing is carried through to the end and the *kerygma* itself treated as a remnant of mythology. Then we looked at the views which Jaspers has expressed on these topics—views which are not very different from Buri's and have also much in common with the older liberal type of theology, except that this new liberalism moves in a context

of existentialist instead of Kantian or Hegelian ideas. We saw
that both Buri and Jaspers conduct a vigorous onslaught on the
position which Bultmann gives to the *kerygma* in his thinking.
But in both cases we judged that the onslaught had failed, or
at least that it had proved much less damaging than Buri
and Jaspers intended. Bultmann's adherence to a *kerygma*
was vindicated, and we found little to commend the alternative
positions put forward by his two left-wing critics; for in talking
of a *kerygma*, Bultmann is doing justice to certain indispensable
aspects of Christian experience which are inadequately
recognized by Buri and Jaspers.

Buri's attack, as we have seen, breaks down especially on
his conception of grace. His vague notion of the grace of
existence, a kind of inborn nobility which is part of our natural
endowment, is quite inadequate to the needs of man when a
realistic view is taken of human sinfulness and powerlessness;
and certainly it is far removed from the New Testament understanding of grace. Buri's views are, indeed, much closer to the
teaching of Confucius and Mencius than to that of the New
Testament. If the New Testament is anywhere near the truth,
then only an act from beyond man, such as Bultmann finds
proclaimed in the *kerygma*, will be adequate to effect salvation
for those who are fallen and unable to lift themselves.

Jaspers' attack breaks down especially on his conception of
revelation. Once again, it is a vague notion which is offered to
us—that of a revelation which can be everywhere and always,
and which claims no definitive character. As we have seen,
however, Jaspers himself acknowledges that men remain
largely unmoved by those situations which might be expected
to reveal the transcendent and that for the majority of men a
philosophical faith is powerless compared with a living historical
religion. There is little or nothing of a genuine revelatory
character in that vague general awareness of transcendence
which may from time to time break in on our human existence.
If there is an adequate revelation of God, with power to
make an impact on human lives, it must be something more
concrete, such as is the *kerygma* whose importance Bultmann
maintains.

It is worth quoting what Bultmann has to say on these two
themes of grace and revelation. He makes both of them

concrete. On grace, he says: 'The New Testament speaks, and faith knows, of an act of God through which man becomes capable of self-commitment, capable of faith and love, of his authentic life.'[1] On revelation, he says: 'Revelation is something which God does, an event . . . Christ is the deed of the divine love.'[2] Thus Bultmann relates both grace and revelation to a concrete event which for him is what he calls an 'act of God', making its impact on human existence but originating beyond such existence. In so far as this act brings men to self-commitment and authentic life, it is experienced as grace; in so far as it brings to them a new self-understanding, it is experienced as revelation. We have already seen that concreteness does not imply exclusiveness. That the grace of God and the knowledge of God may come to some men in other ways, we would not wish to deny. But we have to remember that in these matters we have to do not with shadowy generalities but with men in definite situations. As a Christian apologist, Bultmann is thinking of the ordinary fallen man of our Western civilization, with all his perplexities and temptations, and Bultmann knows very well that if grace and revelation are ever to reach such a man, they are much less likely to come through those vague indefinite channels of which Buri and Jaspers speak than through a saving decisive act such as the Christian *kerygma* proclaims.

The discussion of Buri and Jaspers was then supplemented by a consideration of the bearing of logical empiricism upon demythologizing. When Bultmann, as over against Jaspers and Buri, talks of an 'act of God', what does he mean? Although the term 'act' refers to human existence, when we talk of an 'act of God' we are not talking existentially but analogically, for we are employing the term 'act' of someone—God—who is not a human existent. Nor can we do anything else if we wish to think of God—as Bultmann certainly does—as a reality transcending human existence, and not just, let us say, as man's ideal of himself or as a focus of value. Thus demythologizing, understood as the translation of mythological into existential statements, is limited by the need to supplement such existential statements by analogical statements, as Bultmann certainly does. Yet these analogical statements are themselves a kind of

---

[1] *Kerygma and Myth*, p. 33.   [2] *Begriff der Offenbarung*, p. 40.

demythologizing, in so far as the immediate naïve relation to the symbol which characterizes myth is replaced by a conscious awareness that the symbol is a symbol. The myth is 'broken', and though the symbols are retained, the criticism and assessment of them becomes possible. Thus demythologizing involves more than existential interpretation. The various limits to existential interpretation all go back in one way or another to the limit constituted by 'a transcendent God present and active in history',[1] to quote Bultmann's own words. Talk of such a transcendent God, even if it is expressed in language drawn from human existence, carries a reference which points to a reality beyond the confines of any existential analysis.

Now that we have glanced over the various results which have emerged from our investigations into the crucial points at issue between Bultmann and his critics, and have seen these results as a whole, we have to ask whether the elucidation of them has really enabled us to advance very far from our starting-point. Are we any nearer to vindicating Bultmann's combination of demythologizing and *kerygma*? It may fairly be claimed that in one respect a considerable advance has been made, for we have seen that both sides of Bultmann's theology have stood up remarkably well to the criticisms directed against them. As far as the right-wing critics are concerned, we have seen the strength and the value of demythologizing and existential interpretation. To show the limits of any point of view is also to demonstrate its scope. While we have conceded that the critics of the right legitimately draw attention to the limits of an existentialist theology, we have also seen that within these limits such an approach to theological problems has a most important contribution to make. Even the claim that Christianity has, in some sense, a definitive (though not an exclusive) character was seen to be tenable only from an existential standpoint, to mention only one topic. If there is anything like a *kerygma*, it must be a proclamation addressed to man as existing, and it must be unfolded in its existential significance. Thus the scope of demythologizing is vindicated. But we have also seen good reason for rejecting some of the attacks made upon Bultmann from the left, and it has become clear to us that the *kerygma* is quite essential to Christian

[1] *Kerygma and Myth*, p. 44.

theology. Without a *kerygma*, it is no doubt possible to construct some kind of religious philosophy of existence, but not a theology which would do justice to the factors of grace and revelation in Christian experience. Thus the place of the *kerygma* is also vindicated. Both sides of Bultmann's theology are still standing, and this marks a real advance on our starting-point because it provides confirmation for what, to begin with, was for us only a charitable supposition—namely, that the bifurcation in Bultmann's thought is to be understood as paradox and not as radical inconsistency. This bifurcation goes back to living Christian experience itself. Neither side can be suppressed without falsification of the whole picture, and if it is the business of theology to give us an account of what Christianity is, then any adequate theology must have room for both sides.

In another respect, however, it cannot be claimed that we have made much advance at all. At an earlier stage,[1] it was maintained that the theologian should never be content to glory in a paradox, so to speak, but that he should work patiently upon it, removing needless mystifications and superfluous contradictions. Such vindicating of a paradox, as we called the procedure, would seek to show not only that the two apparently opposing elements genuinely correspond to the living experience which is being interpreted, but also that they are related as polarities within a whole. In this direction, our examination of Bultmann's thought has so far made less progress than we would have liked to see. We may have shown that both sides of his theology have their right, and are rooted in Christian experience, but they still stand somewhat in-congruously alongside one another, and there remains the task of trying to bring out more fully the relation between them.

But before we embark directly upon this task, we must ask why there is all this difficulty in reconciling the two sides of Bultmann's thought. Is there something in his approach to theological problems which aggravates the difficulties? The alarm and despondency which the orthodox feel as they visual-ize Bultmann sliding towards the dissolution of the Christian faith, and the acute disappointment which the philosophers feel

[1] See above, pp. 27ff.

when Bultmann brings the *kerygma* on to the scene, are evidences of something that is highly misleading in Bultmann himself. Why should his appeal to the *kerygma* seem so arbitrary as to be almost an afterthought, and the limit which he sets to de-mythologizing so abrupt and incongruous?

We noted at an early stage in the discussion[1] that Bultmann's demythologizing involves something more than simple existen-tial interpretation. The extra element consists in negations which are not demanded by existential interpretation itself. But the difficulty in reconciling the two sides of Bultmann's thought arises very largely from these negations which, as they mount up, seem to be driving his theology inevitably in the direction of becoming a philosophy of existence—or, as Buri would express it, in the direction of dekerygmatizing. What, then, is the source of these negative attitudes, if it does not lie in existential interpretation? The answer to this question is not far to seek. The source lies in Bultmann's conception of modernity, and of the modern man. This conception plays an important, if sometimes hidden, part in determining the direction of Bultmann's thinking. Jaspers is one critic who has clearly discerned the influence which the conception of modernity exercises upon Bultmann, and has declared that together with existentialism, it is one of the twin foundations on which Bultmann's whole theology is built up.[2] But this conception of modernity in Bultmann is a most confused and confusing one, and is in large measure responsible for the difficulties which we encounter when we try to understand how existential interpretation and belief in a *kerygma* can be satis-factorily held together in his theology.

In order, therefore, to remove some of the obstacles which stand in the way of vindicating Bultmann's paradoxical position, it will be well worthwhile to begin with an examination of how he understands modernity and how he uses the con-ception of the modern man (Section 34). Then we shall be free to show that the paradoxical elements in Bultmann's thought are related as polarities within a whole, and we shall seek to do this by passing in review some of the key-concepts of his theology (Section 35). The chapter will end with a few con-cluding remarks (Section 36).

[1] See above, pp. 15ff.   [2] *Die Frage der Entmythologisierung*, p. 9.

34 *Bultmann's Conception of Modernity*

It will be recalled that Father George Tyrrell defined a modernist as 'a churchman, of any sort, who believes in the possibility of a synthesis between the essential truth of his religion and the essential truth of modernity'.[1] This definition, however, occurs in a passage in which Tyrrell made it clear that, speaking as a churchman, his attachment was more to his religion than to modernity, that he was critical of modernity as well as of tradition, and that his 'concessions to modernity are reluctant'. Presumably Bultmann, who has so much to say about making Christianity intelligible to the modern man, is a modernist in the wide sense which Tyrrell attaches to the term. But one sometimes fears that Bultmann is too uncritical of modernity, and that he is inclined to ascribe to the outlook of 'the modern man'—we have not yet asked who exactly this modern man is—something of a normative character.

In some ways, there need be no quarrel at all over Bultmann's preoccupation with the modern man—on the contrary, we must welcome it. There always has been and always will be the task of re-interpreting the gospel for the needs of successive generations, and Bultmann applies himself to this task in our time. While we agreed with Bultmann that the cosmologies of the ancient myths are not primarily to be interpreted as primitive science,[2] we also maintained that something like an objective world-picture was implicit in the mythical matrix. Bultmann seems to be conceding as much when he stresses the difference between modern conceptions of the universe and ancient ones. He points out, quite rightly, that men today have a quite different picture of the world from that which was current in New Testament times. The compact universe, with the earth in the middle, the heavenly region not very far above, and the underworld beneath men's feet, has been dissolved away. As a consequence, there are many things of which the New Testament speaks which have become remote and unintelligible to us. They belong to another world of thought. What, for instance, can a man with a modern picture of the world make of the idea that the Son of man shall return on the clouds, or that the faithful shall meet him in the air?[3]

---

[1] *Christianity at the Crossroads*, p. 5.   [2] See above, pp. 211ff.
[3] Mark 13.26; I Thess. 4.17.

Bultmann is right also in saying that it is science which has been primarily responsible for giving us a new picture of the world, and he is right in stressing the important part which science and its way of thinking occupy in the modern world. All this may be conceded, and it follows that there is clearly a need for the work of re-interpretation. Bultmann himself has made valuable contributions towards this work.

We are told that we need not regret in the slightest the passing of the old world-picture, for there was nothing specifically Christian about it. It was in no sense a part of the gospel—it just happened to be the picture current at the time when the New Testament was written, and inevitably it coloured the thought and language of the writers. This is true up to a point. Yet Bultmann is inclined to overlook the fact that some world-pictures may be more hospitable to religion than others. The old geocentric pictures, whether Babylonian or Ptolemaic, gave men a highly privileged position and might predispose them to the belief that they were the special concern of such powers as might govern the universe. A world in which one can, so to speak, take one's bearings is also a world which gives some sense of security. No doubt it was the threat to this security which lay behind the violence with which the churches reacted against the ideas of Copernicus and his followers, so that the Roman Catholic Church persecuted Galileo and Luther said about Copernicus that 'the fool would turn the whole science of astronomy upside down'.[1] We can see the same anxiety manifesting itself in the nostalgic longing for a more homely kind of world among those of our own contemporaries who try to seal off their religion from contact with modern thought. For the modern world-picture makes men pilgrims and strangers far more than they could ever have been in a geocentric universe.

Bultmann, however, maintains that the essential message of the New Testament is independent of the world-picture with which it is entangled. The message is not dissolved with the

---

[1] Quoted by A. C. Lovell in his Reith Lecture, 'Astronomy Breaks Free', *The Listener*, LX, p. 762. Cf. Harnack's comment on Luther: 'This genius had a faith as robust as Paul's . . . but he was not abreast of the knowledge accessible even in his own time' (*What is Christianity?*, trans. Thomas B. Saunders, Williams & Norgate, London, 1901, p. 289).

dissolution of the world-picture. It can still speak to us when the New Testament is interpreted not as offering an objective picture of events which happened in the past or would happen in the future in a world which is not ours, but as presenting an understanding of our existence in our world, for which we can decide now. In all this, Bultmann's use of the concept of modernity is unimpeachable. We all accept the modern picture of the world in our everyday lives, and—unless we are to have split minds—we cannot cling to a different world-picture in our religious lives. But religion is neither to be encapsulated nor rejected just because the world-picture has changed. There is very great need for restatement and reinterpretation, and Bultmann can only be commended for facing up to this task, even by those who do not think that he has had much success.

There are other ways, however, in which we can discern Bultmann's preoccupation with the idea of modernity, and sometimes his concern with it is questionable. When we speak of modern man, we often—indeed, more often than not—mean considerably more than just a man with a modern picture of the world. We mean the man of the modern age in all his aspects—the man whom we often call secularized man. Such a man has not only a picture of the world. He has also a picture of himself, a self-understanding, and it is a secularized one. The question which we must ask is whether Bultmann sometimes takes the conception of modernity in this much wider sense. Is he sometimes trying not only to interpret the gospel in terms of the modern world-picture, but also to present it in relation to the modern secularized self-understanding? If this is the case, then we are immediately shown the source of many of Bultmann's difficulties. If the modern self-understanding is secularized, then it can never understand anything to be an act of God. If it can understand the teaching of the New Testament at all, this teaching must be transformed for it into a humanistic philosophy. The teaching would have to be expressed purely in terms of the possibilities of human existence, and never as a *kerygma* or proclamation of some decisive saving act of God. If it is the modern self-understanding as well as the modern world-picture which is demanding a reinterpretation of the New Testament, then we cannot be surprised if the idea of a *kerygma* seems like a foreign body which cannot by any means be related to an existential interpretation.

First of all, let us look at some very pertinent criticisms of Bultmann's concept of the modern man, which have been put forward by Karl Jaspers.[1] He sees clearly that it is Bultmann's preoccupation with a certain idea of modernity rather than his concern with Heidegger's existentialism that gives to the theology of demythologizing its apparently negative character. Jaspers sees also—and this is the main value of his criticism— that Bultmann's conception of modernity is a very confused one. On the one hand, it is represented as the scientific view of the world. But on the other hand, it is found to be just the average outlook of the man of today. And this average outlook is decidedly not scientific, even if it often likes to think of itself as such. The implied contrast in Bultmann's thought between the mythical and the scientific is quite misleading. The modern man certainly has a high regard for science and constantly appeals to it, but then, as Jaspers says, everyone appeals to science and very few are really acquainted with it. The scientists themselves would seem to support Jaspers here, for in spite of the scientific temper of the modern world and the prevalence of scientific ways of talking, the scientists are continually complaining about lack of understanding on the part of the public. They have their problem of communication as much as the theologians have theirs.

The modern outlook is determined in many ways by science —for instance, it may include a superstitious and uncritical reverence for science—but this is far from saying that it is scientific. A prejudice against religion may not be particularly scientific, even when it appeals to science. After all, unbelief is not peculiar to a scientific age. There were people just as unbelieving in former times, like the Athenians who laughed when Saint Paul mentioned the resurrection of the dead.[2] Equally, there are at all times credulous people. Jaspers mentions as an example the fact that there seem to be many people in the modern Western world who believe in such absurdities as astrology. Although we agreed that myth, in the sense in which we have agreed to use the term, belonged to former times, we saw that modern man has his quasi-myths, as we called

[1] See *Die Frage der Entmythologisierung*, pp. 9ff.   [2] Acts 17.32.

them, corresponding in many ways to the myths of former generations. When we compare modern man with men of other times, it is not therefore a case of setting science over against myth, but rather of comparing with myth the average modern outlook in which scientific and non-scientific factors are confounded together. If Bultmann is right in his view that the meaning of a myth consists primarily in the self-understanding which it brings to expression, what we have to do is to compare one self-understanding with another.

What then is the average self-understanding of the modern man? We may hope to find it in some of his typical quasi-myths. We shall not speak of those which are on the grand scale, such as the 'ideologies', as Bultmann calls them, of National Socialism or Communism, though these are the examples which Jaspers mentions in his critique of Bultmann's idea of modernity. Let us look instead at the popular science-fiction which is so prominent on our bookstalls. Does not this kind of writing—at least, in its more popular forms—have most of the important properties of myth? It moves in the realm of fancy and day-dream, and its situations are often far removed from the sober realities of life—further even than some of the stories of miracle and magic that have come down to us from the past. But this type of writing is certainly the vehicle of a self-understanding. It is one way of expressing that superstitious reverence for science of which mention was made earlier. It gives a vivid and concrete embodiment to the popular belief in the omni-competence of science. Yet such a belief is clearly not itself scientific. It leads back in turn to a deeper belief, which is the modern secular man's understanding of himself as self-sufficient.[1] All things are possible to him, he has taken the place of God, he can master the universe and subject it to his power. Though he has not yet done this in actual fact, he believes himself on the way to it, and he outstrips his already astonishing achievements in those further flights of fancy which science-fiction provides. These concrete pictures confirm his understanding of himself and, almost like the apocalyptic literature of a religion which represents the consummation as already here,

[1] For a discussion of the modern preoccupation with mastery over nature as the expression of an understanding of man, see Emil Brunner, *Christianity and Civilization* (Nisbet, London, 1949), II, pp. 1-15.

encourage him along the path he has chosen—the path towards
godlike power.[1] This self-understanding has been well expressed by Reinhold Niebuhr in the following terms: 'There is a
pride of power in which the human ego assumes its self-sufficiency and self-mastery and imagines itself secure against all
vicissitudes. It does not recognize the contingent and dependent
character of its life and believes itself to be the author of its
own existence, the judge of its own values, and the master of
its own destiny.'[2] We could say that science-fiction of the kind
which we have been discussing is the reverse of the biblical myth
of the Tower of Babel. The biblical myth shows self-sufficiency
leading to frustration, but science-fiction shows it as triumphant.
The quasi-mythology of modern times, unlike the ancient
myths, makes no reference to God or to any power more
ultimate than man himself. Such quasi-myth expresses a secular
self-understanding.

All this, however, is of considerable interest from our
special point of view. If the New Testament message is to be
reinterpreted not only with regard to the modern world-picture
but also with regard to the modern self-understanding, then
there can be no place for a *kerygma* in it. If it can be reinterpreted for such a self-understanding at all, then it can be
presented only as a human possibility—a turning from the world
and from preoccupation with the mastery of things. This is
indeed the teaching of some secular existentialist philosophers,
but to represent it as the teaching of the New Testament is so to
impoverish the New Testament as positively to falsify it. Yet
Bultmann himself clearly recognizes this, as is shown from his
disputes with his left-wing critics.

We have therefore to distinguish two quite different things.
There is a modern world-picture, which we have learned from
science, and which differs from the world-picture (or world-
pictures) assumed by the writers of the New Testament. We
can, and indeed we must, reinterpret the New Testament
teaching in relation to our modern world-picture. We all
accept this picture, we know that there was nothing specifically
Christian about the older ones, and we believe that the New

[1] Of course, science-fiction can be written and read purely for pleasure, and some
of it has a definitely satirical purpose. But these obvious truths do not affect the
general tenor of our remarks.

[2] *The Nature and Destiny of Man* (Nisbet, London, 1941), I, p. 201.

Testament has something vital to say to men whatever their world-picture may be. There is also, however, an average modern self-understanding, which is not scientific, and which differs completely from the self-understanding of the Bible. This modern self-understanding is a secular one, with man as ultimate, whereas in the biblical self-understanding man is a creature dependent upon God. There can be no possibility of trying to reinterpret the New Testament message in a way which would accommodate this average modern self-understanding, for here we are dealing not with an attendant circumstance of the New Testament teaching, as the ancient world-picture is, but with the very heart of this teaching. It is here that the temptation arises to present Christianity in humanistic guise as just a possible way for man to exist, without any reference to a decisive activity of God, since such an activity does not come within the purview of secularized man. But such a presentation falls far short of biblical teaching. Sin is not just alienation from oneself, it is alienation from God. Authentic existence is not just coming to oneself, it is coming to God. Bultmann in his most typical utterances acknowledges all this and it is undoubtedly the point of view which he holds, but sometimes he appears to make concessions to the modern self-understanding which drive his thought in the direction of becoming a human philosophy, and which make it difficult to see how he finds a place for the *kerygma* in it except through a *tour de force*.

This discussion may be carried a little further. In writing about Bultmann's rejection of the healing miracles of the New Testament, I pointed out on a previous occasion that 'in this scientific age thousands go to Lourdes every year', and that 'there seems to be nothing inacceptable about it to many modern minds'.[1] Bultmann's reply to this comment is quite simple and very interesting. He says: 'But these are not modern men.'[2] The concept of modernity implied in Bultmann's remark seems to be a pretty thorough-going one, and seems, moreover, to be used as a norm for what we may or may not believe. It seems to include not just the modern world-picture but also the average modern self-understanding which, as a secular understanding, rules out anything like an act of God. How then can

[1] *An Existentialist Theology*, p. 168.   [2] In a letter to the present writer.

any human word ever be heard as a word of God, or how can any natural event be revelatory of God? To the educated Christian nowadays, a miracle is not an event which constitutes a breach in the course of nature, but an event in which God reveals himself for faith. 'Miracle' is a religious concept. For the Christian, the supreme miracle is the event of Jesus Christ, for he believes that in the human life of Christ the divine being manifests itself. The secularist not only denies, as a consequence of a world-picture, that there can be events which interrupt the regular course of nature, he also denies, as a consequence of his self-understanding, that there can be any events at all which reveal God. The Christian, along with the secularist, may not believe that Christ literally stilled a storm on a lake by a word, and he may also believe that in course of time a natural explanation will be forthcoming for the pheno- mena known as divine or spiritual healing, if he assumes that such healing occurs. But the Christian will still hear Christ's word of peace in the storm and he will still think of Christ as the bringer of wholeness to men, because he sees God in Christ. Only if he does see God in Christ can such stories or events speak to his existence in a religious way. But the secular man does not see God anywhere, so that to him such stories are just fanciful tales, and such an event as a healing at Lourdes is simply an unexplained occurrence.

It may be worthwhile to recall that almost exactly the same points were made by Adolf Harnack at the beginning of the century when a secular mechanistic outlook was firmly estab- lished in Europe. Harnack accepted the uniformity of nature. 'That a storm was quieted by a word', he wrote, 'we do not believe, and we shall never again believe.' He is less sure about healing miracles. 'That the lame walked, the blind saw, and the deaf heard, will not be so summarily dismissed as an illusion'. Yet Harnack believes that natural events can be to the religious man manifestations of God. To believe that things happen 'naturally' is not 'to be shut up within a blind and brutal course of nature'. The religious man has the experience of escaping 'from the power and the service of transitory things'. This experience 'is always felt afresh to be a miracle each time that it occurs; it is inseparable from every higher religion, and were it to be surrendered, religion would be at an end'.[1] If we are to accept a conception of modernity which rules out such experiences from the beginning, then we may as well give up the attempt to bring about a synthesis between the essential truth of religion and the essential truth of modernity.

To the secularized man, it may seem as if his religious contemporary is not a modern man at all, but a survival from past times. The comparison which comes to mind is with the coelacanth, a type of fish which flourished away back in the Devonian Period. A considerable stir was caused in biological circles when a specimen of this fish was caught off the coast of South Africa in 1938, and a few more have been found since. The fish was supposed to have become extinct some sixty million years ago, but apparently some of them still live on in the depths of the Indian Ocean. The religious man may look like a coelacanth in the modern world—he really ought to be extinct! Yet presumably the coelacanth can have survived so long after most of its contemporaries became extinct because there is something fundamentally sound in its constitution. Indeed, in these days when the future of the human race has become so precarious, it is not inconceivable that the coelacanth may still be pursuing its archaic ways in the ocean after *Homo sapiens* has effaced himself from the planet's side! Be that as it may, the religious man may be possessed of some valuable endowment which enables him to survive in the life of faith even in a secularized and sophisticated age. As Bultmann himself says, 'It may well happen that truths which a shallow enlightenment had failed to perceive are later rediscovered in ancient myths.'[2] The endowment of the religious man is not his credulity for myth and miracle, in the popular sense of these terms, but his faith that God makes himself known in events which take place in our world—events which are perfectly natural from one point of view, but which, from another point of view, may be experienced as acts of grace and revelation. In one of his sonnets Wordsworth expressed the wish that he had been born a pagan long ago, so that he might have 'glimpses that would make me less forlorn'. He is not literally wanting to go back to an outmoded and naïve understanding of the world, but in a secular and materialistic age he puts in a plea that man should not, in Harnack's words, be 'shut up in a blind and brutal

---

[1] See *What is Christianity?*, pp. 26-8.   [2] *Kerygma and Myth*, p. 3.

course of nature', but that he should be open to the intimations of the divine.

Incidentally, it seems obvious that Heidegger would not qualify as a 'modern man' on the conception of modernity which we have just discussed. This conception of modernity is rather the outlook of *das Man*, against whose dominance Heidegger makes such a powerful protest. His whole philosophy is a reaction against rather than an expression of the average self-understanding of the modern man.[1] This comes out clearly in his teaching that science is one way of knowing among others, that an existence which is absorbed in concern with things is an inauthentic existence, and above all in his preoccupation with the question of being, a question which the typical modern man evades. This is not just the question of the being of man but of being as a whole, and the over-riding concern with being gives to Heidegger's philosophy its unmistakably religious character.

We may now sum up this discussion of the conception of modernity in Bultmann. We have agreed that the Christian theologian has a duty to reinterpret the Christian faith in the light of the changed world-picture so that it may be intelligible in modern times, and we believe that he can do this without violence to anything that is essential to the faith, because no particular world-picture is an indispensable part of it. But it is no duty of the theologian to accommodate Christian teaching to the modern secularized self-understanding, and indeed he cannot do this. No doubt he could extract from the New Testament a secularized conception of an authentic existence in terms of human possibilities, as Buri has come near to doing in his dekerygmatized theology. But this would be an impoverishment or rather a travesty of the New Testament. It loses the kerygmatic element altogether because it excludes God's activity towards men.

Bultmann's own position is needlessly ambiguous. In some passages he makes concessions to the modern secularized self-understanding as well as to the modern world-picture. His position would have been greatly strengthened if he had shown less deference to modernity and criticized its assumptions more thoroughly. The concessions which he makes do not represent

---

[1] See e.g., *Sein und Zeit*, p. 311, and the essay 'Die Zeit des Weltbildes' in *Holzwege*, pp. 69ff.

his own typical view, which holds firmly to the *kerygma*, but arise from the confusions in his conception of modernity— the confusions to which Jaspers has drawn attention. The concessions which Bultmann makes explain why his orthodox critics fear that he is going to sell out some of the essentials of the faith which he is purporting to expound; they explain why Buri cannot understand Bultmann's reason for setting a limit to demythologizing, and thus they explain why there is so much difficulty in justifying Bultmann's position. His use of the conception of modernity calls for the closest scrutiny, since it is sometimes quite uncritical. But if it is purged of concessions to a secularized point of view which could never see anything like an act of God anywhere, his typical view does emerge, and we can see why Bultmann himself can talk of an act of God.

35 *God, Act of God, Existence*

We are now in a position to come as near as we can towards vindicating the paradox in Bultmann and showing how the two sides of his theology cohere. We shall do this by examining briefly three key-concepts of his thinking, and showing that in each there is a polarity which is faithfully reflected in the combination of demythologizing with the assertion of a *kerygma*. We shall pass these concepts in review, beginning from the Godward side and working towards the manward. The three concepts are: his understanding of God; his understanding of an act of God as mediating between God and man; and his understanding of human existence.

Firstly, we consider his concept of God.[1] 'We must', writes Bultmann, 'clearly distinguish *genuine belief in God* from what is usually termed a world-view. Knowledge about that power which creates and limits our being is not theoretical knowledge, but is the knowledge which breaks in on us in critical moments of our being itself.' In other words, God is not to be objectified, he is not the God of metaphysics such as the God of Descartes, he does not belong to a world-view. But neither is God subjectified, he is not just my ideal of myself in the sense in which Sartre can sometimes speak of God, he comes to me from beyond myself. He is not at my disposal, for I know him

---

[1] See his essay, 'The Crisis in Belief', in *Essays—Philosophical and Theological*, pp. 1ff.

only in so far as he makes himself known to me. Yet I recognize him as a power beyond myself, creating and limiting my being. We might compare with this the teaching of Calvin that 'properly speaking, we cannot say that God is known where there is no religion or piety', and that we do not know 'God as he is in himself, but as he is towards us'.[1] There are therefore always two sides in our thought of God—we recognize him as the being which 'is' beyond our being, but we can speak of him only in so far as he 'speaks' to us in our being. To exaggerate one side or the other is to fall into an objective or a subjective thought of God, and to falsify the living relationship with him.

Next, we may look again at Bultmann's concept of an act of God. 'To speak of an act of God', he says, 'means at the same time to speak of my own existence.'[2] Here again we have two sides to the picture. An act of God is not something purely objective. 'God's act', says Bultmann, 'is concealed for every other eye than the eye of faith.' The cross of Christ, for instance, as we have seen, is an objective fact of history for everyone, but it is a saving act of God only for faith, for the man who makes it his own. But neither is God's activity being considered as something which is purely subjective. To quote again: 'From the statement that the believer, when he speaks of an act of God speaks also of himself, it does not follow in the least that God is not real outside of the believer or his act of faith.' Bultmann talks here of the paradox of faith, and says that this paradox consists in the fact that faith understands as an act of God an event to which a place can be assigned also in the context of natural and historical happening. Again, we cannot exaggerate either side without distortion. We would fall either into an objectivism which would cut off the event from my existence so that it could not be a saving event, or into a subjectivism which would exclude the reality of God's dealing with men. The cross affords the clearest example of the way in which Bultmann conceives an act of God. It is only in so far as we accept the possibility of making it our own that it can become for us an atonement, and yet, unlike the events narrated in Hellenistic mythology, it did happen. The possibility is not one

---

[1] *Institutes*, I, ii.

[2] See his essay, 'Zum Problem der Entmythologisierung' in *K.u.M.*, II, especially pp. 196ff.

which we merely imagine, but one which has been presented to us within the horizons of actual historical existence.

Thirdly, we consider the concept of existence itself. Existentialism is not subjectivism. Again and again, Heidegger protests against the idea of an isolated subject which somehow has to be brought into relation with a world. For him, existence is always being-in-the-world. It is neither subjective nor objective, for it holds both sides together. Bultmann thinks of existence in much the same way, but expresses it slightly differently when he says that existence is encounter.[1] And as we have insisted before, 'encounter' must be understood in the widest sense, to include encounters with the world, with other selves, and with God.[2] Thielicke's well-known accusation that nothing happens in Bultmann except consciousness[3] rests on a misunderstanding of the concept of existence. It would need to be expressed, 'Nothing happens except encounter', but as soon as this is understood, the point of the objection is gone. The objection was intended to imply subjectivism on Bultmann's part, but for encounter of any kind, there must always be two sides. It is not

[1] Loc. cit., pp. 198ff.

[2] It is one of the merits of Owen's book on Bultmann that he clearly recognizes that personal encounter is an 'image' or an 'analogue' when applied to man's relationship with God. See *Revelation and Existence*, pp. 24-29, 32-36.

[3] See his essay, 'The Restatement of New Testament Mythology', in *Kerygma and Myth*, pp. 138ff. Thielicke and others associate the subjectivism which they attribute to Bultmann with an alleged neglect of epistemology on his part (loc. cit., pp. 158ff.). This charge can be read in two ways, according to the meaning which we give to 'epistemology'. (*a*) If Bultmann's supposed neglect of epistemology means that he has failed to make an adequate analysis of myth as a possible religious way of knowing, then we have already seen that this is the case, or rather, that he has only slowly got round to making a detailed examination of the nature and function of myth (see Section 31 above, pp. 198ff.). While Thielicke himself has grasped this problem in the essay quoted, he provides no adequate distinction between 'myth' and 'symbolism'. (*b*) If it is meant that Bultmann neglects the epistemological problem in general, this may be true, but as usual we can find an explanation for it by looking beyond Bultmann to Heidegger. This philosopher speaks somewhat disparagingly of the 'theory of knowledge' (*Erkenntnistheorie*), but he makes it clear that what he has in mind is the traditional formulation of the problem of knowledge, or perhaps we should say, the traditional formulation as he understands it to have been: namely, how can an 'inner' subject of experience emerge from its box, so to speak, to grasp an 'outer' world of objects? Heidegger has his own theory of knowledge, according to which knowing is a mode of Being-in (*Insein*). He sets out from the concept of 'existence' as already a 'Being-in-the-world', within the unity of which the distinction of subject and object emerges. Thus for him the problem of relating an inner knowing subject to an external world is a pseudo-problem. He quotes Kant's statement that it is a scandal to philosophy that there is lacking a cogent proof of an external world, and comments that the scandal is rather that philosophers have busied themselves looking for such a proof. See *Sein und Zeit*, Section 13, pp. 59ff.; and the writer's earlier book, *An Existentialist Theology*, pp. 37-9.

a question of choosing between subjectivism and objectivism, but of holding two sides in proper balance, and this is something which Bultmann succeeds in doing much better than most of his critics.

But with this short survey of some of Bultmann's key-concepts, we have enough for our purpose. Christian faith is always involved in the polarities of the relation between God and man—indeed, *religio* just is this relation. The polarities must be reflected in any theological account of the Christian faith. They are truthfully reflected in the paradox of existential interpretation and kerygmatic proclamation. It is this paradox which we have found to be characteristic of Bultmann's thought, and we now claim that it is a paradox rather than a contradiction, and that the paradox is vindicated. It is unfortunate that by his somewhat dubious use of a certain conception of modernity Bultmann sometimes obscures the genuine intention of his theology. But once this source of trouble has been tracked down, and once suitable adjustments have been made to meet the various criticisms, there is no difficulty in seeing how the two sides of his thinking belong naturally together.

36 *Concluding Remarks*

Discussions between theology and philosophy are usually profitable, and we may even venture to say that each needs the other. Without the corrective of philosophical analysis, theology tends to run into unrestrained paradox and even into sheer superstition; whilst a philosophy which ignores or dismisses the intimations of the religious consciousness is surely leaving out of its purview something of the most vital importance. Yet such discussions are always attended by danger to both sides. There have been times when philosophy has lost its independence and become the handmaid of ecclesiasticism; and equally there have been times when theology has been in danger of losing its distinctive contribution in philosophical speculation. We cannot be surprised at the suspicion which has grown up between the two disciplines—a suspicion which seems to have become particularly pronounced in the present century.

In this study of Bultmann and his critics, we have tried to avoid making any exaggerated claims. But this claim may be made—that Bultmann has gone a considerable way towards working out a properly balanced relation between theology and philosophy, and is reaching towards a synthesis of the rival claims of those two ancient factions within the Christian Church, the pro-philosophical and the anti-philosophical theologians. He recognizes the need for a conceptual framework which is philosophically sound, yet he also holds that theology has its own distinctive contributions to make. His discussion with existentialism has been profitable in many ways, and has helped to make the New Testament teaching understandable as a living issue for the twentieth century. There is plenty of scope for demythologizing and existential interpretation. The Church cannot afford to go on talking an unexamined mythology in an age when this kind of discourse has ceased to be meaningful for most thoughtful people. Demythologizing looks like being one of the most promising ways forward for theology in our time. Yet there is always the danger that Christianity may be represented not as a religion in which God addresses man but as just another possibility of human existence to be set alongside those held out to us by Heidegger, Kamlah,[1] Jaspers and the rest. Sometimes Bultmann seems to have come pretty close to this danger. But with a wisdom which surpasses that of Buri, he has known where to set the limit and to preserve to the Christian religion its essentially kerygmatic character, in virtue of which it is a religion. The limit to demythologizing is nothing other than the recognition of the difference between a philosophy of human existence and a religion of divine grace.

[1] Wilhelm Kamlah well illustrates the danger mentioned. He began as a disciple of Bultmann, but now teaches a doctrine of natural self-commitment which has affinity with Christianity but claims to be independent of it. See his book, *Christentum und Selbstbehauptung* (V. Klostermann, Frankfurt, 1940), and the comments of Bultmann and Thielicke in *Kerygma and Myth*, pp. 25ff. and p. 150.

ADDITIONAL NOTE

The Jesus of History

EARLIER in the course of this book[1] I have stated and defended at some length a view of the relation of Christian faith and theology to history. While I have welcomed the existential interpretation of the sacred history, it seems clear that it is essential to Christian faith and theology that such an existential interpretation needs to be supplemented by some factual historical assertions. But it seems equally clear that faith and theology cannot be made to depend on the detailed historical researches of a handful of experts who rarely agree together for five minutes on end. So the solution which I have proposed so that the *kerygma* may have some empirical anchor is that of a 'minimal core of factuality', the overwhelming probability of which may, prior to any research, be claimed on the basis of a rational inference from the presence before our eyes of the Christian community with its documents and traditions.

I do not pretend that this view is free from difficulties, and in particular the precise relation between the existential significance of the Christian story and the core of factuality needs to be more clearly defined. But I take some encouragement from the fact that this view—which I first adumbrated in 1955[2]—is rather similar to the conclusions towards which other students of Bultmann are moving, especially in Germany. It was mentioned above[3] that in what J. M. Robinson has called the 'post-Bultmannian' phase of German theology, a new interest has arisen in the Jesus of history. The purpose of this note is briefly to compare the views put forward on the preceding pages with those which are emerging in Germany, and

[1] See above, pp. 58ff. [2] *An Existentialist Theology*, pp. 159-92.
[3] See p. 91 n. 1.

to point out that there are differences as well as similarities.[1]

Paul Althaus seems to be saying something very similar to the view which I have put forward when he acknowledges that existential interpretation of the sacred history is important, but that it has a limit and needs supplementing.[2] We can agree with Althaus when he says that some factual history is needed, and we can still agree when he says that Christian faith cannot be made dependent on the researches of historical critics—we cannot admit a 'papacy of the scholars', as he calls it. We can further agree when he denies that our knowledge of the past 'is exclusively mediated through the inductive work of the historian on the sources'.[3] According to Althaus, there is 'an immediate pre-scientific relationship to past history', but we must part company with him when he tells us that this pre-scientific knowledge of the past is found in an 'intuition' or an 'imaginative encounter', which, he alleges, can carry 'absolute certainty'.[4]

Before criticizing this last point, we may mention alongside Althaus a younger theologian who has come from Bultmann's school, Günther Bornkamm. He may be considered as fairly typical of the so-called post-Bultmannian outlook in Germany. He agrees that we do not have detailed biographical material

---

[1] It should perhaps also be pointed out that these problems—like most problems in philosophy and theology—are not really new, for in different forms they have been the subject of past controversies. Back in the nineteenth century, the German scholar Martin Kähler anticipated some of the main points raised by Bultmann's treatment of the historical element in Christianity. Kähler anticipated even Bultmann's distinction of 'historisch' and 'geschichtlich' in the title of the book which he published in 1892: Der sogenannte historische Jesus und der geschichtliche biblische Christus (reissued in 1956 by Kaiser Verlag, Munich). Kähler, quite in the manner of Bultmann, insisted that 'the real Christ is the preached Christ' —op. cit., p. 44. Yet he also maintained that Jesus was a real person belonging to world-history. He supported this view with the contention that the figure of Jesus in the New Testament carries such an overwhelming impression of reality that we cannot suppose him to have been the product of human invention. He is 'so full of life, so real, it is as if we had seen him before our eyes. This is not the idealizing poetry of a human mind; his own essence has stamped itself here imperishably'—op. cit., p. 58.

[2] See his book, The So-called Kerygma and the Historical Jesus, trans. David Cairns (Oliver & Boyd, Edinburgh, 1959). Althaus in this book maintains that the teaching of the New Testament 'as well as being a message of salvation is at the same time a report about a historical event which happened'—p. 48. He says also: 'While it was necessary for Martin Kähler in his day, in reaction against the writers of the "lives" of Jesus, to emphasize the fact that the gospels are not primarily sources but testimonies of faith, today the emphasis must be placed elsewhere; the gospels are also narratives and sources'—p. 25.

[3] Op. cit., p. 69.   [4] Ibid.

about Jesus, that important points concerning him are left in darkness, and that the gospels are largely concerned to present a kerygmatic and existential interpretation of his person and work. Yet he insists that 'we must look for the history in the *kerygma*'. The gospels do not entitle us to be resigned or sceptical about the historical Jesus. In terms not unlike those used by Althaus, Bornkamm claims that the historical figure of Jesus 'is made visible to us in immediate power'. There is said to be 'a genuineness, freshness and particularity' about the picture in the gospels 'which refer back immediately to the earthly figure of Jesus'.[1]

Both Althaus and Bornkamm arrive at results rather similar to my own and try to safeguard themselves against a purely mythical Lord,[2] but they arrive by a different route. I am bound to say frankly that their route is less satisfactory, with its appeal to 'intuition', 'imaginative encounter' and 'immediacy', and its vague talk of 'immediate power'. For surely not everyone on reading the New Testament will get an intuition or be immediately persuaded that it contains truths about facts of past history. Since in this context we are dealing with the question of fact, not with the response of faith, I prefer my own view of a 'minimal core of factuality' ascertainable by a rational inference which can be tested by anyone. A further important difference is that whereas Althaus boldly lays claim to 'absolute certainty' on the basis of his intuition, I have been content with claiming 'overwhelming probability' on the basis of rational inference. It seems to me that the craving for certainty on such matters is quite mistaken.

Exactly where does Bultmann himself stand in this discussion? We have already seen how ambiguous is his thought on these matters, for sometimes he speaks as if the question of historical factuality is entirely foreign to Christian theology, while at other times he wants to claim that the story of Jesus is not simply a myth. We have rejected the view that Bultmann turned to the existential interpretation of the New Testament because his own historical researches had yielded such negative results.[3] Yet we can see how obscure Bultmann's position

[1] See his book, *Jesus von Nazareth* (Kohlhammer, Stuttgart, 1956), pp. 20-2. The very fact that a book with this title has come out of Bultmann's school is a significant indication of the way in which things are moving.

[2] See above, p. 91.   [3] See above, p. 64.

is from the fact that now a precisely opposite charge is being made against him. Hermann Diem brings forward the startling suggestion that Bultmann, so far from being driven into an existential interpretation of history by the negative results of his research, deliberately sought negative results in order to show that only an existential interpretation is possible! Diem says that Bultmann conducted his investigations into Christian origins 'not in order to base faith on the historical conclusions attained, but on the contrary in order to make impossible any such basis for faith, and thus he has greater scope for the most radical results than any of his predecessors. Always, for him, faith must be made insecure, and all historical foundations withdrawn from it'.[1] Whether the extraordinary charge which Diem makes can be substantiated is, to say the least, doubtful. But there is no doubt that Bultmann's thought on the historical nature of Christianity has many obscurities and ambiguities, and needs the kind of clarification and reconstruction which students of his writings are, in various ways, seeking to provide for it.

---

[1] *Dogmatics*, trans. Harold Knight (Oliver & Boyd, Edinburgh, 1959), p. 90. It is interesting to note that Althaus, who is an old adversary of Bultmann, took the view away back in 1927 that the negative results of Bultmann's historical research were forcing him into kerygmatic and existential theology. Bultmann wrote at that time: 'Wiser persons such as Paul Althaus have even detected that I have saved myself from scepticism (by a flight to kerygmatic and existential theology). They must excuse me if their wisdom strikes me as funny. I have never felt uncomfortable in my critical radicalism, but instead quite comfortable'— *Glauben und Verstehen*, Band I (J. C. B. Mohr, Tübingen, 1933), p. 101. Now, however, Althaus seems to have swung round to the same view as Diem, and he maintains that Bultmann's seeming indifference to the questions of factual history and his comfort in the face of negative results spring from an exaggerated misuse of the Lutheran principle of *sola fide*—see *The So-called Kerygma and the Jesus of History*, pp. 43-4. It may be added that it is presumably an exaggeration of the same Lutheran principle which makes Bultmann—and Althaus along with him—deny that any reasons can be given for recognizing the *kerygma* as a *kerygma*, or for holding that it is a genuine 'word' of God—see above, p. 217 n. 1.

GENERAL INDEX AND BIBLIOGRAPHY

SCRIPTURE REFERENCES